MASTER RETREAT

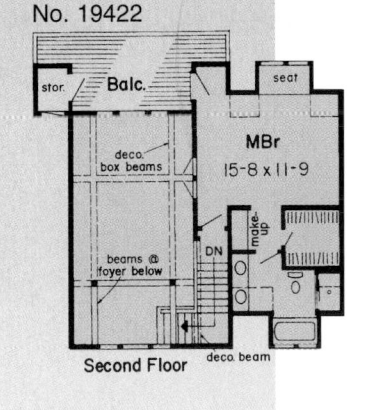

REFER TO PRICE CODE B

✕

No. 19422

Second Floor

stor. | Balc. | seat

deco. box beams

MBr
15-8 x 11-9

beams @ foyer below

DN

make-up

deco. beam

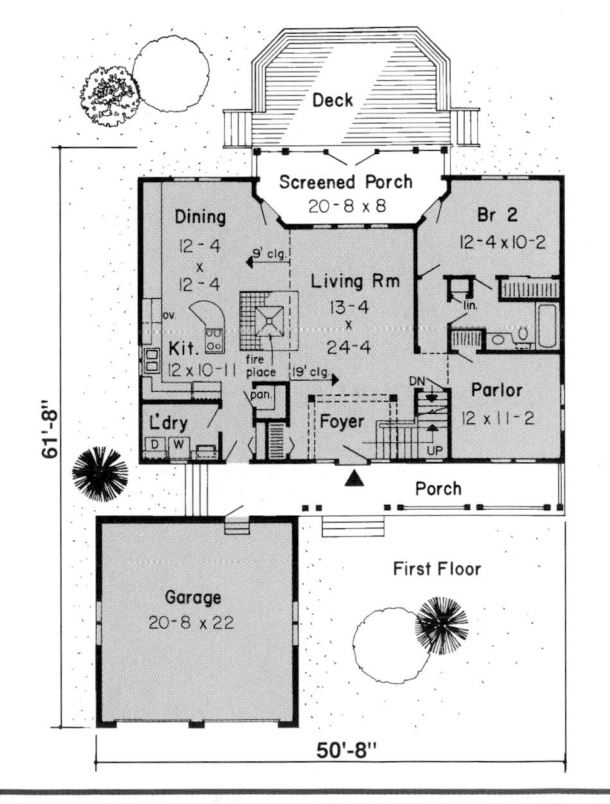

Deck

Screened Porch
20-8 x 8

Dining
12-4
x
12-4

9' clg.

Br 2
12-4 x 10-2

Living Rm
13-4
x
24-4

fire place

lin.

Kit.
12 x 10-11

ov.

19' clg.

pan.

Parlor
12 x 11-2

L'dry

D W

Foyer

DN

UP

61'-8"

Porch

Garage
20-8 x 22

First Floor

50'-8"

Small Home Plans

8th Edition

Publisher
James D. McNair III

Chief Operating Officer
Bradford J. Kidney

Staff Writers
Debra Cochran/Sue Barile

Front Cover Design
Judy-Ann Konopkas

**Back Cover Design &
4/C Layout**
Josephine Panno

Email us at:
http://www.garlinghouse.com

ALL CREDIT CARD TRANSACTIONS ARE
SECURED WITH VERISIGN ENCRYPTION.

TABLE OF CONTENTS

Library of Congress No.: 97-77621
ISBN: 0-938708-82-1

Submit all Canadian plan orders to:
The Garlinghouse Company
60 Baffin Place, Unit #5
Waterloo, Ontario N2V 1Z7

Canadian Orders Only: 1-800-561-4169
Fax No. 1-800-719-3291
Customer Service No.: 1-519-746-4169

Cover Photography By
John Ehrenclou

GARLINGHOUSE

OLD-FASHIONED COUNTRY PORCH

The old-fashioned country porch on the front of this home warmly wel-comes all who visit. As you enter the home, the warm glow of the fireplace in the living room encourages you to move further into the home. The dining room is close at hand for an elegant dinner party or an inti-mate evening. The U-shaped kitchen efficiently services both the formal dining room and the informal breakfast area. A first floor master suite ensures privacy for parents by sending the children to bed on the second floor. The master suite includes a luxurious master bath with a double vanity, walk-in closet, oval tub and step-in shower. A convenient half-bath with a laundry center is located on the first floor. On the second floor the full hall bath is flanked by the two additional bedrooms. The second floor bedrooms are large and have ample closet space.

REFER TO PRICE CODE B

PLAN INFO

FIRST FLOOR	1,057 sq. ft.
SECOND FLOOR	611 sq. ft.
BASEMENT	511 sq. ft.
GARAGE	546 sq. ft.
BEDROOMS	3
BATHROOMS	2(Full), 1(Half)
FOUNDATION	Basement

Total Living Area
1,668 sq. ft.

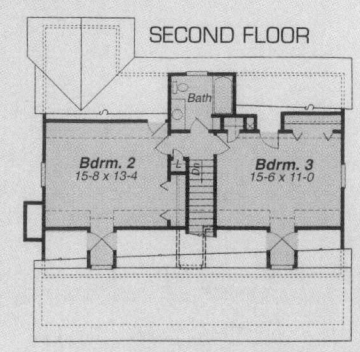

SECOND FLOOR

Bath

Bdrm. 2
15-8 x 13-4

Bdrm. 3
15-6 x 11-0

Deck

Brkfst.
9-0 x 8-0

Kit.
9-0 x 9-6

Dining
9-10 x 11-4

Lav.
W. D.

M.Bath

Living
18-0 x 13-6

Mstr.
Bdrm.
15-6 x 13-6

Porch

38'-0"

FIRST FLOOR
No. 93219

design 93219

Here's a compact beauty with a wide-open feeling. Step past the inviting front porch and savor a breathtaking view of active areas: the columned entry with its open staircase and windows high overhead; the soaring living room, divided from the kitchen and dining room by the towering fireplace chimney; the screened porch beyond the triple living room windows. Tucked behind the stairs, you'll find a cozy parlor. And, across the hall, a bedroom with an adjoining full bath features access to the screened porch. Upstairs, the master suite is an elegant retreat you'll want to come home for, with its romantic dormer window seat, private balcony, and double vanity bath. The photographed home has been modified to suit individual tastes.

PLAN INFO

FIRST FLOOR   1,290 sq. ft.
SECOND FLOOR   405 sq. ft.
SCREENED PORCH   152 sq. ft.
GARAGE   513 sq. ft.
BEDROOMS   2
BATHROOMS   2 (Full)
FOUNDATION   Basement/Crawl
                     Space Combo

Total Living Area   1,695 sq. ft.

design 19422

SKYLIGHT BRIGHTNESS

REFER TO PRICE CODE B

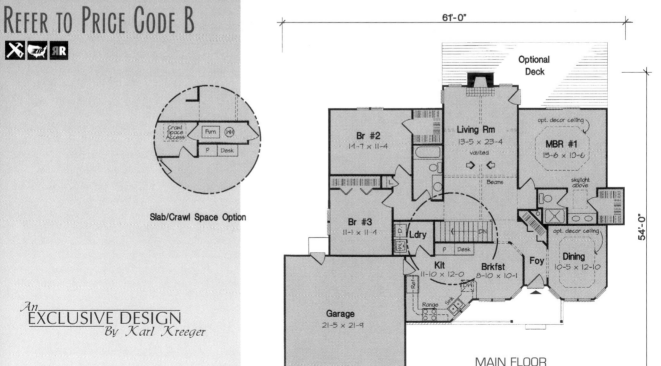

Crawl Space Access | Furn | HH
P | Desk

Slab/Crawl Space Option

An
EXCLUSIVE DESIGN
By Karl Kreeger

61'-0"

Optional Deck

Br #2
14-7 x 11-4

Living Rm
13-5 x 23-4
vaulted

opt. decor ceiling

MBR #1
15-6 x 13-6

Beams

skylight above

Br #3
11-1 x 11-4

Ldry

opt. decor ceiling

P | Desk

Foy

Dining
10-5 x 12-10

Kit
11-10 x 12-0

Brkfst
8-10 x 10-1

Garage
21-5 x 21-9

Range | Sink

54'-0"

MAIN FLOOR
No. 34029

4

Keep dry during the rainy season under the covered porch entry way of this gorgeous home. A foyer separates the dining room with a decorative ceiling from the breakfast area and the kitchen. Off the kitchen is the laundry room, conveniently located. The living room features a vaulted beamed ceiling and a fireplace. A full bath is located between the living room and two bedrooms, both with large closet. On the other side of the living room is the master bedroom. The master bedroom has a decorative ceiling, and a skylight above the entrance of the private bath. The double vanity bathroom features a large walk-in closet. For those who enjoy outdoor living, an optional deck is offered; accessible through sliding glass doors off of the wonderful master bedroom. The photographed home has been modified to suit individual tastes.

PLAN INFO

MAIN FLOOR	1,686 sq. ft.
BASEMENT	1,676 sq. ft.
GARAGE	484 sq. ft.
BEDROOMS	3
BATHROOMS	2 (Full)
FOUNDATION	Basement, Crawl Space or Slab
Total Living Area	1,686 sq. ft.

design 34029

FARM-TYPE TRADITIONAL

REFER TO PRICE CODE B

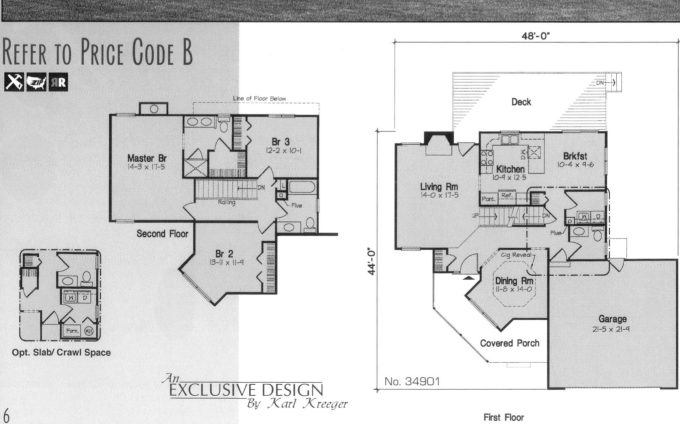

Line of Floor Below

Master Br
14-3 x 17-5

Br 3
12-2 x 10-1

DN

Railing

Flue

Second Floor

Br 2
13-11 x 11-9

Opt. Slab/ Crawl Space

W   D

Furn.

An
EXCLUSIVE DESIGN
By Karl Kreeger

48'-0"

DN

Deck

Kitchen
10-4 x 12-5

Brkfst
10-4 x 9-6

Living Rm
14-0 x 17-5

Pant.   Ref.

UP   DN

44'-0"

Flue

Clg Reveal

Dining Rm
11-8 x 14-0

Garage
21-5 x 21-9

No. 34901

Covered Porch

First Floor

6

This pleasant Traditional design has a farmhouse flavor exterior that incorporates a covered porch and features a circle wood louver on its garage, giving this design a feeling of sturdiness. Inside, on the first level to the right of the foyer, is a formal dining room complete with a bay window and an elevated ceiling. To the left of the foyer is the living room with a wood-burning fireplace. The kitchen is connected to the breakfast room and there is also a room for the laundry facilities. A half-bath is also featured on the first floor. The master bedroom, located on the second floor, has its own private bath and walk-in closet. The other two bedrooms share a full bath. A two-car garage is also added into this design. The photographed home has been modified to suit individual tastes.

PLAN INFO

FIRST FLOOR	909 sq. ft.
SECOND FLOOR	854 sq. ft.
BASEMENT	899 sq. ft.
GARAGE	491 sq. ft.
BEDROOMS	3
BATHROOMS	2 (Full), 1 (Half)
FOUNDATION	Basement, Crawl Space or Slab
Total Living Area	1,763 sq. ft.

design 34901

SIMPLE LINES

REFER TO PRICE CODE A

56'-0"

MAIN FLOOR
No. 34150

Deck
(Optional)

Optional Clg Reveal

Dining
10-10 x 11-4

W.P. Tub

Step

Master Br
13-8 x 13-6

Living Rm
14-6 x 20-10

Sloped Ceiling

Kit.
10-10
x
10-0

DW

P.

Desk

Ref

Railing

Pantry

DN

Br #2
13-8 x 11-6

Den/
Br #3
10-6 x 12-0
Flat Clg
@ 10'

48'-0"

Garage
20-5 x 21-8

W. D. HW Furn

Slab/Crawlspace Option

An
EXCLUSIVE DESIGN
By Karl Kreeger

8

Consider this plan if you work at home and would enjoy a homey, well-lit office or den. The huge, arched window floods the front room with light. This house offers a lot of other practical details for the two-career family. Compact and efficient use of space means less to clean and organize. Yet the open plan keeps the home from feeling too small and cramped. Other features like plenty of closet space, step-saving laundry facilities, easily-cleaned kitchen and a window wall in the living room make this a delightful plan. The photographed home has been modified to suit individual tastes.

PLAN INFO

MAIN FLOOR	1,492 sq. ft.
BASEMENT	1,486 sq. ft.
GARAGE	462 sq. ft.
BEDROOMS	3
BATHROOMS	2 (Full)
FOUNDATION	Basement, Crawl Space or Slab
Total Living Area	1,492 sq. ft.

design 34150

DORMERED DELIGHT

PHOTOGRAPHY BY John Riley of Riley and Riley Photographers

The growing family will appreciate the flexibility offered by an unfinished bonus room and an optional basement in this three-bedroom country cottage that lives bigger than it looks. An elegant palladian window in a clerestory dormer washes the two-story foyer in natural light. Columns between the Great room and dining room add drama and accent nine foot ceilings. A luxurious first level master suite makes a great parent get-away. The master bath features a cheery skylight above the whirlpool tub. Please specify a basement or crawl space foundation when ordering. The photographed home has been modified to suit individual tastes.

PLAN INFO

FIRST FLOOR	1,289 sq. ft.
SECOND FLOOR	542 sq. ft.
BONUS ROOM	393 sq. ft.
GARAGE & STORAGE	521 sq. ft.
BEDROOMS	3
BATHROOMS	2(Full), 1(Half)
FOUNDATION	Basement or Crawl Space

Total Living Area 1,831 sq. ft.

REFER TO PRICE CODE C

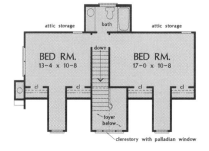

SECOND FLOOR PLAN

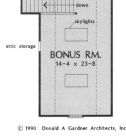

© 1990 Donald A Gardner Architects, Inc.

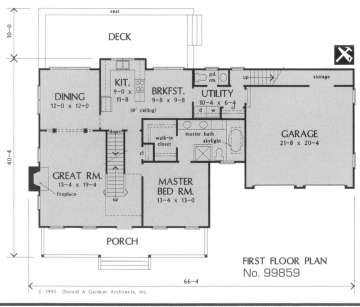

FIRST FLOOR PLAN No. 99859

© 1990 Donald A Gardner Architects, Inc.

10

CHARMING RANCH STYLE

PHOTOGRAPHY SUPPLIED BY Ron & Donna Kolb of Exposures Unlimited

The appeal of this ranch style home is not only in its charm and exterior style. The Great room and the dining room, accented by a sloped ceiling, columns and custom moldings, work together with the corner fireplace to create an outstanding space. People will naturally want to gather in the breakfast area where the sloped ceiling continues, and the light permeates through the rear windows and the French doors, which lead to the spacious screened porch. Convenience was the order of the day when this kitchen was designed. Relaxing in the master suite enhanced by the ultra bath with a whirlpool tub, a double vanity and a large walk-in closet. No materials list is available for this plan. The photographed home has been modified to suit individual tastes.

PLAN INFO

MAIN FLOOR	1,782 sq. ft.
BASEMENT	1,735 sq. ft.
GARAGE	407 sq. ft.
BEDROOMS	3
BATHROOMS	2(Full)
FOUNDATION	Basement

Total Living Area
1,782 sq. ft.

REFER TO PRICE CODE B

Floor Plan — MAIN FLOOR NO. 92630

- Master Bedroom 14'5" x 14'5" (tray ceiling)
- Bath
- walk-in closet
- Bath
- Bedroom 13'10" x 9'11"
- Study/Bedroom 10'3" x 11'11"
- Hall
- Foyer
- Great Room 15'8" x 18'6"
- Breakfast 11'7" x 9'6"
- Screened-in Porch 10'6" x 17'4"
- Kitchen 11'7" x 13'4"
- Dining Room 10'8" x 11'9"
- pantry
- Laun.
- Two-car Garage 20'2" x 20'1"

67'-2"
47'0"

SLEEK LINES

Brick and stucco enhance this dramatic front elevation showcased by sleek lines and decorative windows. The inviting entry has a view into the Great room. The fireplace in the Great room is framed by sunny windows with transoms above. The dining room, accented by a bay window, is nestled between the Great room and the superb kitchen/breakfast area. The design of sleeping areas places a buffer between secondary bedrooms and the master suite. The peaceful master suite enjoys a vaulted ceiling, roomy walk-in closet and a sunlit master bath with a double vanity and a whirlpool tub. The photographed home has been modified to suit individual tastes.

PLAN INFO

MAIN FLOOR	1,666 sq. ft.
BASEMENT	1,666 sq. ft.
GARAGE	496 sq. ft.
BEDROOMS	3
BATHROOMS	1(Full), 1(3/4)
FOUNDATION	Basement

Total Living Area
1,666 sq. ft.

REFER TO PRICE CODE B

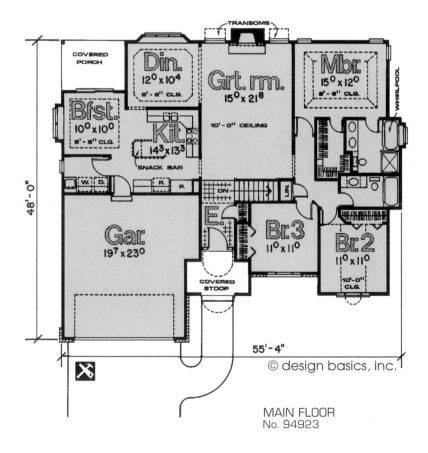

MAIN FLOOR
No. 94923

© design basics, inc.

design 93269

PHOTOGRAPHY BY John Ehrenclou

From the cozy front porch, enter into an inviting living room with a large fireplace. The dining area is open to the living room, giving a spacious feeling to both rooms. The efficient kitchen includes ample counter and cabinet space as well as a double sink. A sunny breakfast area is available for informal eating. The sun deck expands your living area to the outdoors in the warmer weather. The master suite is located on the first floor insuring privacy from the other sleeping quarters. The private master bath is equipped with an oval tub and a double vanity. The first floor powder room includes a hide-away laundry center. The second floor bedrooms have ample closet space and share a full hall bath. The photographed home has been modified to suit individual tastes.

SECOND FLOOR
No. 93269

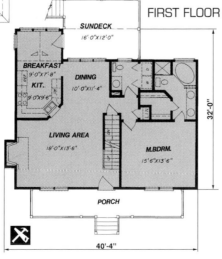

FIRST FLOOR

PLAN INFO

FIRST FLOOR	1,045 sq. ft.
SECOND FLOOR	690 sq. ft.
BASEMENT	465 sq. ft.
GARAGE	580 sq. ft.
BEDROOMS	3
BATHROOMS	2(Full), 1(Half)
FOUNDATION	Basement

Total Living Area
1,735 sq. ft.

REFER TO PRICE CODE B

An EXCLUSIVE DESIGN
By Jannis Vann & Associates, Inc.

13

Extra Touches of Style

Y ou don't have to sacrifice style when buying a smaller home. Notice the palladian window with a fan light above at the front of the home. The entrance porch includes a turned post entry. Once inside, the living room is topped by an impressive vaulted ceiling. A fireplace accents the room. A decorative ceiling enhances both the master bedroom and the dining room. Efficiently designed, the kitchen includes a peninsula counter and serves the dining room with ease. A private bath and double closet highlight the master suite. Two additional bedrooms are served by a full hall bath.

Plan Info

MAIN FLOOR	1,312 sq. ft.
BASEMENT	1,293 sq. ft.
GARAGE	459 sq. ft.
BEDROOMS	3
BATHROOMS	2(Full)
FOUNDATION	Basement, Crawl Space or Slab

Total Living Area
1,312 sq. ft.

Refer to Price Code A

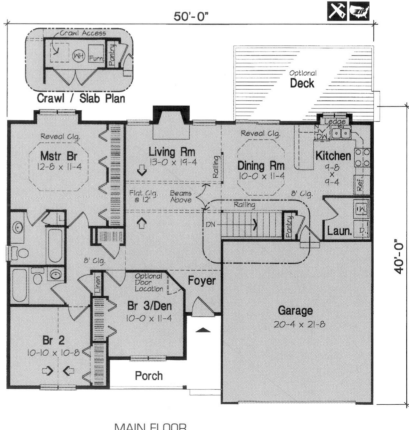

MAIN FLOOR
No. 24700

NATIONAL TREASURE

This delightful home's wrap-around covered porch recalls the warmth and charm of days past - lounging in the porch swing, savoring life. Inside, a spacious foyer welcomes guests and provides easy access to the formal dining room, secluded den/guest room (which might serve as your home office), and the large living room. Ceilings downstairs are all 9' high, with decorative vaults in the living and dining rooms. The kitchen, with its island/breakfast bar, is large enough for two people to work in comfortably. The adjacent laundry room also serves as a mud room and leads directly to the garage, which features an ample storage/shop area at the rear. Upstairs, three bedrooms, each with cathedral ceilings, share a cheery, sunlit sitting area. For privacy, the master bedroom is separated from the other bedrooms, and boasts a palatial bathroom, complete with a whirlpool tub. If room to relax is what you're after, this home is loaded with irresistible features.

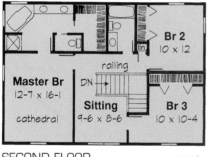

Master Br
12-7 x 16-1
cathedral

Sitting
9-6 x 8-6

Br 2
10 x 12

Br 3
10 x 10-4

railing

DN

SECOND FLOOR

crawl access

Dining

Furn. w/h

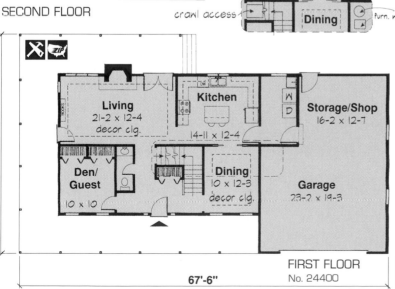

Living
21-2 x 12-4
decor clg.

Kitchen
14-11 x 12-4

Storage/Shop
16-2 x 12-7

Den/Guest
10 x 10

Dining
10 x 12-3
decor clg.

Garage
23-2 x 19-3

39'-6"

67'-6"

FIRST FLOOR
No. 24400

PLAN INFO

FIRST FLOOR	1,034 sq. ft.
SECOND FLOOR	944 sq. ft.
BEDROOMS	3
BATHROOMS	2(Full), 1(Half)
FOUNDATION	Basement, Crawl Space or Slab

Total Living Area
1,978 sq. ft.

REFER TO PRICE CODE C

An EXCLUSIVE DESIGN
By Upright Design

15

EASY LIVING

Here's a pretty, one-level home designed for carefree living. The central foyer divides active and quiet areas. Step back to a fireplaced living room with dramatic, towering ceilings and a panoramic view of the backyard. The adjoining dining room features a sloping ceiling crowned by a plant shelf, and sliders to an outdoor deck. Just across the counter, a handy, U-shaped kitchen features abundant cabinets, a window over the sink overlooking the deck, and a walk-in pantry. You'll find three bedrooms tucked off the foyer. Front bedrooms share a handy full bath, but the master suite boasts its own private bath with both shower and tub, a room-sized walk-in closet, and a bump-out window that adds light and space.

PLAN INFO

MAIN FLOOR	1,456 sq. ft.
BASEMENT	1,448 sq. ft.
GARAGE	452 sq. ft.
BEDROOMS	3
BATHROOMS	2 (Full)
FOUNDATION	Basement, Crawl Space or Slab

Total Living Area
1,456 sq. ft.

REFER TO PRICE CODE A

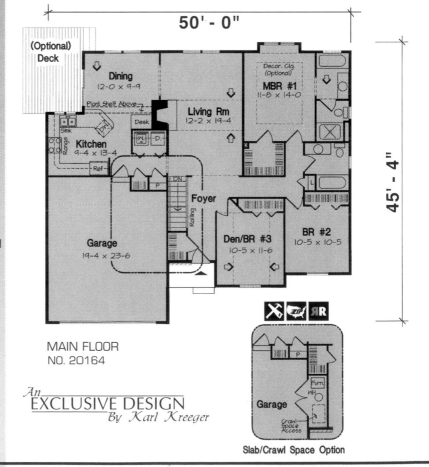

MAIN FLOOR
NO. 20164

An
EXCLUSIVE DESIGN
By Karl Kreeger

Slab/Crawl Space Option

16

DELIGHTFUL HOME

Hanging plants would make for a magnificent entrance to this charming home. Walk into the fireplaced living room brightened by a wonderful picture window. The kitchen and dining area are separated by a counter island featuring double sinks. In the hallway, toward the bedrooms, is a linen closet and full bath. The master bedroom features its own private bath and double closets. The two other bedrooms have good-sized closets, keeping clutter to a minimum. Many windows throughout this home illuminate each room, creating a warm cozy atmosphere.

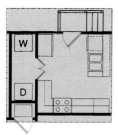

slab/crawlspace option

PLAN INFO

MAIN FLOOR	1,146 sq. ft.
BEDROOMS	3
BATHROOMS	2 (Full)
FOUNDATION	Basement, Crawl Space or Slab

Total Living Area
1,146 sq. ft.

REFER TO PRICE CODE A

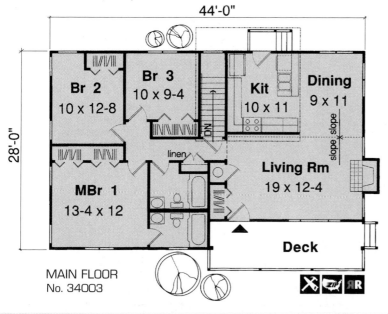

44'-0"

28'-0"

Br 2
10 x 12-8

Br 3
10 x 9-4

Kit
10 x 11

Dining
9 x 11

MBr 1
13-4 x 12

linen

Living Rm
19 x 12-4

Deck

MAIN FLOOR
No. 34003

TRADITIONAL RANCH

This traditional ranch home adds a bit of drama to the convenience of a single level. The large front palladium window gives great curb appeal as well as a view of the front yard from the living room. The vaulted ceiling in the living room adds to the architectural interest and to the spacious feel of the room. The dining room adjoins the living room and has sliders to the wood deck. A built-in pantry, double sink and breakfast bar highlight the efficient kitchen. The private master suite is located at the opposite end of the house from the other bedrooms. A large walk-in closet and a private bath with a double vanity add to the convenience of the suite. The two additional bedrooms share the full hall bath.

PLAN INFO

MAIN FLOOR	1,568 sq. ft.
BASEMENT	1.568 sq. ft.
GARAGE	509 sq. ft.
BEDROOMS	3
BATHROOMS	2 (Full)
FOUNDATION	Basement, Crawl Space or Slab

Total Living Area
1,568 sq. ft.

REFER TO PRICE CODE B

An EXCLUSIVE DESIGN
By Karl Kreeger

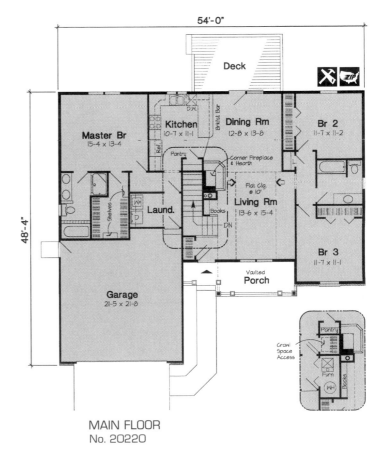

MAIN FLOOR
No. 20220

18

SIMPLE AND MODEST DESIGN

This simple and inexpensive ranch design has a brick and vertical siding exterior. The interior has a well set-up kitchen with its own breakfast area by a large picture window. A formal dining room is located near the kitchen. The living room has one open beam across a sloping ceiling. A large hearth is in front of a wood burning fireplace. Inside the front entrance, a tiled foyer incorporates closet space and has many different room entrances. Three bedrooms are offered in this design. The master bedroom has an extremely large bath area with its own walk-in closet, two other bedrooms share a full bath. There is also a linen closet and a closet for the washer and dryer area. A two-car garage is offered in this plan.

MAIN FLOOR
NO. 20062

PLAN INFO

MAIN FLOOR	1,500 sq. ft.
BASEMENT	1,500 sq. ft.
GARAGE	482 sq. ft.
BEDROOMS	3
BATHROOMS	2(Full)
FOUNDATION	Basement, Crawl Space or Slab

Total Living Area
1,500 sq. ft.

REFER TO PRICE CODE A

An
EXCLUSIVE DESIGN
By Karl Kreeger

COMPACT RANCH

This Ranch home features a large sunken Great room, centralized with a cozy fireplace. The master bedroom has an unforgettable bathroom with a super skylight. The huge three-car plus garage can include a work area for the family carpenter. In the center of this home, the kitchen includes an eating nook for family gatherings. The porch at the rear of the house has easy access from the dining room. One other bedroom and a den, which can easily be converted to a bedroom, are on the opposite side of the house from the master bedroom.

PLAN INFO

MAIN FLOOR	1,738 sq. ft.
BASEMENT	1,083 sq. ft.
GARAGE	796 sq. ft.
BEDROOMS	2
BATHROOMS	2 (Full)
FOUNDATION	Basement/ Crawl Space Combo, Crawl Space or Slab

Total Living Area
1,738 sq. ft.

REFER TO PRICE CODE B

Crawl / Slab Option

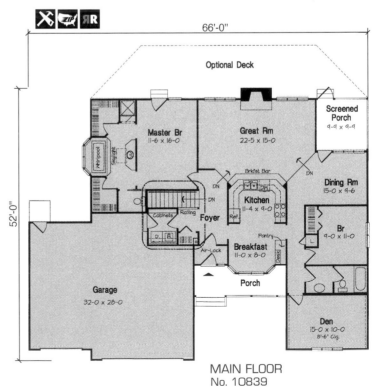

MAIN FLOOR
No. 10839

20

design 24701

This home features a well designed floor plan, offering convenience and style. The roomy living room includes a two-sided fireplace shared with the dining room. An efficient U-shaped kitchen, equipped with a peninsula counter/breakfast bar, is open to the dining room. An entrance from the garage into the kitchen eliminates tracked in dirt and affords step-saving convenience when unloading groceries. The private master suite includes a whirlpool tub, a double vanity and a step-in shower. A large walk-in closet adds ample storage space to the suite. The secondary bedroom and the den/guest room share use of the full hall bath.

MAIN FLOOR
No. 24701

Alternate Foundation Plan

PLAN INFO

MAIN FLOOR	1,625 sq. ft.
BASEMENT	1,625 sq. ft.
GARAGE	455 sq. ft.
BEDROOMS	3
BATHROOMS	2(Full)
FOUNDATION	Basement, Crawl Space or Slab

Total Living Area
1,625 sq. ft.

REFER TO PRICE CODE B

MULTIPLE GABLES

An enchanting one level home with grand openings between rooms creates a spacious effect. The functional kitchen provides an abundance of counter space. Additional room for quick meals or serving an oversized crowd is provided at the breakfast bar. Double hung windows and angles add light and dimension to the dining area. The bright and cheery Great room with a sloped ceiling and a wood burning fireplace opens to the dining area and the foyer, making this three bedroom ranch look and feel much larger than its actual size. No materials list is available for this plan.

PLAN INFO

MAIN FLOOR	1,508 sq. ft.
BASEMENT	1,429 sq. ft.
GARAGE	440 sq. ft.
BEDROOMS	3
BATHROOMS	2 (Full)
FOUNDATION	Basement

Total Living Area
1,508 sq. ft.

REFER TO PRICE CODE B

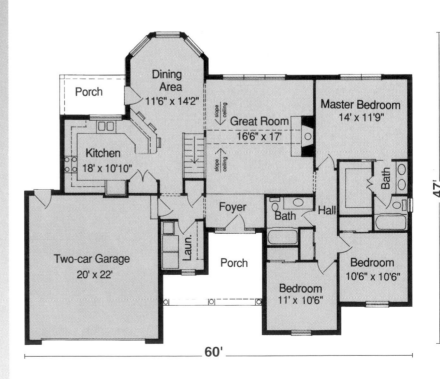

MAIN FLOOR
No. 92649

Dramatic Ranch

The exterior of this ranch home is all wood with interesting lines. More than an ordinary ranch home, it has an expansive feeling to drive up to. The large living area has a stone fireplace and decorative beams. The kitchen and dining room lead to an outside deck. The laundry room has a large pantry, and is off the eating area. The master bedroom has a wonderful bathroom with a huge walk-in closet. In the front of the house, there are two additional bedrooms with a full bathroom. This house offers one floor living and has nice big rooms.

56'-0"

Deck

32'-0"

Kitchen 12 x 11-4

Dining Rm 9 x 11-4

pantry

Ldry

MBr 1 14-2 x 14-4

slope

Living Rm 21-6 x 19-4
decor. beams

lin.

Br 3 12 x 12-6

Br 2 12 x 12-6

slope

MAIN AREA
No. 20198

Plan Info

MAIN AREA	1,792 sq. ft.
BASEMENT	818 sq. ft.
GARAGE	857 sq. ft.
BEDROOMS	3
BATHROOMS	2(Full)
FOUNDATION	Basement

Total Living Area
1,792 sq. ft.

Refer to Price Code B

An
EXCLUSIVE DESIGN
By Karl Kreeger

GENEROUS WINDOWS

This home is a vacation haven with views from every room whether it is situated on a lake or a mountaintop. The main floor features a living room and dining room split by a fireplace. The kitchen flows into the dining room and is gracefully separated by a bar. There is a bedroom and a full bath on the main floor. The second floor has a bedroom or library loft, with clerestory windows, which opens above the living room. The master bedroom and bath are also on the top floor. The lower floor has a large recreation room with a whirlpool tub and a bar, a laundry room and a garage. This home has large decks and windows on one entire side.

PLAN INFO

MAIN FLOOR	728 sq. ft.
UPPER FLOOR	573 sq. ft.
LOWER FLOOR	409 sq. ft.
GARAGE	244 sq. ft.
BEDROOMS	3
BATHROOMS	2(Full)
FOUNDATION	Basement

Total Living Area
1,710 sq. ft.

REFER TO PRICE CODE B

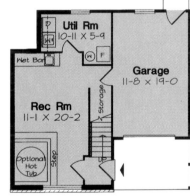

LOWER FLOOR

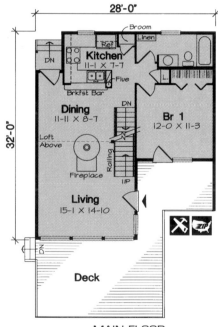

MAIN FLOOR
No. 24319

An
EXCLUSIVE DESIGN
By Marshall Associates

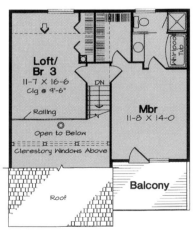

UPPER FLOOR

24

FARMHOUSE FLAVOR

The charm of an old fashioned farmhouse combines with sizzling contemporary excitement in this three-bedroom home. Classic touches abound, from the clapboard exterior with its inviting, wrap-around porch to the wood stove that warms the entire house. Inside, the two-story foyer, crowned by a plant ledge high overhead, affords a view of the soaring, skylit living room and rear deck beyond sliding glass doors. To the right, there's a formal dining room with bay window, just steps away from the kitchen. The well-appointed master suite completes the first floor. Upstairs, you'll find a full bath and two more bedrooms, each with a walk-in closet and cozy gable sitting nook.

An
EXCLUSIVE DESIGN
By Karl Kreeger

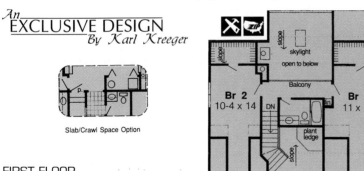

Slab/Crawl Space Option

SECOND FLOOR
No. 10785

FIRST FLOOR

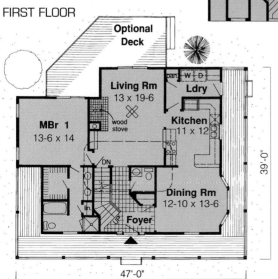

PLAN INFO

FIRST FLOOR	1,269 sq. ft.
SECOND FLOOR	638 sq. ft.
BASEMENT	1,269 sq. ft.
BEDROOMS	3
BATHROOMS	2(Full), 1(Half)
FOUNDATION	Basement, Crawl Space or Slab

Total Living Area
1,907 sq. ft.

REFER TO PRICE CODE C

FAMILY FAVORITE

The elegant half-round windows flanking the clapboard-faced chimney hint at the comfortable atmosphere you'll find inside this easy-care Ranch. An open arrangement with the dining room combines with ten-foot ceilings to make the sunny living room seem even more spacious than its generous size. Glass on three sides overlooking the deck off the dining room adds an outdoor feeling to both rooms. And the compact kitchen, designed for efficiency, is just steps away. You'll appreciate the private location of the bedrooms, tucked away for a quiet atmosphere. The master suite is a special retreat, with its romantic window seat, compartmentalized bath and walk-in closet.

design 20156

PLAN INFO

MAIN FLOOR	1,359 sq. ft.
BASEMENT	1,359 sq. ft.
GARAGE	501 sq. ft.
BEDROOMS	3
BATHROOMS	2 (Full)
FOUNDATION	Basement, Crawl Space or Slab
Total Living Area	1,359 sq. ft.

REFER TO PRICE CODE A

MAIN FLOOR
No. 20156

An
EXCLUSIVE DESIGN
By Karl Kreeger

design 34054

PLAN INFO

MAIN FLOOR	1,400 sq. ft.
BASEMENT	1.400 sq. ft.
GARAGE	528 sq. ft.
BEDROOMS	3
BATHROOMS	2 (Full)
FOUNDATION	Basement, Crawl Space or Slab
Total Living Area	1,400 sq. ft.

REFER TO PRICE CODE A

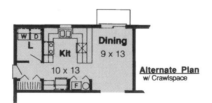

Alternate Plan
w/ Crawlspace

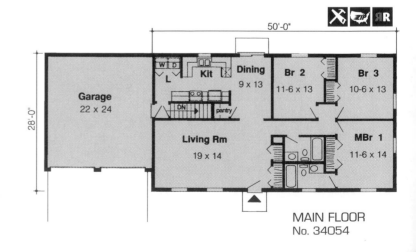

MAIN FLOOR
No. 34054

26

FOR DISCRIMINATING BUYERS

A classic design and spacious interior make this home attractive and exciting to the discriminating buyer. Brick and wood trim, multiple gables, and wing walls enhance the outside; while the interior offers features that are designed for entertaining guests. Sloped ceilings, a corner fireplace, windows across the rear of the Great room and a boxed window in the dining room area are visible as you enter the open foyer. The large kitchen provides plenty of counter space, and a pantry. The breakfast area is surrounded by windows that flood the room with natural light. In the master bedroom suite you will find an ultra bath with a whirlpool tub, double sink, shower and walk-in closet. No materials list is available for this plan.

WIDTH 65'-10"
DEPTH 56'-0"

Patio

Breakfast
10'10" x12'

Great Room
16'2" x 18'4"

Master Bedroom
15' x12'10"

Bath

walk-in closet

Kitchen
11'8" x 14' 4"

Hall

Dining Room
11' x 9'2"

Foyer

Bath

Laun.

Porch

Bedroom
11' x 12'6"

Bedroom
12'6"x11'11"

Two-car Garage
22' x 20'8"

MAIN AREA
No. 92625

design 92625

PLAN INFO

MAIN AREA	1,710 sq. ft.
BASEMENT	1,560 sq. ft.
GARAGE	455 sq. ft.
BEDROOMS	3
BATHROOMS	2 (Full)
FOUNDATION	Basement
Total Living Area	1,710 sq. ft.

REFER TO PRICE CODE B

GREAT KITCHEN AREA

There's a lot of convenience packed into this affordable design. Flanking the kitchen to the right is the dining room which has a sliding glass door to the backyard, and to the left is the laundry room with an entrance to the garage. The master bedroom boasts its own full bathroom and the additional two bedrooms share the hall bath. An optional two-car garage plan is included.

design 34054

FOR TODAY AND TOMORROW

This convenient, one-level plan is perfect for the modern family with a taste for classic design. Traditional Victorian touches in this three-bedroom beauty include a romantic, railed porch and an intriguing breakfast tower just off the kitchen. You will love the step-saving arrangement of the kitchen between the breakfast and formal dining rooms. Enjoy the wide-open living room with sliders out to a rear deck, and the handsome master suite with its skylit, compartmentalized bath. Notice the convenient laundry location in the bedroom hall.

An
EXCLUSIVE DESIGN
By Karl Kreeger

design 34043

PLAN INFO

MAIN AREA   1,583 sq. ft.

BASEMENT   1,573 sq. ft.

GARAGE   484 sq. ft.

BEDROOMS   3

BATHROOMS   2 (Full))

FOUNDATION   Basement, Crawl
                     Space or Slab

Total Living Area   1,583 sq. ft.

REFER TO PRICE CODE B

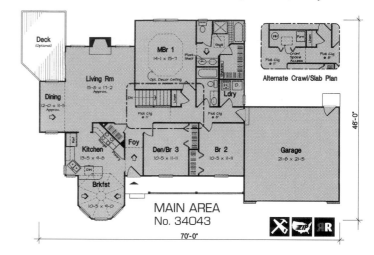

MAIN AREA
No. 34043

design 1074 X

PLAN INFO

MAIN AREA   1,040 sq. ft.

STORAGE   44 sq. ft.

DECK   258 sq. ft.

CARPORT   230 sq. ft.

BEDROOMS   3

BATHROOMS   2 (Full)

FOUNDATION   Crawl Space

Total Living Area   1,040 sq. ft.

REFER TO PRICE CODE A

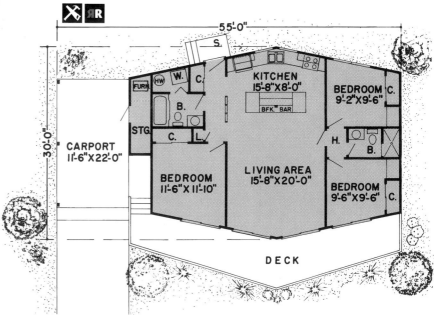

MAIN AREA
No. 1074

SOUTHERN TRADITIONAL

This charming southern traditional styled home has all the features and looks of a much larger home. The covered front porch with its striking columns, brick quoins, and dentil moulding add a rich elegance to this stately design. Entering the foyer we find the sqacious Great room with its vaulted ceilings and fireplace as well as built-in cabinets. The dining room is open to the Great room which opens up to the whole middle of the plan. The utility room is adjacent to the kitchen and this leads to the two car garage with storage rooms. To the right of the foyer is the bedroom wing with bedrooms two and three having their own walk-in closets and a hall bath to serve them. The master bedroom is located to the rear of the hall and features a large walk-in closet and compartmentalized bath. Please specify a crawl space or slab foundation when ordering.

design 92503

PLAN INFO

MAIN AREA	1,271 sq. ft.
GARAGE	506 sq. ft.
BEDROOMS	3
BATHROOMS	2 (Full)
FOUNDATION	Crawl Space or Slab
Total Living Area	1,271 sq. ft.

garage 21 x 21

kit 12 x 9
ref rng dw

dining 11 x 11

mbr 14 x 12

util d w b shvs cab

living 15⁶ x 16

shvs

br 2 11 x 11

sto

porch 20¹⁰ x 5

br 3 11 x 11

shvs

WIDTH 63'-10"
DEPTH 38'-10"

MAIN AREA
No. 92503

REFER TO PRICE CODE B

SIX-SIDED DESIGN

Simple lines flow from this six-sided design. It's affordably scaled, but sizable enough for a growing family. Active living areas are snuggled centrally between two quiet bedroom and bath areas in the floor plan. A small hallway, leading to two bedrooms and a full bath on the right side may be completely shut off from the living room, providing seclusion. Another bath lies behind a third bedroom on the left side, complete with washer/dryer facilities and close enough to a stoop and rear entrance to serve as a mudroom.

design 1074

RUSTIC EXTERIOR

Although rustic in appearance, the interior of this cabin is quiet, modern and comfortable. Small in overall size, it still contains three bedrooms and two baths in addition to a large, two-story living room with exposed beams. As a hunting/fishing lodge or mountain retreat, this compares well.

design 34600

PLAN INFO

MAIN FLOOR	1,013 sq. ft.
UPPER FLOOR	315 sq. ft.
BASEMENT	1,013 sq. ft.
BEDROOMS	3
BATHROOMS	2 (Full)
FOUNDATION	Basement, Crawl Space or Slab
Total Living Area	1,328 sq. ft.

REFER TO PRICE CODE A

Crawl Space / Slab Plan

No. 34600

Master Br
12-0 x 13-4

Upper Floor

Main Floor

design 92525

PLAN INFO

MAIN FLOOR	1,484 sq. ft.
GARAGE & STORAGE	544 sq. ft.
PORCH	110 sq. ft.
BEDROOMS	3
BATHROOMS	2 (Full)
FOUNDATION	Crawl Space or Slab
Total Living Area	1,484 sq. ft.

REFER TO PRICE CODE B

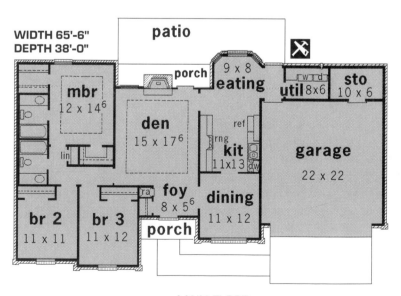

WIDTH 65'-6"
DEPTH 38'-0"

MAIN FLOOR
No. 92525

Spacious and Convenient

Stacked windows fill the wall in the front bedroom of this one-level home, creating an attractive facade and a sunny atmosphere inside. Around the corner, two more bedrooms and two full baths complete the bedroom wing, set apart for bedtime quiet. Notice the elegant vaulted-ceiling in the master bedroom, the master tub and shower illuminated by a skylight, and the double vanities in both baths. Active areas enjoy a spacious feeling. Look at the high, sloping ceilings in the fireplaced living room, the sliders that unite the breakfast room and kitchen with an adjoining deck, and the vaulted-ceilings in the formal dining room off the foyer.

An
EXCLUSIVE DESIGN
By Karl Kreeger

MAIN AREA
No. 20100

design 20100

PLAN INFO

MAIN AREA	1,737 sq. ft.
BASEMENT	1,727 sq. ft.
GARAGE	484 sq. ft.
BEDROOMS	3
BATHROOMS	2 (Full)
FOUNDATION	Basement, Crawl Space or Slab
Total Living Area	1,737 sq. ft.

REFER TO PRICE CODE B

Amenity Packed

Don't let this brick beauty's square footage of only 1,484 square feet fool you. The amenities found in larger homes can be found here. Such as the decorative ceiling and the fireplace in the den. The master bedroom, also with a decorative ceiling, is spacious and has ample storage space between two closets. The private master bath will spoil you. The efficient kitchen has equal access to the sunny breakfast area or the formal dining area. Add two additional bedrooms, another full bath, a utility room, more storage space, a garage and a patio and you can see this is affordability without scrimping. This plan is available with a crawl space or slab foundation. Please specify when ordering.

design 92525

CLASSIC COUNTRY FARMHOUSE

Dual porches, gables, and circle-top windows give this home its special country charm. The foyer, expanded by a vaulted ceiling, introduces a formal colonnaded dining room. The open kitchen features columns and an island for easy entertaining. The vaulted Great room is always bright with light from the circle-top clerestory. Extra room for growth is waiting in the skylit bonus room. The front bedroom doubles as a study for versatility. A tray ceiling adds volume to the private master suite that has a bath with skylight, garden tub, double vanity, and both linen and walk-in closets.

PLAN INFO

MAIN AREA	1,832 sq. ft.
BONUS	425 sq. ft.
GARAGE	562 sq. ft.
BEDROOMS	3
BATHROOMS	2(Full)
FOUNDATION	Crawl Space

Total Living Area
1,832 sq. ft.

REFER TO PRICE CODE C

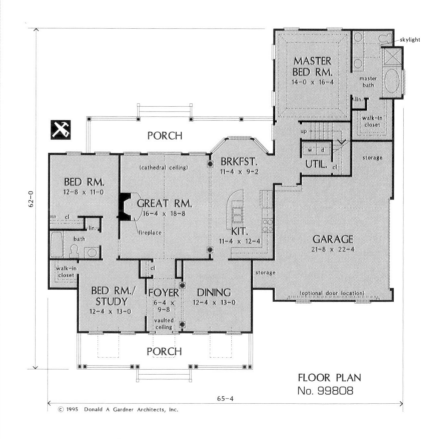

FLOOR PLAN
No. 99808

© 1995 Donald A Gardner Architects, Inc.

32

An
EXCLUSIVE DESIGN
By Karl Kreeger

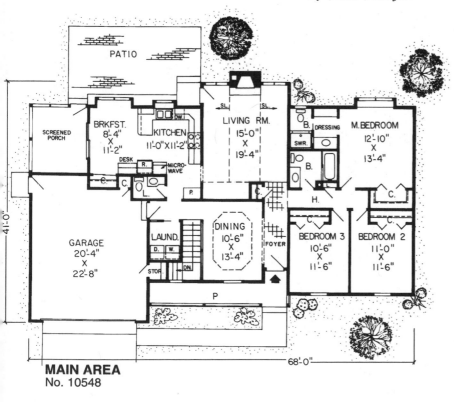

MAIN AREA
No. 10548

Sloped Ceiling Attractive Feature of Ranch Design

■ This plan features:

— Three bedrooms

— Two and one half baths

■ A fireplace and sloped ceiling in the Living Room

■ A Master Bedroom complete with a full bath, shower and dressing area

■ A decorative ceiling in the Dining Room

MAIN AREA — 1,688 SQ. FT.
BASEMENT — 1,688 SQ. FT.
SCREENED PORCH — 120 SQ. FT.
GARAGE — 489 SQ. FT.

TOTAL LIVING AREA:
1,688 SQ. FT.

Wonderful Open Spaces

■ This plan features:

— Three bedrooms

— Two full baths

■ A Family Room, Kitchen and
Breakfast Area that all connects
to form a great space

■ A central, double fireplace adding
warmth and atmosphere to the
Family Room, Kitchen and the
Breakfast area

■ An efficient Kitchen that is highlighted by a peninsula counter
and doubles as a snack bar

■ A Master Suite that includes a
walk-in closet, a double vanity,
separate shower and tub bath

■ Two additional bedrooms sharing
a full hall bath

■ A wooden deck that can be
accessed from the Breakfast Area

■ An optional crawl space or slab
foundation — please specify
when ordering

MAIN FLOOR — 1,388 SQ. FT.
GARAGE — 400 SQ. FT.

An
EXCLUSIVE DESIGN
By Jannis Vann & Associates, Inc.

TOTAL LIVING AREA:
1,388 SQ. FT.

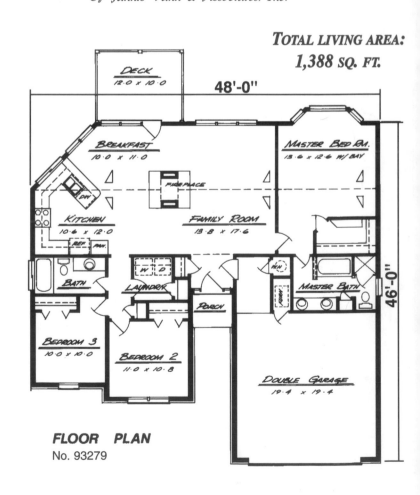

FLOOR PLAN
No. 93279

To order your Blueprints, call 1-800-235-5700

Refer to **Pricing Schedule C** on the order form for pricing information

An EXCLUSIVE DESIGN
By Ahmann Design Inc.

Luxury on One Level

■ This plan features:

— Three bedrooms

— Two full and one half bath

■ Covered front porch leads into Entry and Great Room with vaulted ceilings

■ Huge Great Room perfect for entertaining or family gatherings with cozy fireplace

■ Arched soffits and columns impact the formal Dining Room

■ Country-size Kitchen with a pantry, work island, bright, eating Nook with Screen Porch beyond, and nearby laundry/Garage entry

■ Corner Master Bedroom offers a large walk-in closet and a luxurious bath with a double vanity and spa tub

■ Two bedrooms with over-sized closets share a full bath

■ No materials list is available for this plan

MAIN FLOOR — 2,196 SQ. FT.
BASEMENT — 2,196 SQ. FT.

TOTAL LIVING AREA:
2,196 SQ. FT.

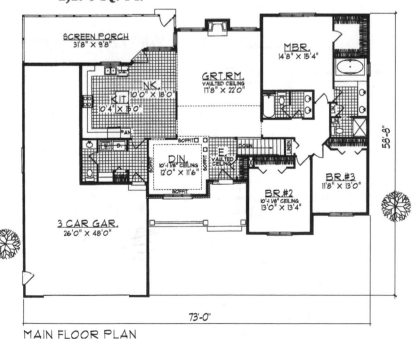

MAIN FLOOR PLAN
No. 93190

Refer to **Pricing Schedule A** on the order form for pricing information

High Impact Angles

■ This plan features:

— Three bedrooms

— Two full baths

■ Soaring ceilings to give the house a spacious, contemporary feeling

■ A fireplaced Great Room adjoining a convenient Kitchen, with a sunny Breakfast Nook

■ Sliding glass doors opening onto an angular Deck

■ A Master Suite with vaulted ceilings and a private bath

MAIN AREA — 1,368 SQ. FT.

TOTAL LIVING AREA: 1,368 SQ. FT.

Main Floor Plan
No. 90357

Mbr
14x12-6
Vaulted Ceiling

Br2
12x10

Patio

Den/Br3
11x9

Kitchen/Brkfst
19x10-8

Dining

Garage
21-4x19-4

Great Room
19x18
Vaulted Ceiling

48'-0"

48'-0"

To order your Blueprints, call 1-800-235-5700

Refer to **Pricing Schedule C** on the order form for pricing information

Master Bedroom
13'6" x 15'1"

Great Room
17'4" x 21'2"

12' high ceiling

Triple French Doors
w/ arched window above

Dining Room
10'10" x 14'0"

Bath

Bath

hanging space

Laun.

walk-in closet

Foyer

pass thru

Kitchen
12'4" x 11'6"

Two-car Garage
22'9" x 22'0"

wood rail

pantry

Breakfast
11' x 9'4"

50'4"

60'

FIRST FLOOR
No. 92642

FIRST FLOOR — 1,524 SQ. FT.
SECOND FLOOR — 558 SQ. FT.
BASEMENT — 1,460 SQ. FT.

**TOTAL LIVING AREA:
2,082 SQ. FT.**

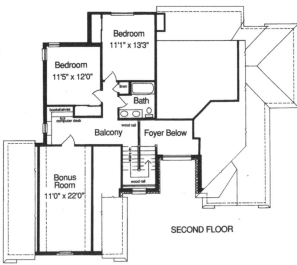

Bedroom
11'1" x 13'3"

Bedroom
11'5" x 12'0"

linen

Bath

bookshelves

computer desk

Balcony

wood rail

Foyer Below

Bonus Room
11'0" x 22'0"

wood rail

SECOND FLOOR

An Extraordinary Home

■ This plan features:

— Three bedrooms

— Two full and one half baths

■ An exciting roof line and textured exterior providing a rich solid look

■ A lovely foyer that views the cozy fireplace and stylish French doors in the Great Room beyond

■ A grand entry into the formal Dining Room with a volume ceiling pulling the Great Room and Dining Room together

■ A roomy well-equipped Kitchen that includes a pass-through to the Great Room

■ Large windows in the Breakfast area flooding the room with natural light, making it a bright and cheery place to start your day

■ Split stairs, graced with wood railings, leading to the versatile second floor

■ No materials list is available for this plan

Refer to **Pricing Schedule D** on the order form for pricing information

Rich Classic Lines

■ This plan features:

— Four bedrooms

— Three full and one half baths

■ A vaulted ceiling in the Great Room and the Master Suite

■ A corner fireplace in the Great Room with French doors to the Breakfast/Kitchen area

■ A center island in the Kitchen with an angled sink and a built-in desk and pantry

■ A tray ceiling and recessed hutch area in the formal Dining Room

■ A Master Suite with a walk-in closet, a whirlpool tub, and a double vanity

■ No materials list is available for this plan

FIRST FLOOR — 1,496 SQ. FT.
SECOND FLOOR — 716 SQ. FT.
BASEMENT — 1,420 SQ. FT.
GARAGE — 460 SQ. FT.

TOTAL LIVING AREA:
2,212 SQ. FT.

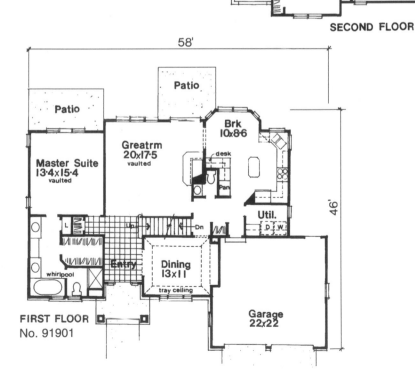

SECOND FLOOR

FIRST FLOOR
No. 91901

To order your Blueprints, call 1-800-235-5700

Refer to **Pricing Schedule B** on the order form for pricing information

Spectacular Traditional

■ This plan features:

— Three bedrooms

— Two full baths

■ The use of gable roofs and the blend of stucco and brick to form a spectacular exterior

■ A high vaulted ceiling and a cozy fireplace, with built-in cabinets in the Den

■ An efficient, U-shaped Kitchen with an adjacent Dining Area

■ A Master Bedroom, with a raised ceiling, that includes a private bath and a walk-in closet

■ Two family bedrooms that share a full hall bath

■ An optional crawl space or slab foundation — please specify when ordering

MAIN AREA — 1,237 SQ. FT.
GARAGE — 436 SQ. FT.

TOTAL LIVING AREA:
1,237 SQ. FT.

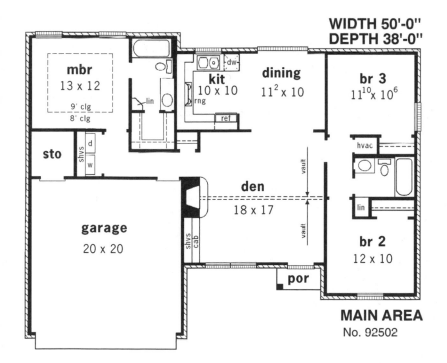

WIDTH 50'-0"
DEPTH 38'-0"

mbr
13 x 12
9' clg
8' clg

kit
10 x 10

dining
11² x 10

br 3
11¹⁰ x 10⁶

sto

den
18 x 17

hvac

garage
20 x 20

br 2
12 x 10

por

MAIN AREA
No. 92502

Refer to **Pricing Schedule A** on the order form for pricing information

Inviting Porch Has Dual Function

■ This plan features:

— Three bedrooms

— One full and one three quarter bath

■ An inviting, wrap-around porch Entry with sliding glass doors leading right into a bayed Dining Room

■ A Living Room with a cozy feeling, enhanced by the fireplace

■ An efficient Kitchen opening to both Dining and Living Rooms

■ A Master Suite with a walk-in closet and private Master Bath

■ An optional basement, slab or crawl space foundation — please specify when ordering

MAIN FLOOR — 1,295 SQ. FT.

TOTAL LIVING AREA:
1,295 SQ. FT.

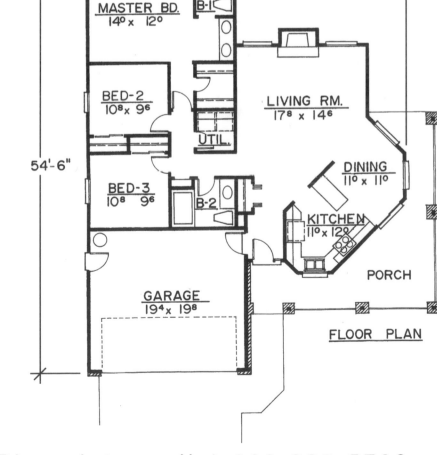

43'-0"

54'-6"

MASTER BD.
14⁰ x 12⁰

B-1

BED-2
10⁸ x 9⁶

UTIL.

LIVING RM.
17⁸ x 14⁶

BED-3
10⁸ 9⁶

B-2

DINING
11⁰ x 11⁰

KITCHEN
11⁰ x 12⁰

PORCH

GARAGE
19⁴ x 19⁸

FLOOR PLAN

To order your Blueprints, call 1-800-235-5700

Refer to **Pricing Schedule A** on
the order form for pricing information

48'-0"

Deck

Brkfst
10-6x14-6

Dining
11x13-4

P

Kitchen

DN

29'-10"

Garage
19-8x23-4

Living Rm
18x12-8
vaulted

UP   DN

FIRST FLOOR

**Loft/
Br 3**
9x11

Br 2
10x9-8

MBr
11-8x13

DN
skylight

open to below

SECOND FLOOR
No. 99315

Lattice Trim Adds Nostalgic Charm

■ This plan features:

— Three bedrooms

— Two full and one half baths

■ Wood and fieldstone exterior

■ A vaulted Living Room with balcony view and floor-to-ceiling corner window treatment

■ A Master Suite with private bath and dressing area

■ A two-car Garage with access to Kitchen

FIRST FLOOR — 668 SQ. FT.
SECOND FLOOR — 691 SQ. FT.

TOTAL LIVING AREA:
1,359 SQ. FT.

Refer to **Pricing Schedule A** on the order form for pricing information

Split Bedroom Plan

■ This plan features:
— Three bedrooms
— Two full baths

■ A tray ceiling giving a decorative touch to the Master Bedroom and a vaulted ceiling topping the five-piece Master Bath

■ A full bath located between the secondary bedrooms

■ A corner fireplace and a vaulted ceiling highlighting the heart of the home, the Family Room

■ A wetbar/serving bar to the Family Room and a built-in pantry add to the convenience of the Kitchen

■ A formal Dining Room crowned in an elegant high ceiling

■ An optional basement, crawl space or slab foundation — please specify when ordering

MAIN FLOOR — 1,429 SQ. FT.
BASEMENT — 1,472 SQ. FT.
GARAGE — 438 SQ. FT.

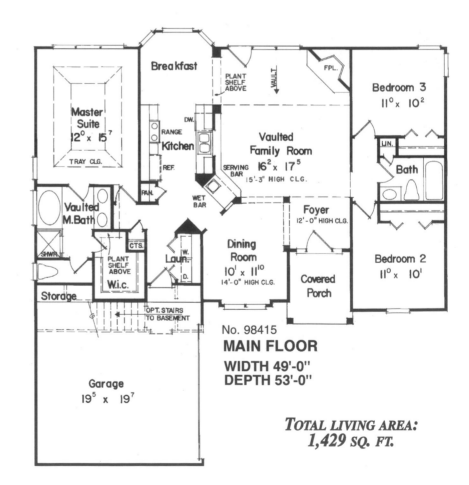

No. 98415
MAIN FLOOR
WIDTH 49'-0"
DEPTH 53'-0"

TOTAL LIVING AREA:
1,429 SQ. FT.

Refer to **Pricing Schedule B** on the order form for pricing information

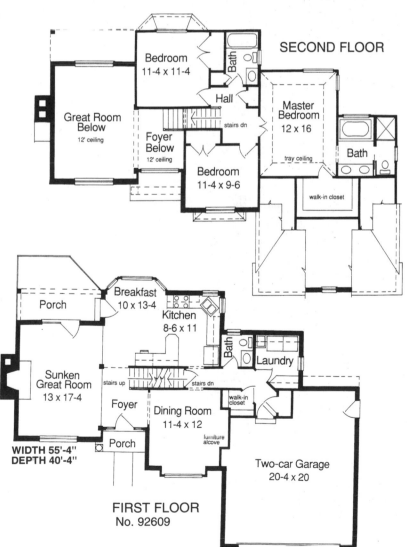

SECOND FLOOR

Bedroom
11-4 x 11-4

Bath

Hall

Great Room
Below
12' ceiling

Foyer
Below
12' ceiling

stairs dn

Master
Bedroom
12 x 16

tray ceiling

Bath

Bedroom
11-4 x 9-6

walk-in closet

Porch

Breakfast
10 x 13-4

Kitchen
8-6 x 11

Bath

Laundry

Sunken
Great Room
13 x 17-4

stairs up

stairs dn

walk-in closet

Foyer

Dining Room
11-4 x 12

furniture alcove

Two-car Garage
20-4 x 20

Porch

WIDTH 55'-4"
DEPTH 40'-4"

FIRST FLOOR
No. 92609

A Little Drama

■ This plan features:

— Three bedrooms

— Two full and one half baths

■ A 12' high Entry with transom and sidelights, multiple gables and a box window

■ A sunken Great Room with a fireplace and access to a rear Porch

■ A Breakfast Bay and Kitchen flowing into each other and accessing a rear Porch

■ A Master Bedroom with a tray ceiling, walk-in closet and a private Master Bath

■ No materials list is available for this plan

FIRST FLOOR — 960 SQ. FT.
SECOND FLOOR — 808 SQ. FT.

TOTAL LIVING AREA:
1,768 SQ. FT.

Refer to **Pricing Schedule A** on the order form for pricing information

Carefree Comfort

- This plan features:
- — Three bedrooms
- — Two full baths
- Cedar shingle siding and flowerboxes
- A heat-circulating fireplace
- A central Foyer separating active areas from the bedroom wing
- A sunny Living Room with an arched window, fireplace, and soaring cathedral ceilings
- A formal Dining Room adjoining the Living Room

MAIN AREA — 1,492 SQ. FT.

TOTAL LIVING AREA:
1,492 SQ. FT.

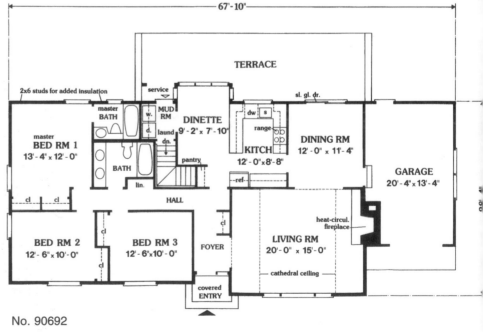

No. 90692

FLOOR PLAN

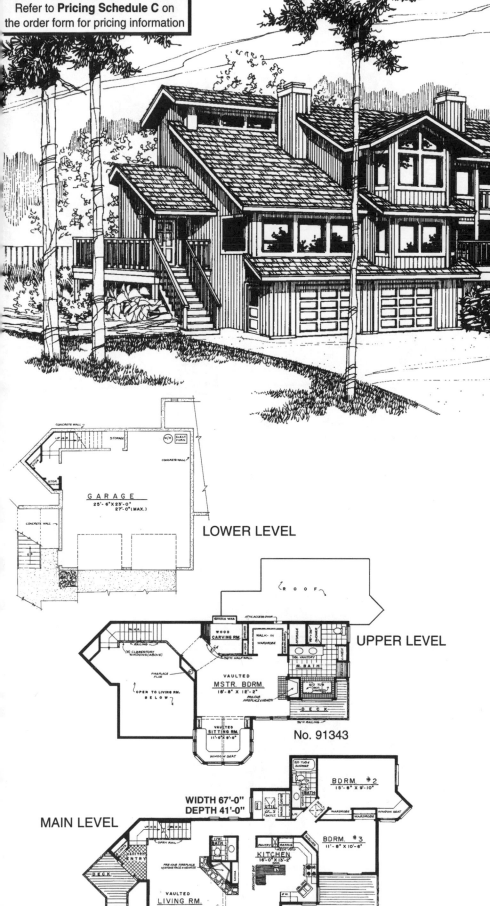

LOWER LEVEL

GARAGE
25'-6" X 23'-0"
27'-0" (MAX.)

UPPER LEVEL

No. 91343

VAULTED
MSTR. BDRM.
18'-8" X 18'-2"

VAULTED
SITTING RM.
11'-0" X 14'-8"

MAIN LEVEL

WIDTH 67'-0"
DEPTH 41'-0"

BDRM. #2
15'-8" X 9'-10"

BDRM. #3
11'-8" X 10'-6"

KITCHEN
16'-0" X 15'-2"

VAULTED
LIVING RM.
15'-4" X 18'-8"

DINING RM.
11'-0" X 11'-0"

DECK

Customized for Sloping View Site

■ This plan features:

— Three bedrooms

— Two full and one half baths

■ A stone-faced fireplace and vaulted ceiling in the Living Room

■ An island food preparation center with a sink and a Breakfast bar in the Kitchen

■ Sliding glass doors leading from the Dining Room to the adjacent deck

■ A Master Suite with a vaulted ceiling, a sitting room, and a lavish Master Bath with a whirlpool tub, skylights, double vanity and a walk-in closet

MAIN LEVEL — 1,338 SQ. FT.
UPPER LEVEL — 763 SQ. FT.
LOWER LEVEL — 61 SQ. FT.

TOTAL LIVING AREA: 2,162 SQ. FT.

Refer to **Pricing Schedule B** on the order form for pricing information

Excellent Choice for First Time Buyer

■ This plan features:

— Three bedrooms

— Two full and one half baths

■ A formal Living Room with a floor-to-ceiling triple window

■ Family Room with a sliding glass door to the backyard, a Utility Closet for washer and dryer and access to the Kitchen

■ Kitchen with a peninsula counter/snackbar

■ Master Bedroom with a recessed dormer window, an oversized, walk-in closet and a private Bath

■ Two bedrooms on the second floor, sharing a full bath and a Playroom

FIRST FLOOR — 805 SQ. FT.
SECOND FLOOR — 961 SQ. FT.
GARAGE — 540 SQ. FT.

TOTAL LIVING AREA: 1,766 SQ. FT.

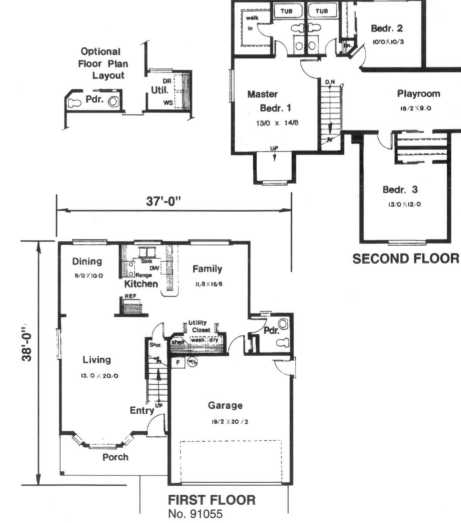

Optional Floor Plan Layout

SECOND FLOOR

FIRST FLOOR
No. 91055

Refer to **Pricing Schedule B** on the order form for pricing information

MAIN AREA
No. 99610

Floor plan showing:

77'-0"

26'-8"

2x6 studs for added insulation

steps — PRIVATE TERRACE — privacy fence — TERRACE

sl. gl. dr.

MASTER BED RM 15' x 12'-8"

master BATH

whirlpool tub

DINING RM 13'-4" x 10'

s. — dw — range — KITCH.

sl. gl. dr.

DINETTE 17' x 11'-4"

MUD RM laundry — w. d. — cl.

STORAGE bicycles etc.

dn.

ref.

cl.

BATH

cl.

HALL

high ceiling

shelves and cabinets

TWO CAR GARAGE 20'-4" x 19'-4"

cl. lin.

BED RM #2 13' x 10'-8"

BED RM #3 12' x 10'-8"

cl.

LIVING RM 20'-6" x 14'

cl. cl.

FOYER divider

heat-circulating fireplace

storage

brick edge

PORCH

columns

TOTAL LIVING AREA:
1,528 SQ. FT.

Greek Revival

■ This plan features:

— Three bedrooms

— Two full baths

■ A large front porch with pediment and columns

■ A stunning, heat-circulating fireplace flanked by cabinetry and shelves in the Living Room

■ A formal Dining Room enhanced by a bay window

■ An efficient, U-shaped Kitchen with a peninsula counter and informal Dinette area

■ A Master Suite with a private Master Bath and direct access to the private terrace

■ Two additional bedrooms sharing a full hall bath

MAIN AREA — 1,528 SQ. FT.
BASEMENT — 1,367 SQ. FT.
GARAGE & STORAGE — 494 SQ. FT.

Refer to **Pricing Schedule B** on the order form for pricing information

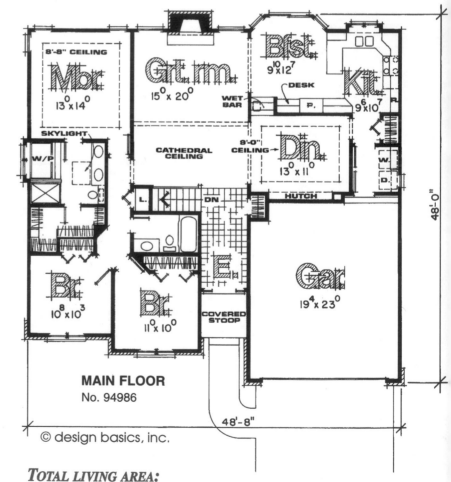

Ten Foot Entry

■ This plan features:

—Three bedrooms

—Two full baths

■ Large volume Great Room highlighted by a fireplace flanked by windows

■ See-through wetbar enhancing the Breakfast area and the Dining Room

■ Decorative ceiling treatment giving elegance to the Dining Room

■ Fully equipped Kitchen with a planning desk and a pantry

■ Roomy Master Bedroom suite has a volume ceiling and special amenities; a skylighted dressing bath area, plant shelf, a large walk-in closet, a double vanity and a whirlpool tub

■ Secondary bedrooms with ample closets sharing a convenient hall bath

MAIN FLOOR — 1,604 SQ. FT.
GARAGE — 466 SQ. FT.

MAIN FLOOR
No. 94986

© design basics, inc.

TOTAL LIVING AREA:
1,604 SQ. FT.

To order your Blueprints, call 1-800-235-5700

Refer to **Pricing Schedule C** on the order form for pricing information

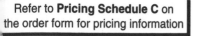

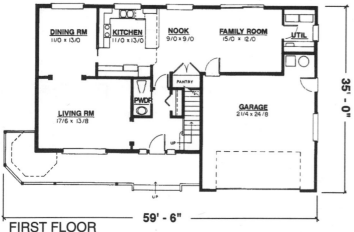

FIRST FLOOR
No. 91053

FIRST FLOOR — 1,150 SQ. FT.
SECOND FLOOR — 949 SQ. FT.
GARAGE — 484 SQ. FT.

TOTAL LIVING AREA:
2,099 SQ. FT.

SECOND FLOOR

Updated Victorian

■ This plan features:

— Three bedrooms

— Two full and one half baths

■ Classic Victorian exterior design accented by a wonderful turret room and second floor covered porch

■ Spacious formal Living Room leading into a formal Dining Room for ease in entertaining

■ Efficient, U-shaped Kitchen with loads of counter space and a peninsula snackbar, opens to an eating Nook and Family Room for informal gatherings and activities

■ Elegant Master Suite with a unique, octagon Sitting area, a private Porch, an oversized, walk-in closet and private bath with a double vanity and a window tub

■ Two additional bedrooms with ample closets share a full bath

Refer to **Pricing Schedule A** on the order form for pricing information

A Stylish, Open Concept Home

■ This plan features:

— Three bedrooms

— Two full baths

■ An angled Entry creating the illusion of space

■ Two square columns that flank the bar and separate the Kitchen from the Living Room

■ A Dining Room that may service both formal and informal occasions

■ A Master Bedroom with a large walk-in closet

■ A large Master Bath with a dual vanity, linen closet and whirlpool tub/shower combination

■ Two additional bedrooms that share a full bath

■ No materials list available for this plan

MAIN FLOOR — 1,282 SQ. FT.
GARAGE — 501 SQ. FT.

TOTAL LIVING AREA:
1,282 SQ. FT.

WIDTH 48–10

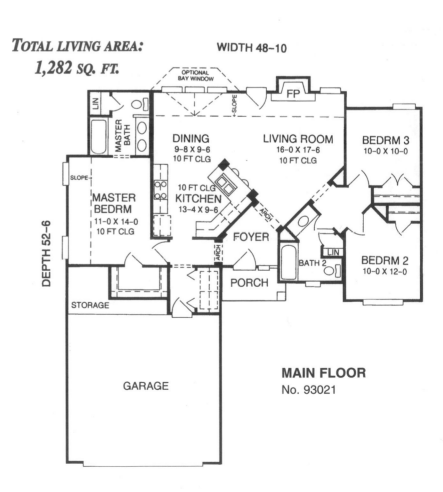

MAIN FLOOR
No. 93021

Refer to **Pricing Schedule B** on the order form for pricing information

© design basics, inc.

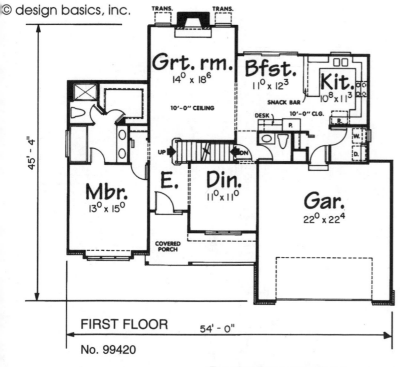

TRANS.   TRANS.

Grt. rm.
14⁰ x 18⁶

10'-0" CEILING

Bfst.
11⁰ x 12³

SNACK BAR

Kit.
10⁸ x 11³

DESK   10'-0" CLG.

UP   DN

Mbr.
13⁰ x 15⁰

E.   **Din.**
11⁰ x 11⁰

Gar.
22⁰ x 22⁴

COVERED PORCH

FIRST FLOOR   54' - 0"

45' - 4"

No. 99420

TOTAL LIVING AREA:
1,694 SQ. FT.

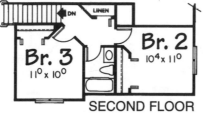

DN   LINEN

Br. 3
11⁰ x 10⁰

Br. 2
10⁴ x 11⁰

SECOND FLOOR

Simplicity at it's Finest

■ This plan features:

— Three bedrooms

— Two full and one half baths

■ Covered porch providing a nostalgic feel for the elevation

■ Volume Great Room offering a fireplace with transom windows to either side

■ Built-in planning desk and pantry in the Breakfast Area

■ Snack bar for informal meals highlighting the Kitchen

■ Formal dining room overlooking the porch with easy access to the Kitchen

■ Isolated Master Suite with private five-piece bath and walk-in closet

FIRST FLOOR — 1,298 SQ. FT.
SECOND FLOOR — 396 SQ. FT.
BASEMENT — 1,298 SQ. FT.
GARAGE — 513 SQ. FT.

Refer to **Pricing Schedule A** on the order form for pricing information

Contemporary Traditions

■ This plan features:

— Three bedrooms

— Two full baths

■ A vaulted ceiling in the Living Room with a half-round transom window and a fireplace

■ A Dining area flowing into either the Kitchen or the Living Room with sliders to the Deck

■ A main floor Master Suite with corner windows, walk-in closet, and private access to a full bath

■ Two additional bedrooms on the second floor, one with a walk-in closet, having use of a full bath

MAIN FLOOR — 857 SQ. FT.
UPPER FLOOR — 446 SQ. FT.

TOTAL LIVING AREA:
1,303 SQ. FT.

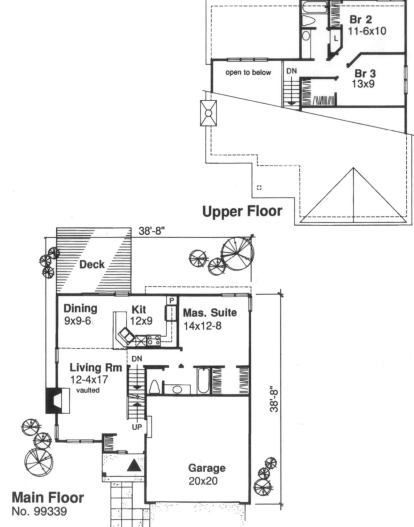

Upper Floor

Br 2
11-6x10

Br 3
13x9

open to below   DN

38'-8"

Deck

Dining
9x9-6

Kit
12x9

Mas. Suite
14x12-8

P

Living Rm
12-4x17
vaulted

DN

UP

Garage
20x20

38'-8"

Main Floor
No. 99339

An
EXCLUSIVE DESIGN
By Independent Designs

MAIN FLOOR
No. 93909

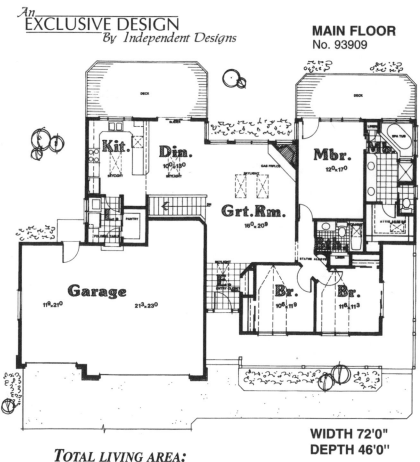

WIDTH 72'0"
DEPTH 46'0"

TOTAL LIVING AREA:
1,716 SQ. FT.

Inviting Wrap-Around Porch

■ This plan features:

— Three bedrooms

— Two full baths

■ A warm and inviting welcome, achieved by a wrap-around porch

■ A corner gas fireplace and two skylights in the Great Room

■ The Dining Room naturally lighted by the sliding glass doors to a rear deck and a skylight above

■ U-shaped Kitchen separated from the Dining Room by a breakfast bar and including another skylight

■ Luxurious Master Bedroom equipped with a plush Bath and access to a private deck

■ Two additional bedrooms sharing the full bath in the hall

■ No materials list is available for this plan

MAIN FLOOR — 1,716 SQ. FT.

Refer to **Pricing Schedule B** on the order form for pricing information

Compact Victorian
Ideal for Narrow Lot

- This plan features:

— Three bedrooms

— Three full baths

- A large, front Parlor with a raised hearth fireplace

- A Dining Room with a sunny bay window

- An efficient galley Kitchen serving the formal Dining Room and informal Breakfast Room

- A beautiful Master Suite with two closets, an oversized tub and double vanity, plus a private sitting room with a bayed window and vaulted ceiling

- An optional basement, crawl space or slab foundation — please specify when ordering

FIRST FLOOR — 954 SQ. FT.
SECOND FLOOR — 783 SQ. FT.

TOTAL LIVING AREA:
1,737 SQ. FT.

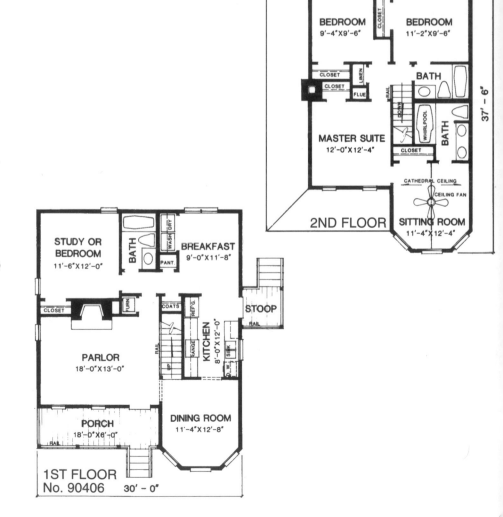

Refer to **Pricing Schedule C** on the order form for pricing information

Cozy Traditional with Style

- This plan features:
  — Three bedrooms
  — Two full baths
- A convenient one-level design
- A galley-style Kitchen that shares a snack bar with the spacious Gathering Room
- A focal point fireplace making the Gathering Room warm and inviting
- An ample Master Suite with a luxury Bath which contains a whirlpool tub and separate Dressing Room
- Two additional bedrooms, one that could double as a Study, located at the front of the house

MAIN AREA — 1,830 SQ. FT.
BASEMENT — 1,830 SQ. FT.

TOTAL LIVING AREA: 1,830 SQ. FT.

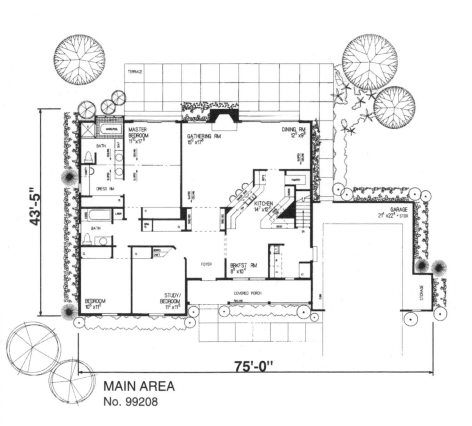

MAIN AREA
No. 99208

75'-0"

43'-5"

Refer to **Pricing Schedule B** on the order form for pricing information

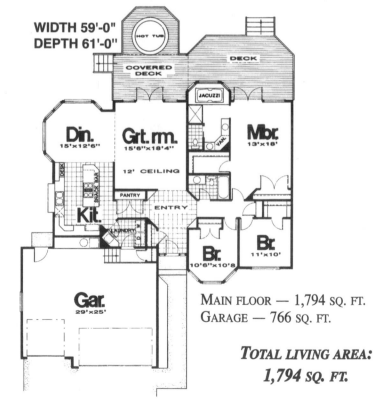

Style All The Way Around

■ This plan features:

— Three Bedrooms

— Two full baths

■ Great Room with twelve foot ceilings and dormer window

■ Dining Room with double bay windows

■ Center island/snack bar in the large Kitchen

■ Ample pantry located across from the laundry room, just steps away from Kitchen

■ Bay window accents the front bedroom

■ Master Suite enhanced by a bayed whirlpool tub area, a wrap around vanity, a private toilet and a separate shower

■ A grand covered deck with hot tub accessed from the Great room or the Master Suite

■ No materials list is available for this plan

WIDTH 59'-0"
DEPTH 61'-0"

MAIN FLOOR — 1,794 SQ. FT.
GARAGE — 766 SQ. FT.

TOTAL LIVING AREA:
1,794 SQ. FT.

MAIN FLOOR
No. 94024

An
EXCLUSIVE DESIGN *By*
CRANE DESIGN inc.

To order your Blueprints, call 1-800-235-5700

Refer to **Pricing Schedule C** on the order form for pricing information

An
EXCLUSIVE DESIGN
By Jannis Vann & Associates, Inc.

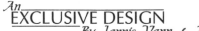

SECOND FLOOR
No. 93212

STUDY
11·2 x 11·1

BEDROOM 2
13·6 x 13·4

BATH

BEDROOM 3
12·0 x 13·4

BONUS ROOM
11·8 x 21·10

TOTAL LIVING AREA:
2,091 SQ. FT.

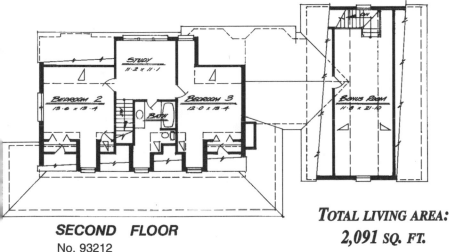

72'-0"

SUN DECK
16·8 x 14·0

DINING ROOM
13·0 x 13·6

BREAKFAST
10 x 9·4

LAUNDRY

STOR.

KITCHEN
12·0 x 8·0

DOUBLE GARAGE
21·4 x 21·8

MASTER BATH

MASTER BEDROOM
13·6 x 17·0

LIVING AREA
20·0 x 13·6

FOYER

PORCH

38'-0"

FIRST FLOOR

Modern Conveniences

- This plan features:
  — Three bedrooms
  — Two full and one half baths
- Living Room with a cozy fireplace
- Formal Dining Room with a bay window
- A sunny Breakfast Nook with a bay window overlooking the deck
- Master Suite with jacuzzi and a step-in shower, double vanity, and a walk-in closet
- A second floor study or hobby room overlooking the deck
- A future Bonus Room
- No materials list is available for this plan
- An optional basement, slab or crawl space foundation — please specify when ordering

FIRST FLOOR — 1,362 SQ. FT.
SECOND FLOOR — 729 SQ. FT.
BONUS ROOM — 384 SQ. FT.
BASEMENT — 988 SQ. FT.
GARAGE — 559 SQ. FT.

Refer to **Pricing Schedule B** on the order form for pricing information

© 1995 Donald A Gardner Architects, Inc.

Tremendous Curb Appeal

- This plan features:
  — Three bedrooms
  — Two full baths
- Wrap-around porch sheltering entry
- Great Room topped by a cathedral ceiling and enhanced by a fireplace
- Great Room, Dining Room and Kitchen open to each other for a feeling of spaciousness
- Pantry, skylight and peninsula counter add to the comfort and efficiency of the Kitchen
- Cathedral ceiling crowns the Master Suite and has many amenities; walk-in and linen closets, luxurious private bath
- Bedroom/Study topped by a cathedral ceiling
- Skylight over full hall bath naturally illuminates the room

MAIN FLOOR — 1,246 SQ. FT.
GARAGE — 420 SQ. FT.

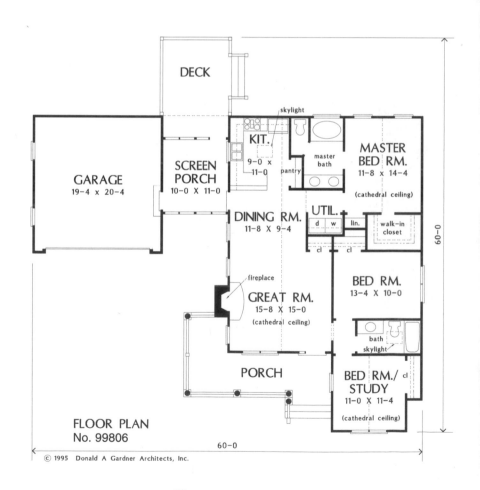

FLOOR PLAN
No. 99806

© 1995 Donald A Gardner Architects, Inc.

TOTAL LIVING AREA:
1,246 SQ. FT.

To order your Blueprints, call 1-800-235-5700

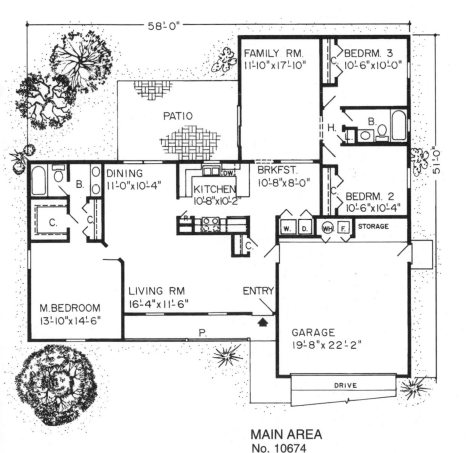

MAIN AREA
No. 10674

Carefree Convenience

■ This plan features:

— Three bedrooms

— Two full baths

■ A galley Kitchen, centrally located between the Dining, Breakfast and Living Room areas

■ A huge Family Room which exits onto the Patio

■ A Master Suite with double closets and vanity with two additional bedrooms share a full-half bath

MAIN AREA — 1,600 SQ. FT.
GARAGE — 465 SQ. FT.

TOTAL LIVING AREA:
1,600 SQ. FT.

Refer to **Pricing Schedule B** on the order form for pricing information

Charming, Compact and Convenient

■ This plan features:

— Three bedrooms

— Two full and one half bath

■ Double dormer, arched window and Covered Porch add light and space

■ Open Foyer graced by banister staircase and balcony

■ Spacious Activity Room with a pre-fab fireplace opens to formal Dining Room

■ Country-size Kitchen/Breakfast area with island counter and access to Sun Deck and Laundry/Garage entry

■ First floor bedroom highlighted by lovely arched window below a tray ceiling and a pampering bath

■ Two upstairs bedrooms share a dual vanity bath

■ An optional basement or crawl space foundation — please specify when ordering

FIRST FLOOR — 1,165 SQ. FT.
SECOND FLOOR — 587 SQ. FT.
GARAGE — 455 SQ. FT.
BASEMENT — 1165 SQ. FT.

TOTAL LIVING AREA: 1,752 SQ. FT.

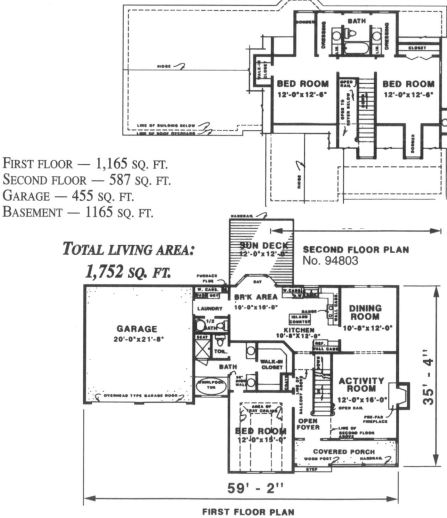

SECOND FLOOR PLAN
No. 94803

FIRST FLOOR PLAN

To order your Blueprints, call 1-800-235-5700

Lots of Light

■ This plan features:

— Three bedrooms

— One full and one three quarter bath

■ Skylight brightens entry into Living Room with vaulted ceiling, palladian window and an inviting fireplace

■ Convenient Dining area with decorative window extends from Living Room for easy entertaining

■ Efficient Kitchen with pantry, corner sink and eating Nook with an arched window and Patio access

■ Vaulted ceiling tops Master Suite containing a decorative window, double vanity and walk-in closet

■ Two additional bedrooms with ample closets share a full bath

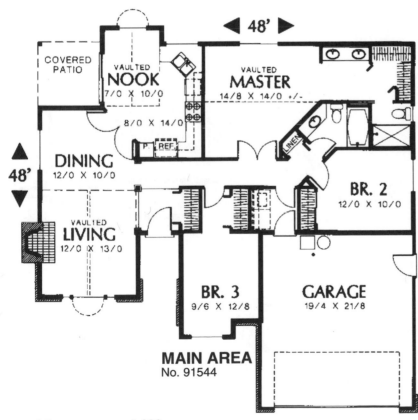

MAIN FLOOR — 1,338 SQ. FT.

TOTAL LIVING AREA:
1,338 SQ. FT.

Refer to **Pricing Schedule B** on the order form for pricing information

Open Space Living

■ This plan features:

— Three bedrooms

— Two full and one half baths

■ A wrap-around Deck providing outdoor living space, ideal for a sloping lot

■ Two and a half-story glass wall and two separate atrium doors providing natural light for the Living/Dining Room area

■ An efficient galley Kitchen with easy access to the Dining area

■ A Master Bedroom suite with a half bath and ample closet space

■ Another bedroom on the first floor adjoins a full hall bath

■ A second floor Bedroom/Studio, with a private Deck, adjacent to a full hall bath and a Loft area

FIRST FLOOR — 1,086 SQ. FT.
SECOND FLOOR — 466 SQ. FT.
BASEMENT — 1,080 SQ. FT.

An
EXCLUSIVE DESIGN
By Westhome Planners, Ltd.

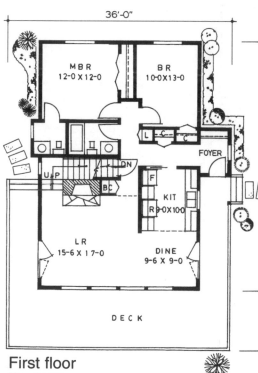

First floor
No. 90844

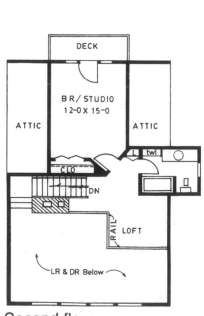

Second floor

TOTAL LIVING AREA:
1,552 SQ. FT.

To order your Blueprints, call 1-800-235-5700

Refer to **Pricing Schedule E** on the order form for pricing information

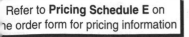

© design basics, inc.

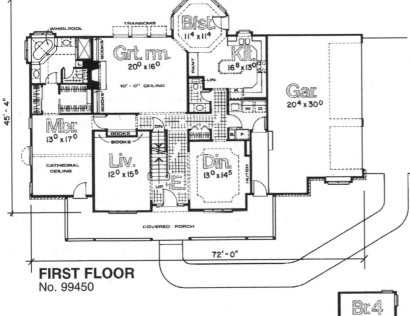

45' - 4"

72' - 0"

FIRST FLOOR
No. 99450

TOTAL LIVING AREA:
2,695 SQ. FT.

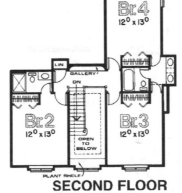

SECOND FLOOR

Fashionable Country Style

■ This plan features:

— Four bedrooms

— Two full, one three quarter and one half baths

■ The large covered front Porch adds old fashioned appeal to this modern floor plan

■ Dining Room with a decorative ceiling and a built-in hutch

■ Kitchen has a center island and access to gazebo shaped Nook

■ Great Room is accented by transom windows and a fireplace with bookcases on each side

■ The Master Bedroom has a cathedral ceiling, a door to the front porch, and a large bath with a whirlpool tub

■ An optional basement or slab foundation — please specify when ordering

FIRST FLOOR — 1,881 SQ. FT.
SECOND FLOOR — 814 SQ. FT.
GARAGE — 534 SQ. FT.

Refer to **Pricing Schedule B** on the order form for pricing information

Carefree Comfort

- ■ This plan features:
- — Three bedrooms
- — Two full baths
- ■ A dramatic vaulted Foyer
- ■ A range top island Kitchen with a sunny eating Nook surrounded by a built-in planter
- ■ A vaulted ceiling in the Great Room with a built-in bar and corner fireplace
- ■ A bayed Dining Room that combines with the Great Room for a spacious feeling
- ■ A Master Bedroom with a private reading nook, vaulted ceiling, walk-in closet, and a well appointed private Bath
- ■ Two additional bedrooms sharing a full hall bath
- ■ An optional basement, slab or crawl space foundation— please specify when ordering

MAIN AREA — 1,665 SQ. FT.
GARAGE — 2-CAR

TOTAL LIVING AREA:
1,665 SQ. FT.

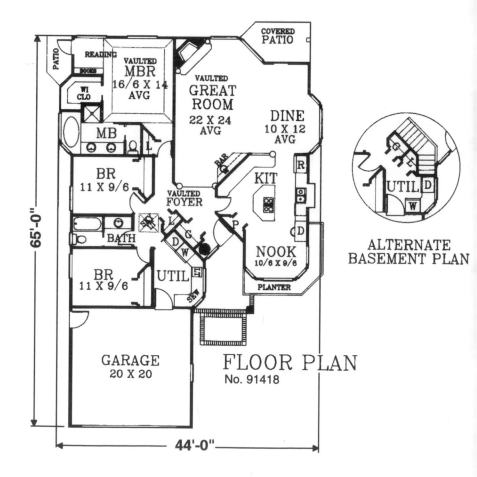

ALTERNATE
BASEMENT PLAN

FLOOR PLAN
No. 91418

To order your Blueprints, call 1-800-235-5700

PLAN NO. 90409

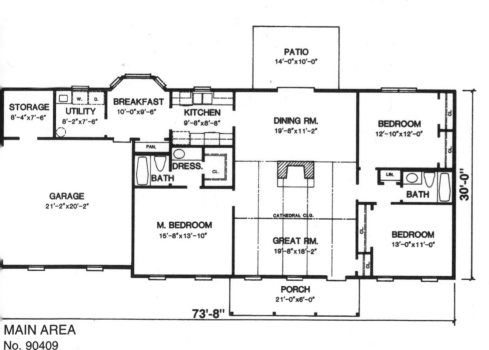

PATIO
14'-0"x10'-0"

STORAGE
8'-4"x7'-6"

UTILITY
8'-2"x7'-6"

BREAKFAST
10'-0"x9'-6"

KITCHEN
9'-8"x8'-8"

DINING RM.
19'-8"x11'-2"

BEDROOM
12'-10"x12'-0"

PAN.

DRESS.

BATH

LIN.

BATH

GARAGE
21'-2"x20'-2"

M. BEDROOM
15'-8"x13'-10"

CATHEDRAL CLG.

GREAT RM.
19'-8"x18'-2"

BEDROOM
13'-0"x11'-0"

30'-0"

PORCH
21'-0"x6'-0"

73'-8"

MAIN AREA
No. 90409

Rocking Chair Living

■ This plan features:

— Three bedrooms

— Two full baths

■ A massive fireplace separating Living and Dining Rooms

■ An isolated Master Suite with a walk-in closet and a helpful compartmentalized bath

■ A galley-type Kitchen between the Breakfast Room and Dining Room

■ An optional basement, slab or crawl space foundation — please specify when ordering

MAIN AREA — 1,670 SQ. FT.

TOTAL LIVING AREA:
1,670 SQ. FT.

Refer to **Pricing Schedule B** on the order form for pricing information

One-Level with a Twist

■ This plan features:

— Three bedrooms

— Two full baths

■ Wide-open active areas that are centrally-located

■ A spacious Dining, Living, and Kitchen area

■ A Master Suite at the rear of the house with a full bath

■ Two additional bedrooms that share a full hall bath and the quiet atmosphere that results from an intelligent design

MAIN AREA — 1,575 SQ. FT.
BASEMENT —1,575 SQ. FT.
GARAGE — 475 SQ. FT.

TOTAL LIVING AREA:
1,575 SQ. FT.

An
EXCLUSIVE DESIGN
By Karl Kreeger

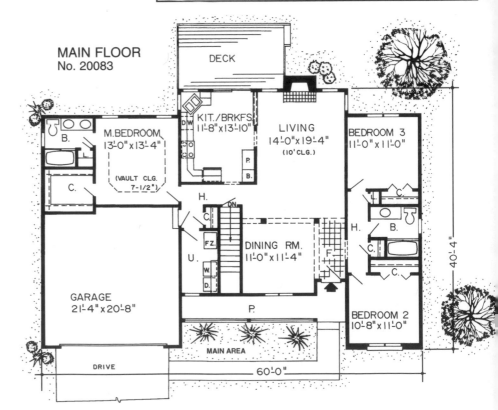

MAIN FLOOR
No. 20083

DECK

KIT./BRKFS.
11'-8"x13'-10"

LIVING
14'-0"x19'-4"
(10' CLG.)

BEDROOM 3
11'-0" x 11'-0"

M. BEDROOM
13'-0"x13'-4"

(VAULT CLG.
7-1/2")

B.

C.

H.

DN

DINING RM.
11'-0"x11'-4"

FZ.

U.

W.

D.

B.

H.

C.

GARAGE
21'-4"x20'-8"

P.

BEDROOM 2
10'-8"x11'-0"

MAIN AREA

DRIVE

60'-0"

40'-4"

To order your Blueprints, call 1-800-235-5700

Refer to **Pricing Schedule C** on the order form for pricing information

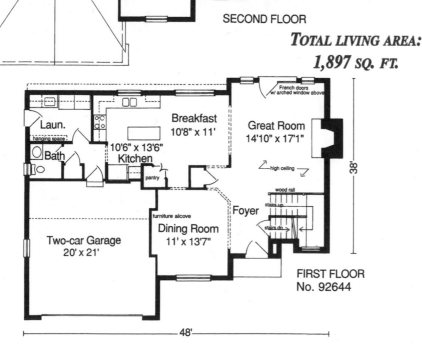

walk-in closet

Master Bedroom
12' x 14'11"

Bedroom
10'6" x 11'2"

Great Room Below

computer desk

Bath

Bath

Balcony

Bedroom
11' x 12'

stairs dn

window seat

SECOND FLOOR

TOTAL LIVING AREA:
1,897 SQ. FT.

Laun.

hanging space

Bath

Breakfast
10'8" x 11'

10'6" x 13'6"
Kitchen

pantry

French doors w/ arched window above

Great Room
14'10" x 17'1"

high ceiling

38'

wood rail

stairs up

Foyer

furniture alcove

stairs dn

Two-car Garage
20' x 21'

Dining Room
11' x 13'7"

FIRST FLOOR
No. 92644

48'

Distinctive Detail and Design

■ This plan features:

— Three bedrooms

— Two full and one half baths

■ Impressive pilaster entry into open Foyer with landing staircase enhanced by decorative windows

■ Great Room with a hearth fireplace, French doors with arched window and a high ceiling

■ Dining Room enhanced by furniture alcove

■ L-shaped Kitchen with work island, walk-in pantry, breakfast area, adjoining Laundry, half bath and Garage entry

■ Master Bedroom offers a walk-in closet, and plush bath with two vanities and whirlpool tub

■ Two additional bedrooms share a full bath and computer desk

■ No materials list is available for this plan

FIRST FLOOR — 1,036 SQ. FT.
SECOND FLOOR — 861 SQ. FT.
GARAGE — 420 SQ. FT.

Refer to **Pricing Schedule A** on the order form for pricing information

A Lovely Small Home

■ This plan features:

— Three bedrooms

— Two full baths

■ A large Living Room with a ten foot ceiling

■ A Dining Room with a distinctive bay window

■ A Breakfast Room located off the Kitchen

■ A Kitchen with an angled eating bar that opens to the Living Room

■ A Master Suite with ten foot ceiling, huge walk-in closets, his-n-her vanities, a combination whirlpool tub and shower

■ Two additional bedrooms that share a full bath

■ No materials list is available for this plan

MAIN AREA — 1,402 SQ. FT.
GARAGE — 437 SQ. FT.

WIDTH 59–10

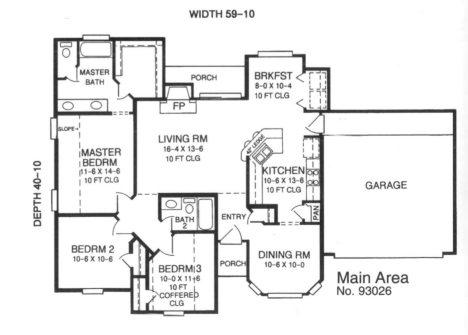

DEPTH 40–10

MASTER BATH

PORCH

BRKFST
8–0 X 10–4
10 FT CLG

FP

SLOPE

MASTER BEDRM
11–6 X 14–6
10 FT CLG

LIVING RM
16–4 X 13–6
10 FT CLG

40" LEDGE

KITCHEN
10–6 X 13–6
10 FT CLG

GARAGE

BEDRM 2
10–6 X 10–6

BATH 2

ENTRY

PAN

BEDRM 3
10–0 X 11–6
10 FT COFFERED CLG

PORCH

DINING RM
10–6 X 10–0

Main Area
No. 93026

TOTAL LIVING AREA:
1,402 SQ. FT.

To order your Blueprints, call 1-800-235-5700

Refer to **Pricing Schedule B** on the order form for pricing information

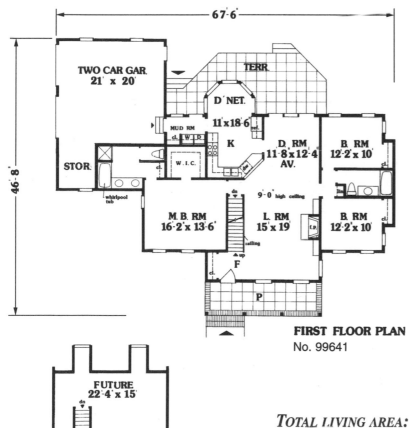

FIRST FLOOR PLAN
No. 99641

67'-6"

46'-8"

TWO CAR GAR.
21' x 20'

TERR.

D´NET.
11'x18-6"

MUD RM

STOR.

K

D. RM
11-8"x12-4"
AV.

B. RM
12-2' x 10'

W.I.C.

whirlpool
tub

9'-0" high ceiling

M. B. RM
16-2' x 13-6'

L. RM
15' x 19'

B. RM
12-2' x 10'

f.p.

F

railing

up

P

FUTURE
22'-4' x 15'

SECOND FLOOR PLAN

TOTAL LIVING AREA:
1,567 SQ. FT.

Southern Traditional Flavor

■ This plan features:

— Three bedrooms

— Two full baths

■ A varied roof line with dormers and a charming colonnaded front porch sheltering the entrance

■ Living Room enhanced by nine foot ceilings and a bookcase flanked fireplace

■ Two mullioned French doors leading from the Dining Room to the rear terrace

■ Laundry area/Mudroom between the Garage and Kitchen

■ Master Suite with walk-in closet and a compartmented bath with a separate stall shower, whirlpool tub and double vanity

■ Two additional bedrooms that share a full hall bath

FIRST FLOOR — 1,567 SQ. FT.
SECOND FLOOR(BONUS) — 462 SQ. FT.
BASEMENT — 1,567 SQ. FT.
GARAGE — 504 SQ. FT.

With Room to Expand

- This plan features:
- — Three bedrooms
- — Two full and one half baths
- An impressive two-story Foyer
- The Kitchen is equipped with ample cabinet and counter space
- Spacious Family Room flows from the Breakfast Bay and is highlighted by a fireplace and a French door to the rear yard
- The Master Suite is topped by a tray ceiling and is enhanced by a vaulted, five-piece master bath
- Two additional bedrooms share the full bath in the hall
- An optional crawl space or basement foundation — please specify when ordering

FIRST FLOOR — 882 SQ. FT.
SECOND FLOOR — 793 SQ. FT.
BONUS ROOM — 416 SQ. FT.
BASEMENT — 882 SQ. FT.
GARAGE — 510 SQ. FT.

TOTAL LIVING AREA:
1,675 SQ. FT.

SECOND FLOOR PLAN

SHWR.
PLANT SHELF ABOVE
Vaulted M.Bath
LINEN
W.i.c.
Laund.
D. W.
TRAY CLG.
Master Suite
17⁰ x 12⁰
LINEN
Bath
OVERLOOK
STAIRS DOWN
Bedroom 3
11⁴ x 10⁰
Foyer Below
SHELF
Bedroom 2
10² x 11⁴

SECOND FLOOR PLAN W/
Opt. Bonus Room

W.i.c.
SHWR.
LINEN
PLANT SHELF ABOVE
Vaulted M.Bath
Opt. Bonus Room
15⁵ x 20³
W.i.c.
D. W.
W.i.c.
Bedroom 3
11⁴ x 10⁰

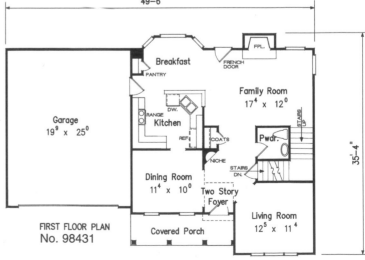

FIRST FLOOR PLAN
No. 98431

49'–6"
35'–4"

Garage
19⁹ x 25⁰
Breakfast
PANTRY
FPL.
FRENCH DOOR
Family Room
17⁴ x 12⁰
RANGE
Kitchen
DW.
REF.
COATS
NICHE
Pwdr.
STAIRS UP
STAIRS DN.
Dining Room
11⁴ x 10⁰
Two Story Foyer
Living Room
12⁵ x 11⁴
Covered Porch

To order your Blueprints, call 1-800-235-5700

Refer to **Pricing Schedule B** on the order form for pricing information

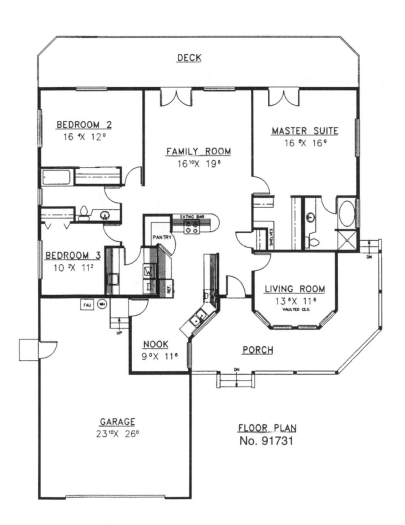

DECK

BEDROOM 2
16⁴X 12⁰

FAMILY ROOM
16¹⁰X 19⁶

MASTER SUITE
16⁶X 16⁶

EATING BAR

PANTRY

SHELVES

BEDROOM 3
10²X 11²

LIVING ROOM
13⁶X 11⁶
VAULTED CLG.

REF.

FAU WH

DN

NOOK
9⁰X 11⁶

PORCH

UP

DN

GARAGE
23¹⁰X 26⁰

FLOOR PLAN
No. 91731

Country Style & Charm

■ This plan features:

— Three bedrooms

— Two full baths

■ Brick accents, front facing gable, and railed wrap-around covered porch

■ A built-in range and oven in a L-shaped Kitchen

■ A Nook with garage access for convenient unloading of groceries and other supplies

■ A bay window wrapping around the front of the formal Living Room

■ A Master Suite with French doors opening to the deck

MAIN AREA — 1,857 SQ. FT.
GARAGE — 681 SQ. FT.
WIDTH — 51'-6"
DEPTH — 65'-0"

TOTAL LIVING AREA:
1,857 SQ. FT.

Refer to **Pricing Schedule B** on the order form for pricing information

Daytime Delight

◼ This plan features:

— Three bedrooms

— Two full baths

◼ Adjoining living and dining rooms enhanced with vaulted ceiling and huge windows

◼ A centrally-located Kitchen with a double sink, and ample cabinet and counter space

◼ A glass-walled eating Nook with access to a covered porch

◼ A vaulted ceiling in the Family Room, with a focal point fireplace

◼ An exciting Master Suite with a vaulted ceiling, a walk-in closet and a private double-vanity bath

◼ Two additional bedrooms, one with French doors, served by a full hall bath

MAIN FLOOR — 1,653 SQ. FT.

TOTAL LIVING AREA:
1,653 SQ. FT.

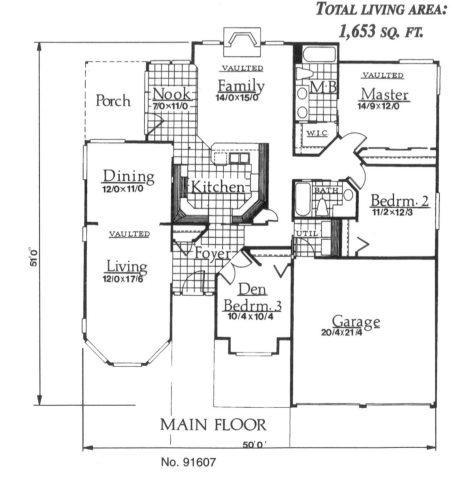

MAIN FLOOR

No. 91607

Refer to **Pricing Schedule C** on the order form for pricing information

© 1994 Donald A Gardner Architects, Inc.

B. NATHAN

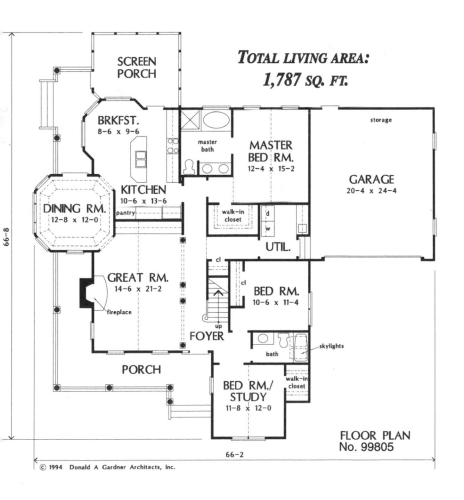

TOTAL LIVING AREA:
1,787 SQ. FT.

SCREEN PORCH

BRKFST.
8-6 x 9-6

master bath

storage

MASTER BED RM.
12-4 x 15-2

GARAGE
20-4 x 24-4

KITCHEN
10-6 x 13-6

DINING RM.
12-8 x 12-0

pantry

walk-in closet

d
w

UTIL.

GREAT RM.
14-6 x 21-2

fireplace

cl

cl

BED RM.
10-6 x 11-4

up

FOYER

PORCH

bath

skylights

BED RM./ STUDY
11-8 x 12-0

walk-in closet

66-8

66-2

FLOOR PLAN
No. 99805

© 1994 Donald A Gardner Architects, Inc.

Enticing Design

■ This plan features:

—Three bedrooms

—Two full baths

■ A Great Room enhanced by a fireplace, cathedral ceiling, and built-in bookshelves

■ A Kitchen designed for efficiency with a food preparation island and a pantry

■ A Master Suite topped by a cathedral ceiling and pampered by a luxurious bath and a walk-in closet

■ Two additional bedrooms, one with a cathedral ceiling and a walk-in closet, sharing a skylit bath

■ A second floor bonus room, perfect for a study or play area

■ An optional basement or crawl space foundation — please specify when ordering

MAIN FLOOR — 1,787 SQ. FT.
GARAGE & STORAGE — 521 SQ. FT.
BONUS ROOM — 326 SQ. FT.

Refer to **Pricing Schedule A** on the order form for pricing information

Spanish Style Affordable Home

■ This plan features:

— Two bedrooms

— Two full baths

■ A large Master Suite with vaulted ceilings and a handicap accessible private bath

■ Vaulted ceilings in the Great Room

■ An open Kitchen area with an eating bar

MAIN AREA — 1,111 SQ. FT.

TOTAL LIVING AREA:
1,111 SQ. FT.

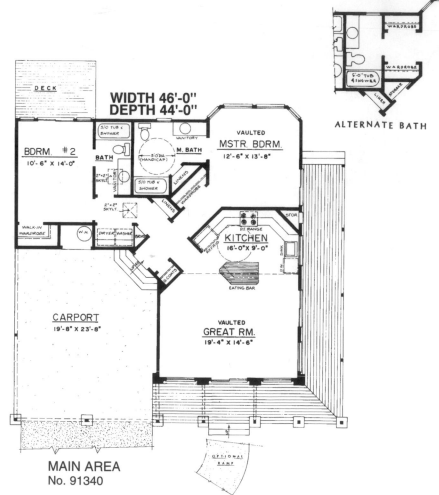

WIDTH 46'-0"
DEPTH 44'-0"

DECK

BDRM. #2
10'-6" X 14'-0"

BATH

5/0 TUB & SHOWER

2'x2' SKYLT.

VANITORY

5'-0" DIA (HANDICAP)

M. BATH

VANITORY

LINENS

5/0 TUB & SHOWER

VAULTED
MSTR. BDRM.
12'-6" X 13'-8"

WARDROBE

LINENS

WALK-IN WARDROSE

W. H.

DRYER WASHER

KITCHEN
16'-0" X 9'-0"

DI RANGE

OTOR

EATING BAR

CARPORT
19'-8" X 23'-8"

VAULTED
GREAT RM.
19'-4" X 14'-6"

OPTIONAL RAMP

MAIN AREA
No. 91340

ALTERNATE BATH

WARDROBE

WARDROBE

5'-0" TUB & SHOWER

To order your Blueprints, call 1-800-235-5700

Turret Master Bedroom

- This plan features:
- — Three bedrooms
- — Two full and one half baths
- Curved glass entry into two-story Foyer with graceful, apron staircase
- Sunken Great Room with focal point fireplace and atrium door
- Efficient U-shaped Kitchen with work island, built-in pantry, Breakfast alcove and adjoining Dining Room with bay window
- Sloped ceiling accents window alcove in Master Bedroom offering a plush bath
- Two bedrooms have private access to a double vanity bath
- No materials list is available for this plan

FIRST FLOOR — 1,625 SQ. FT.
SECOND FLOOR — 475 SQ. FT.
GARAGE — 437 SQ. FT.

TOTAL LIVING AREA:
2,101 SQ. FT.

SECOND FLOOR

Bedroom 15 x 10-8

Great Room Below

Bath

Bedroom 14 x 10-6

Foyer Below

FIRST FLOOR
No. 92610

WIDTH 59'-0"
DEPTH 60'-8"

Deck

Breakfast 9-2 x 16

Sunken Great Room 16-10 x 21

Kitchen 8 x 13-4

Bath

Walk-in closet

Dining Room 16 x 11-8

Foyer

Master Bedroom 14 x 17-4

Bath

Slope ceiling   Slope ceiling

Hall

Laundry

Two-car Garage 21 x 20-8

Refer to **Pricing Schedule C** on the order form for pricing information

Open Plan Accented By Loft, Windows and Decks

- This plan features:
  - Three bedrooms
  - Two and one half baths
- A fireplaced Family Room and Dining Room
- A large Kitchen sharing a preparation/eating bar with Dining Room
- A first floor Master Bedroom featuring two closets and a five-piece bath
- An ample Utility Room designed with a pantry and room for a freezer, a washer and dryer, plus a furnace and a hot water heater

FIRST FLOOR — 1,280 SQ. FT.
SECOND FLOOR — 735 SQ. FT.
GREENHOUSE — 80 SQ. FT.

TOTAL LIVING AREA:
2,015 SQ. FT.

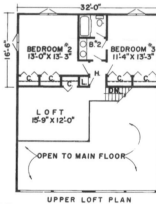

UPPER LOFT PLAN

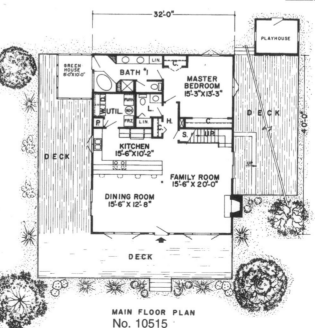

MAIN FLOOR PLAN
No. 10515

To order your Blueprints, call 1-800-235-5700

Refer to **Pricing Schedule A** on the order form for pricing information

An
EXCLUSIVE DESIGN
By Jannis Vann & Associates. Inc.

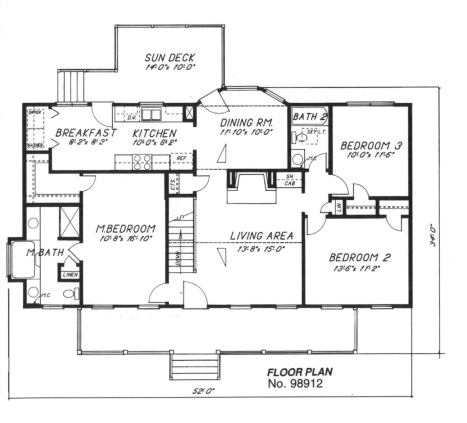

FLOOR PLAN
No. 98912

Simply Cozy

- This plan features:
  — Three bedrooms
  — Two full baths
- Quaint front porch shelters Entry into the Living Area which is showcased by a massive fireplace and built-ins
- Formal Dining Room with Sun Deck access accented by a bay of glass
- Efficient, galley Kitchen with Breakfast area, laundry facilities and outdoor access
- Secluded Master Bedroom offers a roomy walk-in closet and plush bath with two vanities and a garden window tub
- Two additional bedrooms with ample closets share a full bath with a skylight

MAIN FLOOR — 1,325 SQ. FT.

TOTAL LIVING AREA:
1,325 SQ. FT.

77

Refer to **Pricing Schedule B** on the order form for pricing information

© 1993 Donald A. Gardner Architects, Inc.

Economical Three Bedroom

■ This plan features:
— Three bedrooms
— Two full baths

■ Dormers above the covered porch cast light into the Foyer

■ Columns punctuating the entrance to the Great Room/ Dining Room area with a shared cathedral ceiling and a bank of operable skylights

■ Kitchen with a breakfast counter, open to the Dining Area

■ Private Master Bedroom with a tray ceiling and luxurious bath featuring a double vanity, separate shower, and skylights over the whirlpool tub

MAIN FLOOR — 1,322 SQ. FT.
GARAGE & STORAGE — 413 SQ. FT.

TOTAL LIVING AREA:
1,322 SQ. FT.

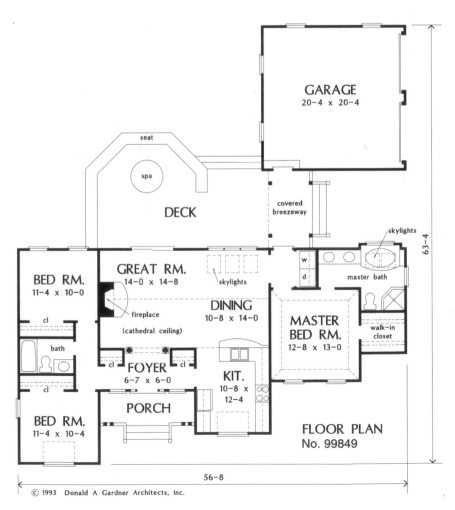

GARAGE
20-4 x 20-4

seat

spa

DECK

covered breezeway

skylights

w
d

master bath

walk-in closet

GREAT RM.
14-0 x 14-8

skylights

fireplace

(cathedral ceiling)

DINING
10-8 x 14-0

MASTER BED RM.
12-8 x 13-0

BED RM.
11-4 x 10-0

cl

bath

cl

cl

FOYER
6-7 x 6-0

cl

KIT.
10-8 x 12-4

BED RM.
11-4 x 10-4

PORCH

FLOOR PLAN
No. 99849

63-4

56-8

© 1993 Donald A Gardner Architects, Inc.

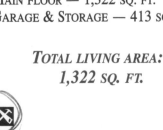

Refer to **Pricing Schedule B** on the order form for pricing information

PLAN NO. 92523

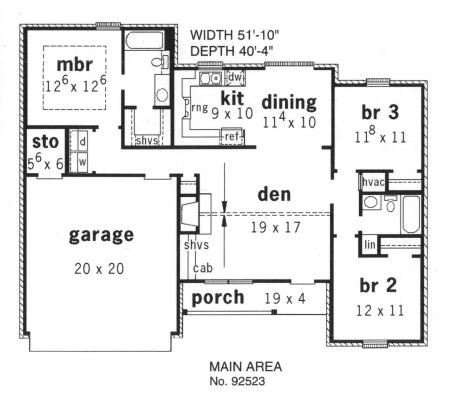

WIDTH 51'-10"
DEPTH 40'-4"

mbr 12⁶ x 12⁶

sto 5⁶ x 6

d
w

shvs

kit 9 x 10

rng   dw
ref

dining 11⁴ x 10

br 3 11⁸ x 11

den 19 x 17

hvac

lin

garage 20 x 20

shvs
cab

porch 19 x 4

br 2 12 x 11

MAIN AREA
No. 92523

Private Master Suite

■ This plan features:

— Three bedrooms

— Two full baths

■ A spacious Great Room enhanced by a vaulted ceiling and fireplace

■ A well-equipped Kitchen with windowed double sink

■ A secluded Master Suite with decorative ceiling, private Master Bath, and walk-in closet

■ Two additional bedrooms sharing hall bath

■ An optional crawl space or slab foundation — please specify when ordering

MAIN FLOOR — 1,293 SQ. FT.
GARAGE — 433 SQ. FT.

TOTAL LIVING AREA:
1,293 SQ. FT.

Refer to **Pricing Schedule C** on the order form for pricing information

Small, Yet Lavishly Appointed

■ This plan features:

— Three bedrooms

— Two full and one half baths

■ The Dining Room, Living Room, Foyer and Master Bath all topped by high ceilings

■ Master Bedroom includes a decorative tray ceiling and a walk-in closet

■ Kitchen open to the Breakfast Room enhanced by a serving bar and a pantry

■ Living Room with a large fireplace and a French door to the rear yard

■ Master Suite located on opposite side from secondary bedrooms, allowing for privacy

■ Please specify basement or crawl space foundation when ordering

MAIN FLOOR — 1,845 SQ. FT.
BONUS — 409 SQ. FT.
GARAGE — 529 SQ. FT.

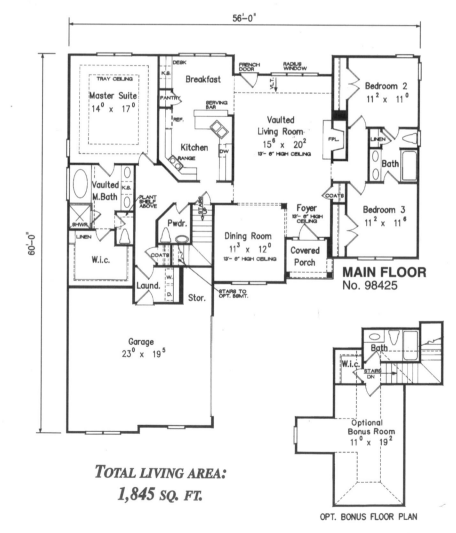

TOTAL LIVING AREA:
1,845 SQ. FT.

MAIN FLOOR
No. 98425

OPT. BONUS FLOOR PLAN

To order your Blueprints, call 1-800-235-5700

Refer to **Pricing Schedule A** on the order form for pricing information

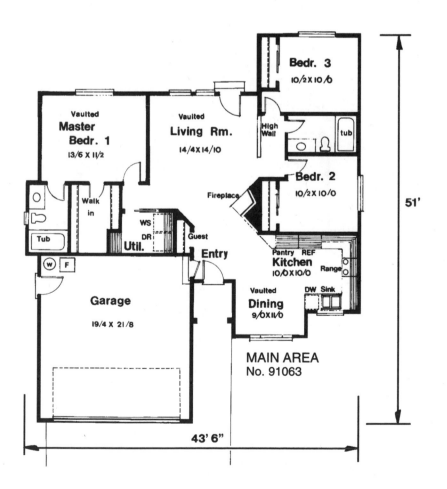

Vaulted
**Master
Bedr. 1**
13/6 X 11/2

Vaulted
Living Rm.
14/4 X 14/10

Bedr. 3
10/2 X 10/6

High Wall

tub

Bedr. 2
10/2 X 10/0

Fireplace

Walk in

Tub

WS

DR

Util.

Guest

Entry

Pantry   REF

Kitchen
10/0 X 10/0

Range

W   F

Garage
19/4 X 21/8

Vaulted
Dining
9/0 X 11/0

DW   Sink

MAIN AREA
No. 91063

51'

43' 6"

Gabled Roofline and Arched Windows Enhance Exterior

■ This plan features:

— Three bedrooms

— Two full baths

■ Vaulted ceilings and an open interior creating a spacious feeling

■ A private Master Bedroom with a generous closet and Master Bath

■ Two additional bedrooms sharing the second full bath

■ A Kitchen with ample storage, countertops, and a built-in pantry

■ No materials list available for this plan

MAIN AREA — 1,207 SQ. FT.
GARAGE — 440 SQ. FT.

TOTAL LIVING AREA:
1,207 SQ. FT.

Refer to **Pricing Schedule C** on the order form for pricing information

Impressive Design

■ This plan features:

— Three bedrooms

— Two full and one half baths

■ Two-story keystone entrance with sidelights leads into Foyer with balcony above

■ Bay windows illuminate formal Dining and Living Rooms

■ Expansive Family Room with cozy fireplace and a wall of windows with access to Patio

■ Efficient, U-shaped Kitchen convenient to both formal and informal dining areas

■ Master Bedroom crowned by decorative ceiling, two vanities and garden tub bath

■ Upstairs, two bedrooms, a full bath and convenient laundry closet

■ No materials list is available for this plan

■ An optional basement or slab foundation — please specify when ordering

An EXCLUSIVE DESIGN
By Jannis Vann & Associates, Inc.

SECOND FLOOR

FIRST FLOOR
No. 93213

FIRST FLOOR — 1,126 SQ. FT.
SECOND FLOOR — 959 SQ. FT
BASEMENT — 458 SQ. FT.
GARAGE — 627 SQ. FT.

TOTAL LIVING AREA:
2,085 SQ. FT.

82

To order your

PLAN NO. 98441

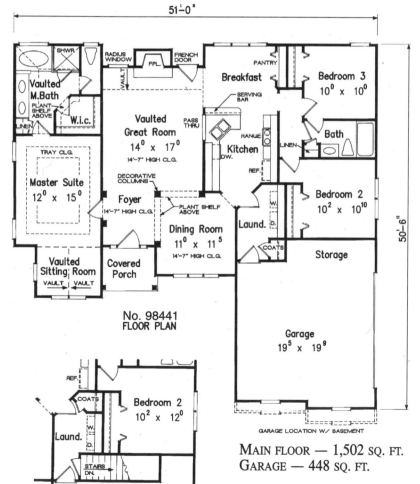

51'-0"

SHWR.

Vaulted M. Bath

RADIUS WINDOW   FPL   FRENCH DOOR   PANTRY

Breakfast

SERVING BAR

PLANT SHELF ABOVE

Bedroom 3
10⁰ x 10⁰

W.i.c.

LINEN

Vaulted Great Room
14⁰ x 17⁰
14'-7" HIGH CLG.

PASS THRU

Kitchen

RANGE

REF.

DW.

Bath

LINEN

TRAY CLG.

DECORATIVE COLUMNS

Master Suite
12⁰ x 15⁰

Foyer
14'-7" HIGH CLG.

PLANT SHELF ABOVE

Bedroom 2
10² x 10¹⁰

Dining Room
11⁰ x 11⁵
14'-7" HIGH CLG.

Laund.

W.

D.

COATS

Vaulted Sitting Room
VAULT   VAULT

Covered Porch

Storage

No. 98441
FLOOR PLAN

Garage
19⁵ x 19⁹

50'-6"

GARAGE LOCATION W/ BASEMENT

REF.

COATS

Bedroom 2
10² x 12⁰

Laund.

W.

D.

STAIRS DN.

OPT. BASEMENT STAIR LOCATION

MAIN FLOOR — 1,502 SQ. FT.
GARAGE — 448 SQ. FT.

TOTAL LIVING AREA:
1,502 SQ. FT.

High Ceilings and Arched Windows

■ This plan features:

— Three bedrooms

— Two full baths

■ Natural illumination streaming into the Dining Room and Sitting area of the Master Suite through large, arched windows

■ Kitchen with pass through to the Great Room and a serving bar for the Breakfast Room

■ Great Room topped by a vaulted ceiling accented by a fireplace and a French door

■ Decorative columns accenting the entrance of the Dining Room

■ Tray ceiling in the Master Suite and a vaulted ceiling over the sitting room and the Master Bath

■ No matcrials list is available for this plan

■ An optional basement or crawl space foundation — please specify when ordering

Refer to **Pricing Schedule A** on the order form for pricing information

Great Room
Heart of Home

■ This plan features:

— Three bedrooms

— Two full baths

■ Sheltered porch leads into the Entry with arches and a Great Room

■ Spacious Great Room with a ten foot ceiling above a wall of windows and rear yard access

■ Efficient Kitchen with a built-in pantry, a laundry closet and a Breakfast area accented by a decorative window

■ Bay of windows enhances the Master Bedroom suite with a double vanity bath and a walk-in closet

■ Two additional bedrooms with ample closets, share a full bath

■ No materials list is available for this plan.

MAIN AREA — 1,087 SQ. FT.

TOTAL LIVING AREA:
1,087 SQ. FT.

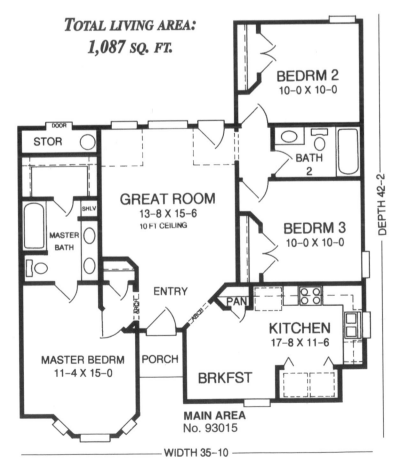

DEPTH 42-2

STOR

DOOR

MASTER BATH

SHLV

GREAT ROOM
13-8 X 15-6
10 FT CEILING

BEDRM 2
10-0 X 10-0

BATH 2

BEDRM 3
10-0 X 10-0

ENTRY

PAN

KITCHEN
17-8 X 11-6

MASTER BEDRM
11-4 X 15-0

PORCH

BRKFST

MAIN AREA
No. 93015

WIDTH 35-10

To order your Blueprints, call 1-800-235-5700

Refer to **Pricing Schedule D** on the order form for pricing information

PLAN NO. 92675

Detailed Brick and Fieldstone Facade

■ This plan features:

— Three bedrooms

— Two full and one half baths

■ Open Foyer enhanced by a graceful, banister staircase

■ Great Room highlighted by a twelve foot ceiling topping an alcove of windows, fireplace, built-in entertainment center and Porch access

■ Spacious Kitchen and Breakfast area with extended counter/snackbar and nearby Pub, walk-in closet, Laundry and Garage

■ Comfortable Master Bedroom with a large walk-in closet and double vanity bath

■ Two additional bedrooms share a double vanity bath

■ No materials list is available for this plan

FIRST FLOOR — 1,192 SQ. FT.
SECOND FLOOR — 1,013 SQ. FT.
BASEMENT — 1,157 SQ. FT.

TOTAL LIVING AREA:
2,205 SQ. FT.

SECOND FLOOR
No. 92675

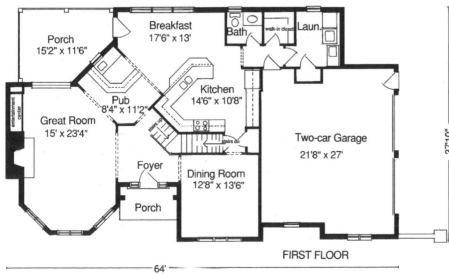

FIRST FLOOR

Refer to **Pricing Schedule D** on the order form for pricing information

Exciting Arched Accents Give Impact

■ This plan features:

— Three bedrooms

— Two full and one half baths

■ Keystone arch accents entrance into open Foyer with angled staircase and sloped ceiling

■ Great Room enhanced by an entertainment center, hearth fireplace and a wall of windows

■ Efficient, angled Kitchen offers work island/snackbar, Breakfast area with access to back yard

■ Master Bedroom wing with a lavish Bath with two vanities, and corner window tub

■ Two bedrooms with walk-in closets share a skylit Study, double vanity bath and a Bonus Room

■ No materials list is available for this plan

FIRST FLOOR — 1,542 SQ. FT.
SECOND FLOOR — 667 SQ. FT.
BONUS ROOM — 236 SQ. FT.
BASEMENT — 1,470 SQ. FT.

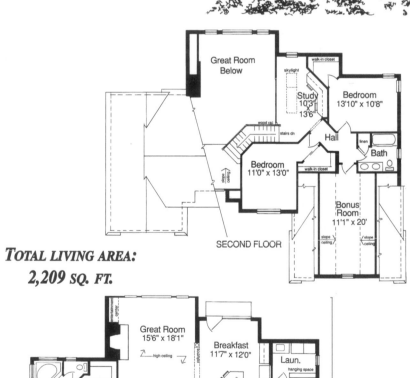

SECOND FLOOR

TOTAL LIVING AREA:
2,209 SQ. FT.

FIRST FLOOR
No. 92643

To order your Blueprints, call 1-800-235-5700

© design basics, inc.

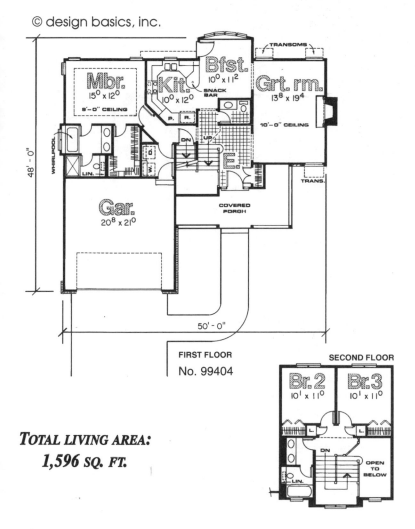

Mbr. 15⁰ x 12⁰
9'-0" CEILING

Kit. 10⁰ x 12⁰

Bfst. 10⁰ x 11²
SNACK BAR

Grt. rm. 13⁸ x 19⁴
10'-0" CEILING

TRANSOMS

WHIRLPOOL
LIN.
P. R.
DN
UP
D.
W.
TRANS.

Gar. 20⁸ x 21⁰

COVERED PORCH

48' - 0"

50' - 0"

FIRST FLOOR
No. 99404

SECOND FLOOR

Br. 2 10¹ x 11⁰

Br. 3 10¹ x 11⁰

DN
OPEN TO BELOW
LIN.

TOTAL LIVING AREA:
1,596 SQ. FT.

Charming Country Style

◼ This plan features:

— Three bedrooms

— Two full and one half baths

◼ Specious Great Room enhanced by a fireplace and transom windows

◼ Breakfast Room with a bay window and direct access to the Kitchen

◼ Snack bar extending work space in the Kitchen

◼ Master Suite enhanced by a crowning in a boxed nine foot ceiling, a compartmental whirlpool bath and a large walk-in closet

◼ Second floor balcony overlooking the U-shaped stairs and Entry

◼ Two second floor bedrooms share a full hall bath

FIRST FLOOR — 1,191 SQ. FT.
SECOND FLOOR — 405 SQ. FT.
BASEMENT — 1,191 SQ. FT.
GARAGE — 454 SQ. FT.

Refer to **Pricing Schedule A** on the order form for pricing information

Easy Living Design

- This plan features:
- — Three bedrooms
- — Two full baths

- A handicaped Master Bath plan is available

- Vaulted Great Room, Dining Room and Kitchen areas

- A Kitchen accented with angles and an abundance of cabinets for storage

- A Master Bedroom with an ample sized wardrobe, large covered private deck, and private bath

MAIN AREA — 1,345 SQ. FT.
WIDTH — 47'-8"
DEPTH — 56'-0"

TOTAL LIVING AREA:
1,345 SQ. FT.

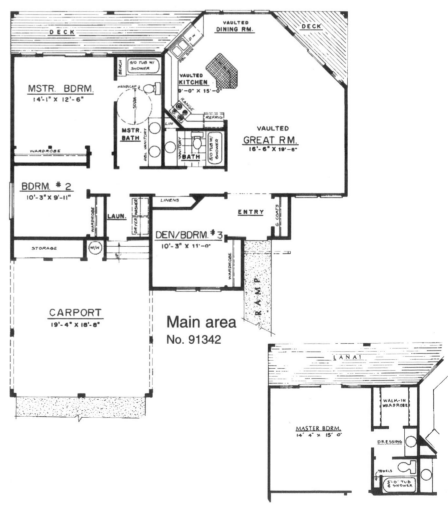

Main area
No. 91342

ALTERNATE BATH

To order your Blueprints, call 1-800-235-5700

Refer to **Pricing Schedule B** on the order form for pricing information

A Comfortable Informal Design

■ This plan features:

— Three bedrooms

— Two full baths

■ Warm, country front Porch with wood details

■ Spacious Activity Room enhanced by a pre-fab fireplace

■ Open and efficient Kitchen/Dining area highlighted by bay window, adjacent to Laundry and Garage entry

■ Corner Master Bedroom offers a pampering bath with a garden tub and double vanity topped by a vaulted ceiling

■ Two additional bedrooms with ample closets, share a full bath

■ An optional slab or crawl space foundation — please specify when ordering

MAIN FLOOR — 1,300 SQ. FT.
GARAGE — 576 SQ. FT.

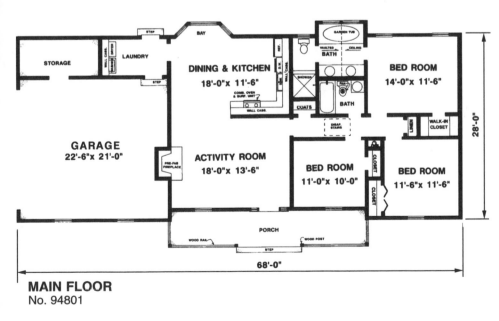

MAIN FLOOR
No. 94801

TOTAL LIVING AREA:
1,300 SQ. FT.

Refer to **Pricing Schedule B** on the order form for pricing information

Outdoor-Lovers' Delight

- ■ This plan features:
- — Three bedrooms
- — Two full baths

- ■ A roomy Kitchen and Dining Room

- ■ A massive Living Room with a fireplace and access to the wrap-around porch via double French doors

- ■ An elegant Master Suite and two additional spacious bedrooms closely located to the laundry area

MAIN FLOOR — 1,540 SQ. FT.
PORCHES — 530 SQ. FT.

TOTAL LIVING AREA:
1,540 SQ. FT.

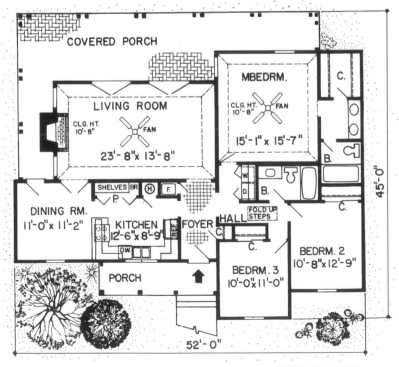

COVERED PORCH

MBEDRM.
CLG. HT.
10'-8"   FAN

15'-1" x 15'-7"

LIVING ROOM
CLG. HT.
10'-8"   FAN

23'-8" x 13'-8"

C.

B.

SHELVES BR H F.
P.

W
D B.

FOLD UP STEPS

DINING RM.
11'-0" x 11'-2"

KITCHEN
12'-6" x 8'-9"

REF. FOYER

HALL

C.

C.

DW

PORCH

BEDRM. 3
10'-0" x 11'-0"

BEDRM. 2
10'-8" x 12'-9"

45'-0"

52'-0"

MAIN FLOOR
No. 10748

To order your Blueprints, call 1 - 8 0 0 - 2 3 5 - 5 7 0 0

© 1995 Donald A. Gardner Architects, Inc.

B. NATHAN

Beautiful From Front to Back

■ This plan features:

— Three bedrooms

— Two full baths

■ Porches front and back, gables and dormers adding charm

■ Central Great Room with a cathedral ceiling, fireplace, and a clerestory window which brings in natural light

■ Columns dividing the open Great Room from the Kitchen and the Breakfast Bay

■ A tray ceiling and columns in the formal Dining Room

■ Skylit Master Bath with shower, whirlpool tub, dual vanity and spacious walk-in closet

MAIN FLOOR — 1,632 SQ. FT.
GARAGE & STORAGE — 561 SQ. FT.

TOTAL LIVING AREA:
1,632 SQ. FT.

FLOOR PLAN

MASTER BED RM. 13-4 x 16-4

skylight

master bath

walk-in closet

lin.

BRKFST. 10-4 x 8-8

cl

PORCH

(cathedral ceiling)
GREAT RM. 15-4 x 18-6

fireplace

w
d

UTIL.

storage

KIT. 11-4 x 12-10

BED RM. 11-4 x 11-0

cl

lin.

bath

walk-in closet

GARAGE 21-0 x 21-8

cl

BED RM./ STUDY 11-0 x 11-8

FOYER 6-0 x 8-4

DINING 11-0 x 11-8

storage

(optional door location)

PORCH

55-2

62-4

No. 99840
FLOOR PLAN

© 1995 Donald A Gardner Architects, Inc.

91

Refer to **Pricing Schedule C** on the order form for pricing information

© 1995 Donald A Gardner Architects, Inc.

Great Room With Columns

■ This plan features:

— Three bedrooms

— Two full baths

■ Great Room crowned with a cathedral ceiling and accented by columns and a fireplace

■ Tray ceilings and arched picture windows accent front bedroom and the Dining Room

■ Secluded Master Suite highlighted by a tray ceiling and contains a bath with skylight, a garden tub and spacious walk-in closet

■ Two additional bedrooms share a full bath

■ An optional crawl space or basement foundation — please specify when ordering

MAIN FLOOR — 1,879 SQ. FT.
GARAGE — 485 SQ. FT.
BONUS — 360 SQ. FT.

FLOOR PLAN
No. 99807

© 1995 Donald A Gardner Architects, Inc.

TOTAL LIVING AREA:

1,879 SQ. FT.

To order your Blueprints, call 1-800-235-5700

Refer to **Pricing Schedule A** on the order form for pricing information

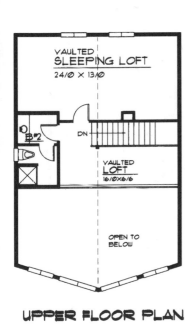

VAULTED SLEEPING LOFT
24/0 X 13/0

B #2

DN

VAULTED LOFT
16/0 X 6/6

OPEN TO BELOW

UPPER FLOOR PLAN

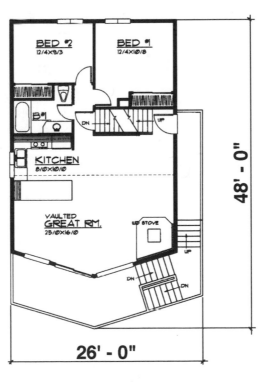

BED #2
12/4X8/3

BED #1
12/4X10/8

B #1

DN

UP

KITCHEN
8/0X10/0

VAULTED GREAT RM.
25/0X16/0

UP STOVE

UP

DN

DN

48' - 0"

26' - 0"

MAIN FLOOR PLAN
No. 91026

Home on a Hill

■ This plan features:

— Two bedrooms

— One full and one three-quarter baths

■ Sweeping panels of glass and a wood stove, creating atmosphere for the Great Room

■ An open plan that draws the Kitchen into the warmth of the Great Room's wood stove

■ A sleeping loft that has a full bath all to itself

FIRST FLOOR — 988 SQ. FT.
SECOND FLOOR — 366 SQ. FT.
BASEMENT — 988 SQ. FT.

TOTAL LIVING AREA:
1,354 SQ. FT.

Refer to **Pricing Schedule A** on the order form for pricing information

PLAN NO. 98434

Expansive Living Room

■ This plan features:
— Three bedrooms
— Two full baths

■ Vaulted ceiling crowns spacious Living Room highlighted by a fireplace

■ Built-in pantry and direct access from the garage adding to the conveniences of the Kitchen

■ Walk-in closet and a private five-piece bath topped by a vaulted ceiling in the Master Bedroom

■ Close proximity to the full bath in the hall from the secondary bedrooms

■ An optional basement, crawl space or slab foundation — please specify when ordering

MAIN FLOOR — 1,346 SQ. FT.
GARAGE — 395 SQ. FT.
BASEMENT — 1358 SQ. FT.

TOTAL LIVING AREA: 1,346 SQ. FT.

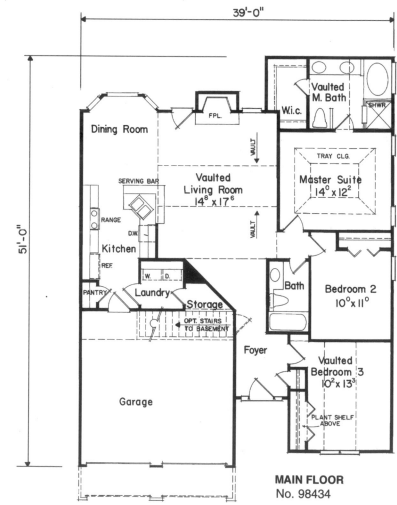

MAIN FLOOR
No. 98434

Refer to **Pricing Schedule B** on the order form for pricing information

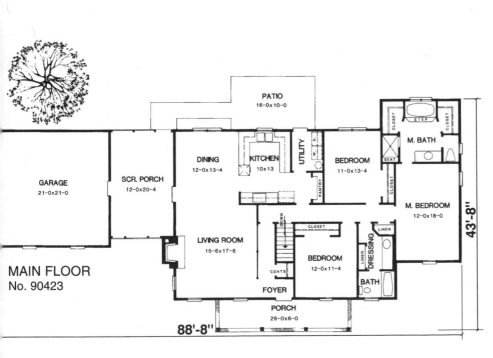

MAIN FLOOR
No. 90423

GARAGE
21-0x21-0

SCR. PORCH
12-0x20-4

DINING
12-0x13-4

KITCHEN
10x13

UTILITY

W. D.

PANTRY

PATIO
16-0x10-0

BEDROOM
11-0x13-4

M. BATH

CLOSET

STEP

CLOSET

SEAT

CLOSET

M. BEDROOM
12-0x18-0

LIVING ROOM
15-6x17-8

DOWN

CLOSET

COATS

BEDROOM
12-0x11-4

LINEN

DRESSING

LINEN

BATH

FOYER

PORCH
26-0x6-0

88'-8"

43'-8"

Expansive, Not Expensive

■ This plan features:

— Three bedrooms

— Two full baths

■ A Master Suite with his-n-her closets and a private Master Bath

■ Two additional bedrooms that share a full hall closet

■ A pleasant Dining Room that overlooks a rear garden

■ A well-equipped Kitchen with a built-in planning corner and eat-in space

■ An optional basement, slab or crawl space foundation — please specify when ordering

MAIN FLOOR — 1,773 SQ. FT.

TOTAL LIVING AREA:
1,773 SQ. FT.

Refer to **Pricing Schedule C** on the order form for pricing information

Small, But Not Lacking

■ This plan features:

—Three bedrooms

— One full and one three quarter baths

■ Great Room adjoining the Dining Room for ease in entertaining

■ Kitchen highlighted by a peninsula counter/snackbar extending work space and offering convenience in serving informal meals or snacks

■ Split bedroom plan allowing for privacy for the Master Bedroom suite with a private bath and a walk-in closet

■ Two additional bedrooms sharing the full family bath in the hall

■ Garage entry convenient to the kitchen

FIRST FLOOR — 1,546 SQ. FT.
GARAGE — 440 SQ. FT.
BASEMENT — 1,530 SQ. FT.

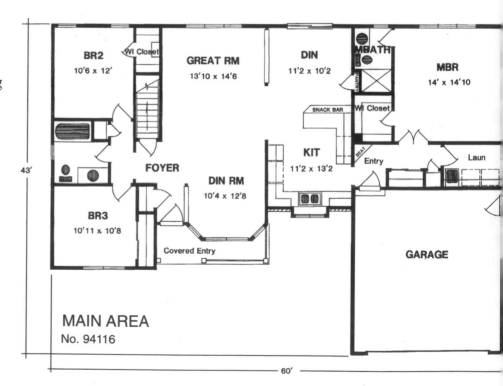

BR2
10'6 x 12'

WI Closet

GREAT RM
13'10 x 14'6

DIN
11'2 x 10'2

MBATH

MBR
14' x 14'10

PANTRY

SNACK BAR

WI Closet

FOYER

KIT
11'2 x 13'2

SEAT

Entry

Laun

DIN RM
10'4 x 12'8

43'

BR3
10'11 x 10'8

Covered Entry

GARAGE

MAIN AREA
No. 94116

60'

TOTAL LIVING AREA:
1,546 SQ. FT.

To order your Blueprints, call 1-800-235-5700

Refer to **Pricing Schedule B** on the order form for pricing information

Ranch with Handicapped Access

■ This plan features:

— Three bedrooms

— Two full baths

■ Ramps into the front Entry from the Porch; the Utility area and the Kitchen from the Garage; and the Family Room from the Deck

■ An open area topped by a sloped ceiling for the Family Room, the Dining Room, the Kitchen and the Breakfast alcove

■ An efficient Kitchen, with a built-in pantry, easily serves both the Breakfast nook and the Dining Room

■ A Master Bedroom suite accented by a sloping ceiling above a wall of windows and access to the Deck

■ Two front bedrooms with sloped ceilings sharing a full hall bath

MAIN FLOOR — 1,734 SQ. FT.
PORCH — 118 SQ. FT.
DECK — 354 SQ. FT.
GARAGE — 606 SQ. FT.

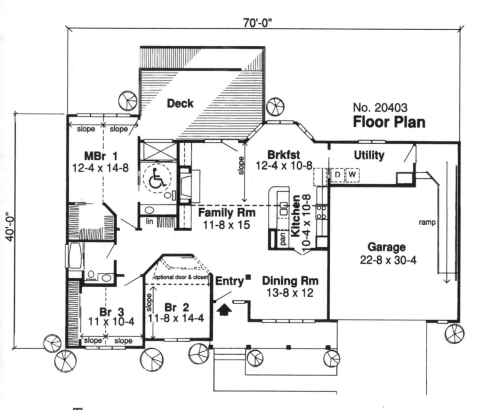

No. 20403
Floor Plan

TOTAL LIVING AREA:
1,734 SQ. FT.

Refer to **Pricing Schedule B** on the order form for pricing information

© 1995 Donald A Gardner Architects, Inc.

Cathedral Ceiling

■ This plan features:

— Three bedrooms

— Two full baths

■ Cathedral ceiling expanding the Great room, Dining Room and Kitchen

■ A versatile bedroom or study topped by a cathedral ceiling accented by double circle-top windows

■ Master Suite complete with a cathedral ceiling, including a bath with a garden tub, linen closet and a walk-in closet

MAIN FLOOR — 1,417 SQ. FT.
GARAGE — 441 SQ. FT.

TOTAL LIVING AREA:
1,417 SQ. FT.

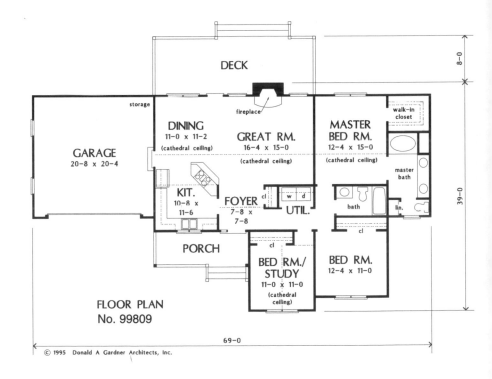

FLOOR PLAN
No. 99809

© 1995 Donald A Gardner Architects, Inc.

To order your Blueprints, call 1-800-235-5700

Refer to **Pricing Schedule B** on the order form for pricing information

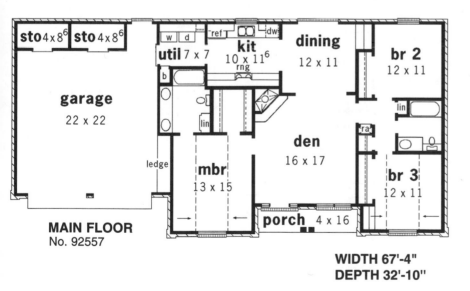

MAIN FLOOR
No. 92557

WIDTH 67'-4"
DEPTH 32'-10"

TOTAL LIVING AREA:
1,390 SQ. FT.

Elegant Brick Exterior

■ This plan features:

—Three bedrooms

—Two full baths

■ Detailing and accenting columns highlighting the covered front porch

■ Den is enhanced by a corner fireplace and adjoins Dining Room

■ Efficient Kitchen well-appointed and has easy access to the utility/laundry room

■ Master Bedroom topped by a vaulted ceiling and has a private bath and walk-in closet

■ Two secondary bedrooms are located at the opposite end of home sharing a full bath

■ An optional slab or crawl space foundation — please specify when ordering

MAIN FLOOR — 1,390 SQ. FT.
GARAGE — 590 SQ. FT.

Refer to **Pricing Schedule B** on the order form for pricing information

Natural Light Gives Bright Living Spaces

■ This plan features:

— Three bedrooms

— One full and one three quarter baths

■ A generous use of windows throughout the home, creating a bright living space

■ A center work island and a built-in pantry in the Kitchen

■ A sunny Eating Nook for informal eating and a formal Dining Room for entertaining

■ A large Living Room with a cozy fireplace to add atmosphere to the room as well as warmth

■ A Master Bedroom with a private bath and double closets

■ Two additional bedrooms that share a full, compartmented hall bath

MAIN AREA — 1,620 SQ. FT.

TOTAL LIVING AREA:
1,620 SQ. FT.

An EXCLUSIVE DESIGN
By Marshall Associates

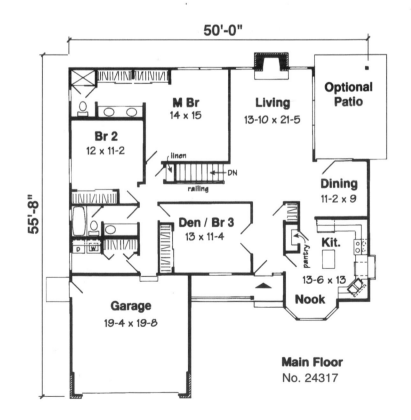

50'-0"

55'-8"

M Br
14 x 15

Living
13-10 x 21-5

Optional Patio

Br 2
12 x 11-2

linen

DN

railing

Dining
11-2 x 9

Den / Br 3
13 x 11-4

pantry

Kit.
13-6 x 13

Garage
19-4 x 19-8

Nook

Main Floor
No. 24317

WIDTH 58'- 0"
DEPTH 48'- 0"

CARPORT
22⁰ x 12⁰

KITCHEN

R.O.

WSH DRY

UTILITY

SINK

WALK-IN CLOSET

WALK-IN CLOSET

SHOWER

SHOWER

REF

DW

EATING BAR

FAU

WH

BEDROOM
15⁸ x 15⁰

BEDROOM
15⁸ x 15⁰

DINING
9⁶ x 10⁶

UP

UP

UP FIREPLACE
RAISED HEARTH

LIVING ROOM
25⁰ x 16⁶

DECK

FIRST FLOOR
No. 98714

DECK
12⁰ x 22⁰

LOFT
11¹⁰ x 20⁶

WALK-IN CLOSET

ATTIC ACCESS

DN

OPEN TO BELOW

SECOND FLOOR

Vacation Living

■ This plan features:

— Three bedrooms

— One full, two three-quarter and one half baths

■ A wrap-around Deck offering views and access into the Living Room

■ A sunken Living Room with a vaulted ceiling, and a raised-hearth fireplace adjoining the Dining area

■ An open Kitchen with a corner sink and windows, an eating bar and a walk-in storage/pantry

■ Two private Bedroom suites with sliding glass doors leading to a Deck, walk-in closets and plush baths

■ A Loft area with a walk-in closet, attic access, a private bath and a Deck

FIRST FLOOR — 1,704 SQ FT
SECOND FLOOR — 313 SQ. FT.

TOTAL LIVING AREA:
2,017 SQ. FT.

Refer to **Pricing Schedule C** on the order form for pricing information

Quality and Diversity

■ This plan features:

— Four bedrooms

— Two full and one half bath

■ Elegant arched entrance from Porch into Foyer and Great Room

■ Corner fireplace and atrium door highlight Great Room

■ Hub Kitchen with walk-in pantry and peninsula counter easily accesses glass Breakfast bay

■ Master Bedroom wing crowned by tray ceiling offers plush bath and walk-in closet

■ Three additional bedrooms with decorative windows and large closets share a full bath

■ No materials list is available for this plan

FIRST FLOOR — 1,401 SQ. FT.
SECOND FLOOR — 621 SQ. FT.
BASEMENT — 1,269 SQ. FT.
GARAGE — 478 SQ. FT.

TOTAL LIVING AREA:
2,022 SQ. FT.

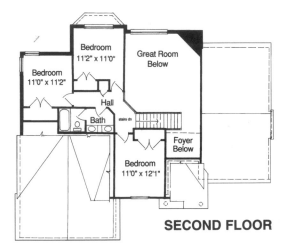

SECOND FLOOR

FIRST FLOOR
No. 92629

To order your Blueprints, call 1-800-235-5700

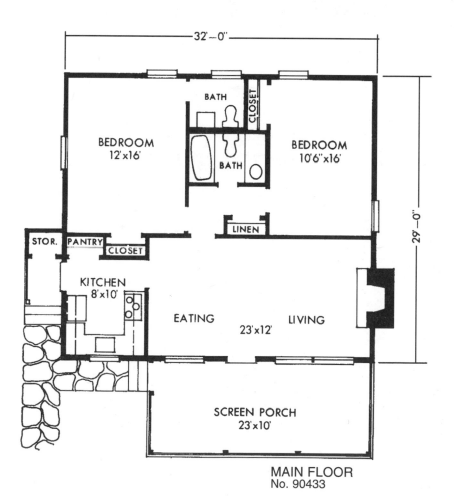

32'—0"

29'—0"

BATH

CLOSET

BEDROOM
12'x16'

BEDROOM
10'6"x16'

BATH

LINEN

STOR. PANTRY

CLOSET

KITCHEN
8'x10'

EATING

23'x12'

LIVING

SCREEN PORCH
23'x10'

MAIN FLOOR
No. 90433

Cabin in the Country

■ This plan features:

— Two bedrooms

— One full and one half baths

■ A Screened Porch for enjoyment of your outdoor surroundings

■ A combination Living and Dining area with cozy fireplace for added warmth

■ An efficiently laid out Kitchen with a built-in pantry

■ Two large bedrooms located at the rear of the home

■ An optional slab or crawl space foundation — please specify when ordering

MAIN FLOOR — 928 SQ. FT.
SCREENED PORCH — 230 SQ. FT.
STORAGE — 14 SQ. FT.

TOTAL LIVING AREA:
928 SQ. FT.

For Today's Sophisticated Homeowner

■ This plan features:

— Three bedrooms

— Two full baths

■ A formal Dining Room that opens off the foyer and has a classic bay window

■ A Kitchen notable for it's angled eating bar that opens to the Living Room

■ A cozy fireplace in the Living Room that can be seen from the Kitchen

■ A Master Suite that includes a whirlpool tub/shower combination and a walk-in closet

■ Ten foot ceilings in the major living areas, including the Master Bedroom

■ No materials list available for this plan

MAIN AREA — 1,500 SQ. FT.
GARAGE — 437 SQ. FT.

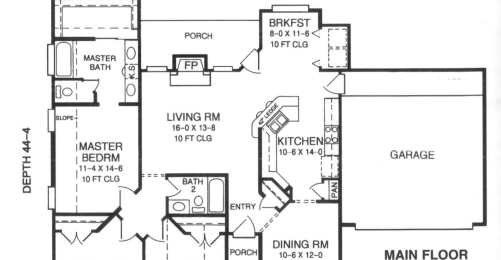

WIDTH 59–10

BRKFST
8-0 X 11-6
10 FT CLG

PORCH

FP

MASTER BATH

LIVING RM
16-0 X 13-8
10 FT CLG

KITCHEN
10-6 X 14-0

GARAGE

DEPTH 44-4

SLOPE

MASTER BEDRM
11-4 X 14-6
10 FT CLG

42" LEDGE

BATH 2

ENTRY

PAN

BEDRM 2
12-0 X 13-0

BEDRM 8
11-0 X 13-6
10 FT COFFERED CLG

PORCH

DINING RM
10-6 X 12-0

MAIN FLOOR
No. 93027

TOTAL LIVING AREA:
1,500 SQ. FT.

To order your Blueprints, call 1-800-235-5700

© 1996 Donald A. Gardner Architects, Inc.

B. NATHAN

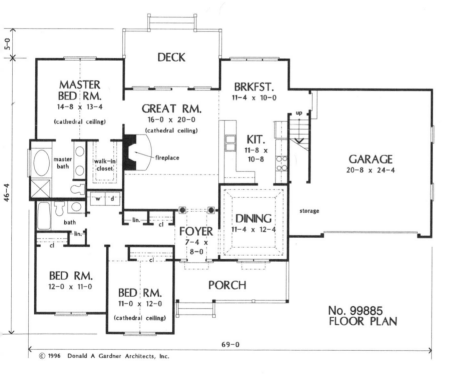

DECK

MASTER BED RM.
14-8 x 13-4
(cathedral ceiling)

master bath

walk-in closet

w d

bath

lin.

GREAT RM.
16-0 x 20-0
(cathedral ceiling)

fireplace

BRKFST.
11-4 x 10-0

up

KIT.
11-8 x 10-8

GARAGE
20-8 x 24-4

storage

lin. cl

FOYER
7-4 x 8-0

DINING
11-4 x 12-4

cl

BED RM.
12-0 x 11-0

BED RM.
11-0 x 12-0
(cathedral ceiling)

PORCH

No. 99885
FLOOR PLAN

69-0

5-0

46-4

© 1996 Donald A Gardner Architects, Inc.

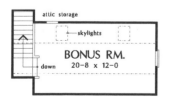

attic storage

skylights

BONUS RM.
20-8 x 12-0

down

**TOTAL LIVING AREA:
1,669 SQ. FT.**

Cathedral Ceilings

■ This plan features:

— Three bedrooms

— Two full baths

■ Living and entertaining space expanding from the Great Room to the Deck

■ Cathedral ceilings adding volume and drama to the Great Room and the Master Bedroom

■ Master Suite including a roomy walk-in closet and bath with garden tub and double vanity

■ A third cathedral ceiling in the front bedroom highlighted by a double window topped off by a half-round window

■ A skylit Bonus Room for expansion in the future

MAIN FLOOR — 1,669 SQ. FT.
GARAGE & STORAGE — 584 SQ. FT.
BONUS ROOM — 314 SQ. FT.

Refer to **Pricing Schedule C** on the order form for pricing information

© 1995 Donald A. Gardner Architects, Inc.

Casually Elegant

■ This plan features:

— Three bedrooms

— Two full baths

■ Arched windows, dormers and charming front and back porches with columns creating country flavoring

■ Central Great Room topped by a cathedral ceiling, a fireplace and a clerestory window

■ Breakfast bay for casual dining is open to the Kitchen

■ Columns accenting the entryway into the formal Dining Room

■ Cathedral ceiling crowning the Master Bedroom

■ Master Bath with skylights, whirlpool tub, shower, and a double vanity

■ Two additional bedrooms sharing a bath located between the rooms

MAIN FLOOR — 1,561 SQ. FT.
GARAGE & STORAGE — 346 SQ. FT.

FLOOR PLAN
No. 96417

© 1995 Donald A Gardner Architects, Inc.

TOTAL LIVING AREA:
1,561 SQ. FT.

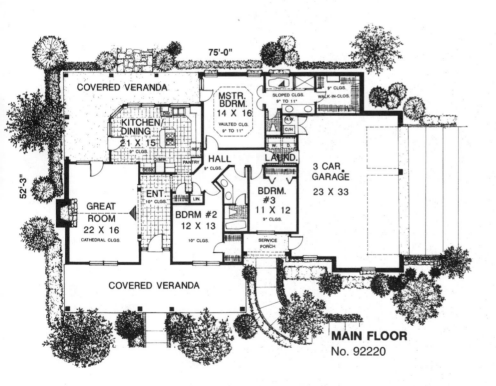

75'-0"

52'-3"

COVERED VERANDA

KITCHEN/
DINING
21 X 15
9" CLGS.

MSTR.
BDRM.
14 X 16
VAULTED CLG.
9" TO 11"

SLOPED CLGS.
9" TO 11"

9" CLGS.

WALK-IN-CLOS.

HALL
9" CLGS.

LAUND.

3 CAR GARAGE
23 X 33

GREAT ROOM
22 X 16
CATHEDRAL CLGS.

ENT.
10" CLGS.

BDRM #2
12 X 13
10" CLGS.

BDRM. #3
11 X 12
9" CLGS.

SERVICE PORCH

COVERED VERANDA

MAIN FLOOR
No. 92220

GARAGE — 759 SQ. FT.

TOTAL LIVING AREA:
1,830 SQ. FT.

Southern Hospitality

■ This plan features:

— Three bedrooms

— Two full baths

■ Welcoming Covered Veranda

■ Easy-care, tiled Entry leads into Great Room with fieldstone fireplace and atrium door to another Covered Veranda topped by a cathedral ceiling

■ A bright Kitchen/Dining Room includes a stovetop island/snackbar, built-in pantry and desk, and access to Covered Veranda

■ Vaulted ceiling crowns Master Bedroom that offers a plush bath and huge walk-in closet

■ Two additional bedrooms with ample closets share a double vanity bath

■ No materials list is available for this plan

MAIN FLOOR — 1,830 SQ. FT.

Refer to **Pricing Schedule A** on the order form for pricing information

Affordable Style

■ This plan features:

— Three bedrooms

— Two full baths

■ A country porch welcomes you to an Entry hall with a convenient closet

■ A well-appointed Kitchen boasts a double sink, ample counter and storage space, a peninsula eating bar and a built-in hutch

■ A terrific Master Suite including a private bath and a walk-in closet

■ A Dining Room that flows from the Great Room and into the Kitchen that includes sliding glass doors to the deck

■ A Great Room with a cozy fireplace that can also be enjoyed from the Dining area

■ Two additional bedrooms share a full hall bath

■ No materials list is available for this plan

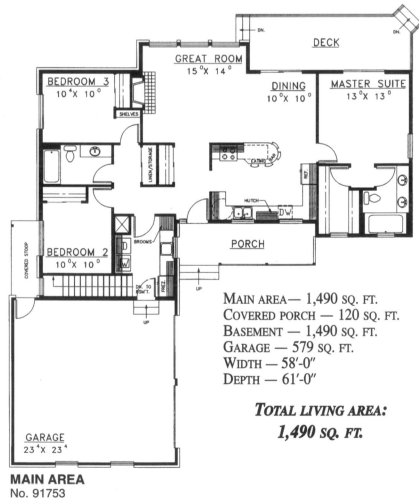

MAIN AREA— 1,490 SQ. FT.
COVERED PORCH — 120 SQ. FT.
BASEMENT — 1,490 SQ. FT.
GARAGE — 579 SQ. FT.
WIDTH — 58'-0"
DEPTH — 61'-0"

TOTAL LIVING AREA:
1,490 SQ. FT.

MAIN AREA
No. 91753

Refer to **Pricing Schedule A** on the order form for pricing information

OPTIONAL
BASEMENT PLAN

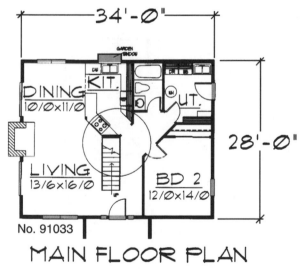

34'-0"

DINING
10/0×11/0

KIT.

UT.

28'-0"

LIVING
13/6×16/0

BD 2
12/0×14/0

GARDEN WINDOW

No. 91033

MAIN FLOOR PLAN

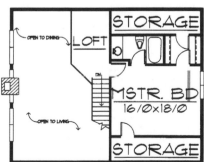

STORAGE

LOFT

OPEN TO DINING

MSTR. BD
16/0×18/0

OPEN TO LIVING

STORAGE

UPPER FLOOR PLAN

Neat and Tidy

- This plan features:
  — Two bedrooms
  — Two full baths
- A two story Living Room and Dining Room with a handsome stone fireplace
- A well-appointed Kitchen with a peninsula counter
- A Master Suite with a walk-in closet and private Master Bath
- A large utility room with laundry facilities
- An optional basement or crawl space foundation — please specify when ordering

FIRST FLOOR — 952 SQ. FT.
SECOND FLOOR — 297 SQ. FT.

TOTAL LIVING AREA:
1,249 SQ. FT.

Refer to **Pricing Schedule G** on the order form for pricing information

The Town House

■ This plan features(per unit):

— Two or three bedrooms

— One full and one three-quarter baths

■ Sheltered entrance leads to spacious Living/Dining area

■ Living area enhanced by a corner fireplace and sliding glass door to Patio with built-in barbecue

■ Efficient, U-shaped Kitchen easily serves Dining area

■ Den/Bedroom with a large closet and easy access to Patio and full bath

■ Spacious Master Bedroom offers three closets, a private Deck and full bath access

■ No materials list is available for this plan

FIRST FLOOR — 722 SQ. FT.
SECOND FLOOR — 512 SQ. FT.

TOTAL LIVING AREA(PER UNIT):
1,234 SQ. FT.

WIDTH 56'-0"
DEPTH 42'-0"

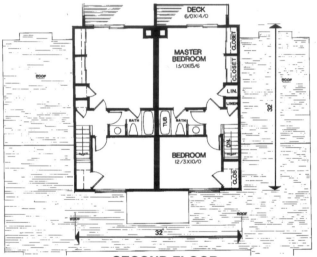

SECOND FLOOR

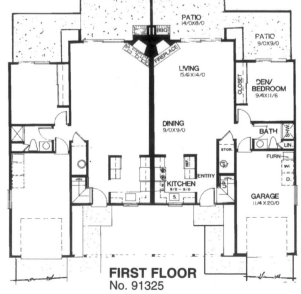

FIRST FLOOR
No. 91325

To order your Blueprints, call 1-800-235-5700

Refer to **Pricing Schedule A** on the order form for pricing information

PLAN NO. 99639

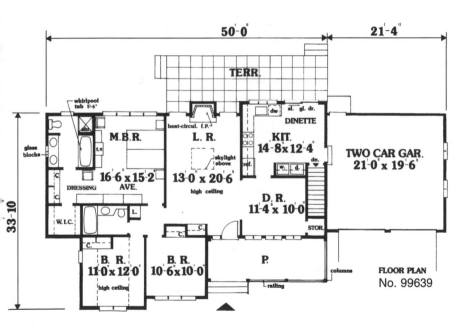

MAIN AREA — 1,367 SQ. FT.
BASEMENT — 1,267 SQ. FT.
GARAGE — 431 SQ. FT.

**TOTAL LIVING AREA:
1,367 SQ. FT.**

One-Story Country Home

■ This plan features:

— Three bedrooms

— Two full baths

■ A Living Room with an imposing, high ceiling that slopes down to a normal height of eight feet, focusing on the decorative heat-circulating fireplace at the rear wall

■ An efficient Kitchen that adjoins the Dining Room which views the front Porch

■ A Dinette Area for informal eating in the Kitchen that can comfortably seat six people

■ A Master Suite arranged with a large dressing area that has a walk-in closet, plus two linear closets and space for a vanity

■ Two family bedrooms that share a full hall bath

Refer to **Pricing Schedule C** on the order form for pricing information

Secluded Master Suite

■ This plan features:

— Three bedrooms

— Two full baths

■ A convenient one-level design with an open floor plan between the Kitchen, Breakfast area and Great Room

■ A vaulted ceiling and a large cozy fireplace in the Great Room

■ A well-equipped Kitchen using a peninsula counter as an eating bar

■ A Master Suite with a luxurious Master Bath

■ Two additional bedrooms having use of a full hall bath

■ An optional crawl space or slab foundation — please specify when ordering

MAIN AREA — 1,680 SQ. FT.
GARAGE — 538 SQ. FT.

TOTAL LIVING AREA:
1,680 SQ. FT.

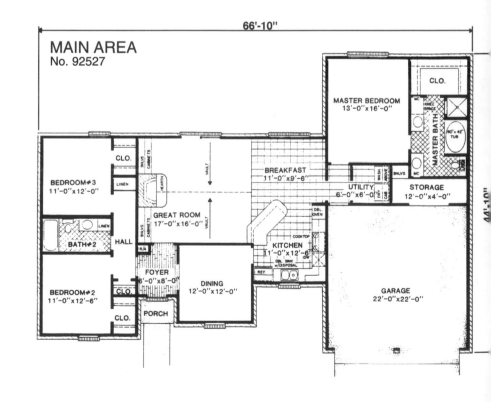

MAIN AREA
No. 92527

66'-10"

MASTER BEDROOM
13'-0"x16'-0"

CLO.

MASTER BATH

60" x 42" TUB

BEDROOM #3
11'-0"x12'-0"

CLO.

LINEN

BREAKFAST
11'-0"x9'-6"

UTILITY
6'-0"x6'-0"

STORAGE
12'-0"x4'-0"

GREAT ROOM
17'-0"x16'-0"

VAULT

VAULT

KITCHEN
11'-0"x12'-6"

LINEN

BATH #2

HALL

FOYER
6'-0"x8'-0"

DINING
12'-0"x12'-0"

GARAGE
22'-0"x22'-0"

BEDROOM #2
11'-0"x12'-6"

CLO.

CLO.

PORCH

WIDTH 54'-0"
DEPTH 47'-6"

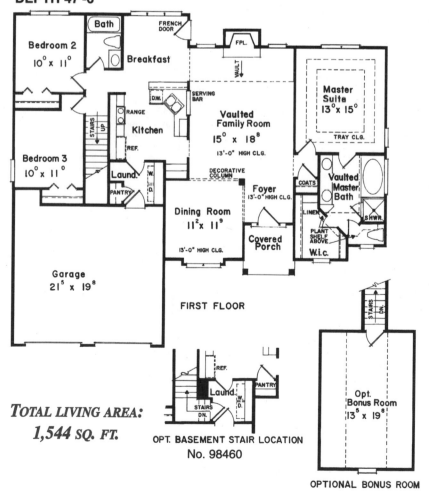

FIRST FLOOR

TOTAL LIVING AREA:
1,544 SQ. FT.

OPT. BASEMENT STAIR LOCATION
No. 98460

OPTIONAL BONUS ROOM

European Flair

■ This plan features:

— Three bedrooms

— Two full baths

■ Large fireplace serving as an attractive focal point for the vaulted Family Room

■ Decorative columns defining the elegant Dining Room

■ Kitchen including a serving bar for the Family Room and a Breakfast area

■ Master Suite topped by a tray ceiling over the bedroom and a vaulted ceiling over the five-piece Master Bath

■ Optional bonus room for future expansion

■ An optional basement or crawl space foundation — please specify when ordering

■ No materials list is available for this plan

MAIN FLOOR — 1,544 SQ. FT.
BONUS ROOM — 284 SQ. FT.
GARAGE — 440 SQ. FT.

Refer to **Pricing Schedule B** on the order form for pricing information

Spacious Family Areas

■ This plan features:

— Three bedrooms

— Two full and one half baths

■ Two-story Foyer with landing staircase leads to formal Living and Dining rooms

■ Open layout for Kitchen/Breakfast area and Family Room

■ Family Room with a focal point fireplace and a wall of windows

■ Master Bedroom has a decorative ceiling and French doors into private bath and walk-in closet

■ Two bedrooms, full bath, laundry closet and Bonus Room complete second floor

■ An optional basement, slab or crawl space foundation — please specify when ordering

FIRST FLOOR — 902 SQ. FT.
SECOND FLOOR — 819 SQ. FT.
FINISHED STAIRCASE — 28 SQ. FT.
BONUS ROOM — 210 SQ. FT.
BASEMENT — 874 SQ. FT.
GARAGE — 400 SQ. FT.

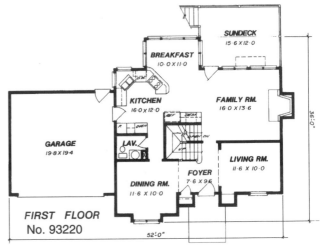

FIRST FLOOR
No. 93220

TOTAL LIVING AREA:
1,749 SQ. FT.

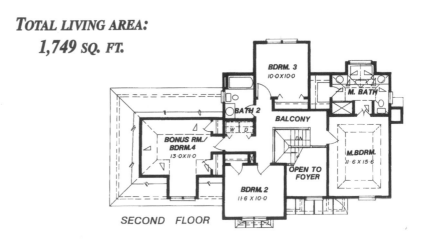

SECOND FLOOR

An
EXCLUSIVE DESIGN
By Jannis Vann & Associates, Inc.

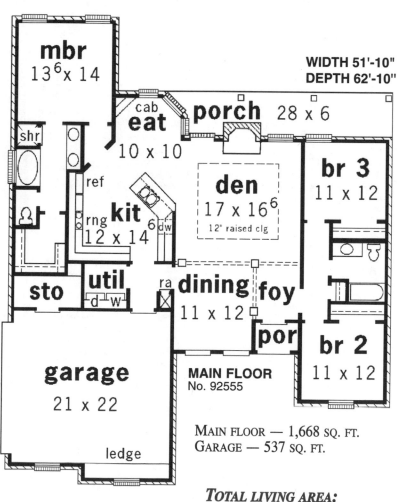

WIDTH 51'-10"
DEPTH 62'-10"

mbr 13⁶ x 14

shr

cab
eat 10 x 10

porch 28 x 6

ref

kit 12 x 14

den 17 x 16⁶
12" raised clg

br 3 11 x 12

rng

dw

util
d w

sto

ra

dining 11 x 12

foy

por

br 2 11 x 12

garage 21 x 22

ledge

MAIN FLOOR
No. 92555

MAIN FLOOR — 1,668 SQ. FT.
GARAGE — 537 SQ. FT.

TOTAL LIVING AREA:
1,668 SQ. FT.

Classic Blend of Brick and Stucco

■ This plan features:

— Three bedrooms

— Two full baths

■ Arched windows on the front of this home combined with brick, stucco, brick quoins and dentil molding

■ Foyer giving access to Den, secondary bedrooms or formal dining room accented by columns

■ Den includes a raised ceiling and a focal point fireplace

■ Kitchen and Breakfast Nook open into the den creating a feeling of spaciousness

■ Master suite is situated to the left, rear corner and features a five piece bath and walk-in closet

■ Two secondary bedrooms sharing a full bath located in the hall between the two rooms

■ An optional crawl space or slab foundation — please specify when ordering

Refer to **Pricing Schedule A** on the order form for pricing information

Easy Maintenance

■ This plan features:

— Two bedroom

— Two three quarter baths

■ Abundant glass and a wrap-around Deck to enjoy the outdoors

■ A tiled entrance into a large Great Room with a fieldstone fireplace and dining area under a sloped ceiling

■ A compact tiled Kitchen open to Great Room and adjacent to the Utility area

■ Two bedrooms, one with a private bath, offer ample closet space

■ No materials list is available for this plan

MAIN AREA — 786 SQ. FT.

TOTAL LIVING AREA:
786 SQ. FT.

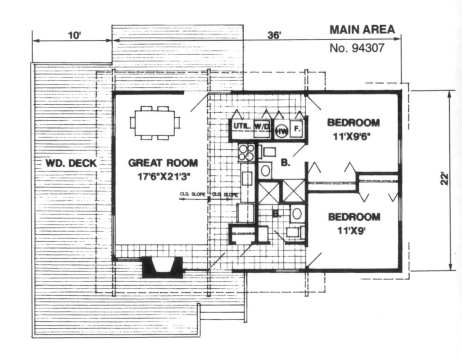

An
EXCLUSIVE DESIGN
By Marshall Associates

To order your Blueprints, call 1-800-235-5700

Refer to **Pricing Schedule A** on the order form for pricing information

47'-0"

54'-0"

PATIO

BDRM-2
11/0 x 10/10

BDRM-3
11/0 x 10/10

KIT.
10/4 x 10/10

VAULTED DINING RM.
10/8 x 11/2

REF.

PANT

LINEN

TUB

VAULTED LIVING RM.
15/10 x 20/8

HEARTH

MASTER
12/10 x 15/2

D

E

S

COVERED PORCH

F

GARAGE
21/4 x 21/8

MAIN AREA
No. 91807

An Affordable, Stylish Floor Plan

■ This plan features:

— Three bedrooms

— One full and one three quarter baths

■ A covered porch entry

■ An old-fashioned hearth fireplace in the vaulted ceiling Living Room

■ A handy Kitchen with U-shaped counter that is accessible from the Dining Room

■ A Master Bedroom with a large walk-in closet and private bath

■ An optional crawl space or slab foundation — please specify when ordering

MAIN FLOOR — 1,410 SQ. FT.
GARAGE — 484 SQ. FT.

TOTAL LIVING AREA: 1,410 SQ. FT.

Refer to **Pricing Schedule C** on the order form for pricing information

© 1996 Donald A. Gardner Architects, Inc.

B. NATHAN

Dramatic Dormers

- This plan features:
  — Three bedrooms
  — Two full baths
- A Foyer open to the dramatic dormer, defined by columns
- A Dining Room augmented by a tray ceiling
- A Great Room expands into the Kitchen and Breakfast Room
- A privately located Master Suite is topped by a tray ceiling and pampered by a garden tub with a picture window as the focal point of the master bath
- Two additional bedrooms, located at the opposite side share a full bath and linen closet

MAIN FLOOR — 1,685 SQ. FT.
GARAGE & STORAGE — 536 SQ. FT.
BONUS — 331 SQ. FT.

TOTAL LIVING AREA:
1,685 SQ. FT.

BONUS RM.
12-0 x 21-8

attic storage   skylights   down

MASTER BED RM.
13-4 x 16-4

skylight

master bath

walk-in closet

lin.

w d

PORCH

cl   up   storage

GREAT RM.
15-4 x 18-6
(cathedral ceiling)

BRKFST.
11-4 x 8-8

BED RM.
11-4 x 11-0

cl   lin.

fireplace

bath

KIT.
11-4 x 12-10

GARAGE
21-0 x 21-8

walk-in closet

cl

BED RM./ STUDY
11-0 x 11-8

FOYER
6-0 x 8-4

DINING
11-0 x 11-8

storage

57-4

PORCH

FLOOR PLAN
No. 99810

62-4

© 1996 Donald A Gardner Architects, Inc.

To order your Blueprints, call 1-800-235-5700

Refer to **Pricing Schedule A** on the order form for pricing information

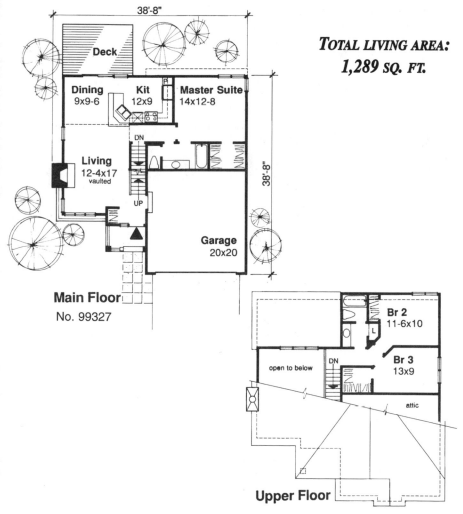

Main Floor
No. 99327

Deck

Dining
9x9-6

Kit
12x9

Master Suite
14x12-8

Living
12-4x17
vaulted

DN

UP

Garage
20x20

38'-8"

38'-8"

Upper Floor

open to below

DN

Br 2
11-6x10

Br 3
13x9

attic

TOTAL LIVING AREA:
1,289 SQ. FT.

Tradition Combined with Contemporary

■ This plan features:

— Three bedrooms

— Two full baths

■ A vaulted ceiling in the Entry

■ A formal Living Room with a fireplace and a half-round transom

■ A Dining Room with sliders to the deck and easy access to the Kitchen

■ A main floor Master Suite with corner windows, a closet and private bath access

■ Two additional bedrooms that share a full hall bath

FIRST FLOOR — 858 SQ. FT.
SECOND FLOOR — 431 SQ. FT.
BASEMENT — 858 SQ. FT.

For First Time Buyers

■ This plan features:

— Three bedrooms

— Two full baths

■ An efficiently designed Kitchen with a corner sink and ample counter space

■ A sunny Breakfast Room with a convenient hide-away laundry center

■ An expansive Family Room that includes a corner fireplace and direct access to the Patio

■ A private Master Suite with a walk-in closet and a double vanity bath

■ Two additional bedrooms, both with walk-in closets, share a full hall bath

■ No materials list available for this plan

MAIN FLOOR — 1,310 SQ. FT.
GARAGE — 449 SQ. FT.

TOTAL LIVING AREA:
1,310 SQ. FT.

WIDTH 49–10

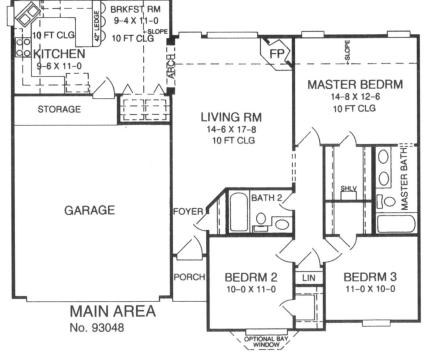

DEPTH 40–6

BRKFST RM
9-4 X 11-0
10 FT CLG
42" LEDGE
SLOPE

10 FT CLG

KITCHEN
9-6 X 11-0

STORAGE

GARAGE

ARCH

FP

SLOPE

MASTER BEDRM
14-8 X 12-6
10 FT CLG

LIVING RM
14-6 X 17-8
10 FT CLG

MASTER BATH

SHLV

FOYER

BATH 2

PORCH

BEDRM 2
10-0 X 11-0

LIN

BEDRM 3
11-0 X 10-0

OPTIONAL BAY
WINDOW

MAIN AREA
No. 93048

Refer to **Pricing Schedule B** on the order form for pricing information

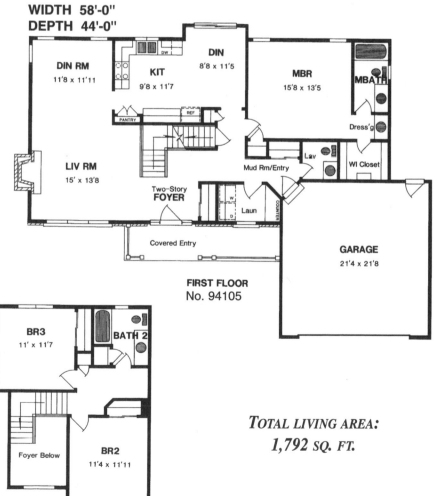

WIDTH 58'-0"
DEPTH 44'-0"

DIN RM
11'8 x 11'11

KIT
9'8 x 11'7

DIN
8'8 x 11'5

MBR
15'8 x 13'5

MBATH

PANTRY

REF

Dress'g

LIV RM
15' x 13'8

Lav

WI Closet

Mud Rm/Entry

Two-Story
FOYER

W
D

Laun

COUNTER

Covered Entry

GARAGE
21'4 x 21'8

FIRST FLOOR
No. 94105

BR3
11' x 11'7

BATH 2

Foyer Below

BR2
11'4 x 11'11

SECOND FLOOR

TOTAL LIVING AREA:
1,792 SQ. FT.

Classic Style and Comfort

■ This plan features:

— Three bedrooms

— Two full and one half bath

■ Covered Entry leads into two-story Foyer with a dramatic landing staircase brightened by decorative window

■ Spacious Living/Dining Room combination with hearth fireplace and decorative windows

■ Hub Kitchen with built-in pantry and informal Dining area with sliding glass door to rear yard

■ First floor Master Bedroom offers a walk-in closet, dressing area and full bath

■ Two additional bedrooms on second floor share a full bath

■ No materials list is available for this plan

FIRST FLOOR — 1,281 SQ. FT.
SECOND FLOOR —511 SQ. FT.
GARAGE — 467 SQ. FT.

Refer to **Pricing Schedule A** on the order form for pricing information

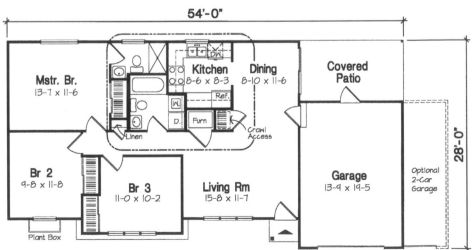

An EXCLUSIVE DESIGN
By Marshall Associates

Champagne Style on a Soda-Pop Budget

■ This plan features:

— Three bedrooms

— One full and one three quarter baths

■ Multiple gables, circle-top windows, and a unique exterior setting this delightful Ranch apart in any neighborhood

■ Living and Dining Rooms flowing together to create a very roomy feeling

■ Sliding doors leading from the Dining Room to a covered patio

■ A Master Bedroom with a private Bath

MAIN AREA — 988 SQ. FT.
BASEMENT — 988 SQ. FT.
GARAGE — 280 SQ. FT
OPTIONAL 2-CAR GARAGE — 384 SQ. FT.

TOTAL LIVING AREA:
988 SQ. FT.

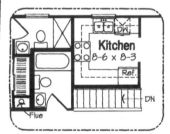

Optional Basement Plan

Main Floor
No. 24302

To order your Blueprints, call 1-800-235-5700

Refer to **Pricing Schedule C** on the order form for pricing information

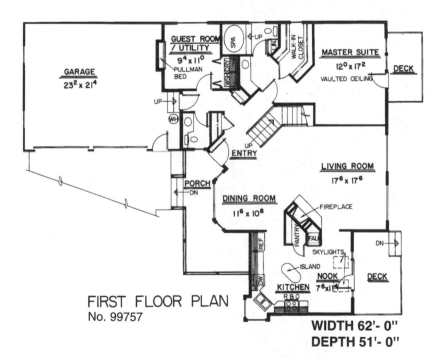

FIRST FLOOR PLAN
No. 99757

GARAGE
23² x 21⁴

GUEST ROOM / UTILITY
9⁴ x 11⁰
PULLMAN BED

SPA

WALK-IN CLOSET

MASTER SUITE
12⁰ x 17²
VAULTED CEILING

DECK

WSH DRY

WH

UP

ENTRY

LIVING ROOM
17⁶ x 17⁶

PORCH
DN

DINING ROOM
11⁶ x 10⁶

FIREPLACE

PANTRY

FAU

SKYLIGHTS

REF

ISLAND

NOOK
7⁶ x 11

DECK

DN

KITCHEN

WIDTH 62'- 0"
DEPTH 51'- 0"

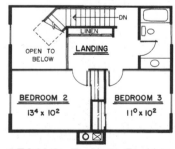

DN

LINEN

OPEN TO BELOW

LANDING

BEDROOM 2
13⁴ x 10²

BEDROOM 3
11⁰ x 10²

SECOND FLOOR PLAN

The Ultimate Kitchen

■ This plan features:

— Three bedrooms

— Two full and one half baths

■ Front Porch leads into an open Entry with an angled staircase

■ Living Room with a wall of windows and an island fireplace opens to Dining Room

■ Kitchen with a work island, walk-in pantry, garden window over sink, skylit Nook and nearby Deck

■ Corner Master Suite enhanced by Deck access, vaulted ceiling, a large walk-in closet and spa bath

■ Guest/Utility Room offers a pullman bed and laundry

■ Two second floor bedrooms with large closets share a full bath

FIRST FLOOR — 1,472 SQ. FT.
SECOND FLOOR — 478 SQ. FT.
GARAGE — 558 SQ. FT.

TOTAL LIVING AREA:
1,950 SQ. FT.

Refer to **Pricing Schedule B** on the order form for pricing information

Large Front Window Provides Streaming Natural Light

■ This plan features:

— Three bedrooms

— Two full and one half baths

■ An outstanding, two-story Great Room with an unusual floor-to-ceiling, corner front window and cozy, hearth fireplace

■ Kitchen with a work island, pantry, a corner, double sink opening to the Great Room, and a bright, bay window eating Nook

■ Master Suite with a vaulted ceiling and a double vanity, spa tub and walk-in closet

■ Two additional bedrooms share a full hall bath and a Bonus area for multiple uses

FIRST FLOOR — 1,230 SQ. FT.
SECOND FLOOR — 477 SQ. FT.
BONUS ROOM — 195 SQ. FT.

TOTAL LIVING AREA:
1,707 SQ. FT.

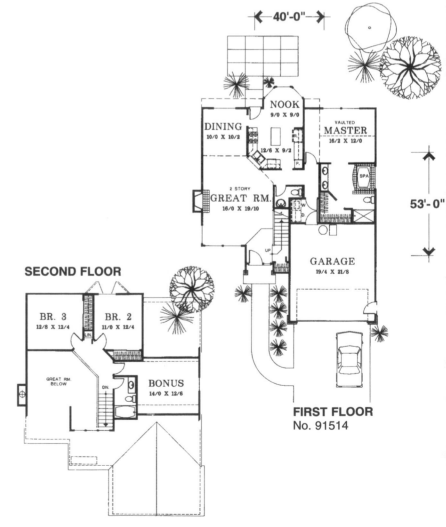

SECOND FLOOR

BR. 3
12/8 X 12/4

BR. 2
11/0 X 12/4

GREAT RM. BELOW

BONUS
14/0 X 12/6

40'-0"

NOOK
9/0 X 9/0

DINING
10/0 X 10/2

12/6 X 9/2

VAULTED
MASTER
16/2 X 12/0

SPA

2 STORY
GREAT RM.
16/0 X 19/10

53'-0"

GARAGE
19/4 X 21/8

FIRST FLOOR
No. 91514

To order your Blueprints, call 1-800-235-5700

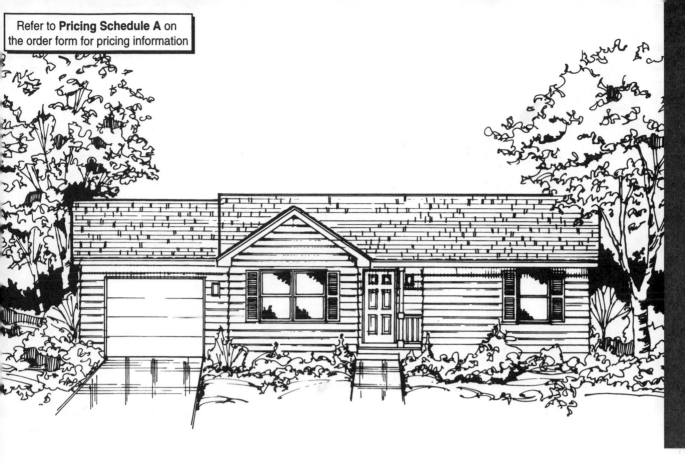

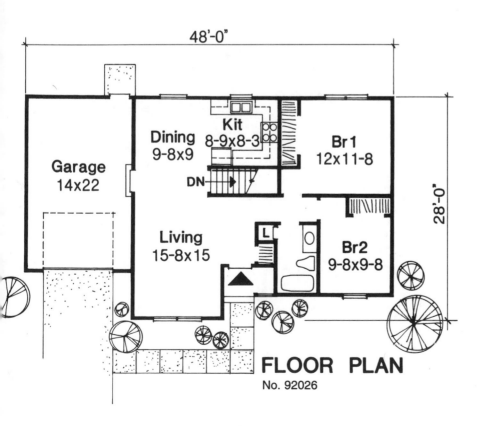

48'-0"

28'-0"

Garage
14x22

Dining
9-8x9

Kit
8-9x8-3

Br 1
12x11-8

DN

Living
15-8x15

L

Br2
9-8x9-8

FLOOR PLAN
No. 92026

Inviting Entrance Welcomes All

■ This plan features:

— Two bedrooms

— One full bath

■ A covered front porch

■ A large Living Room/Dining Room combination

■ An efficient U-shaped Kitchen with a double sink and ample cabinet and counter space

■ Two bedrooms that share the full hall bath and have ample storage space

MAIN FLOOR — 863 SQ. FT.

TOTAL LIVING AREA:
863 SQ. FT.

Refer to **Pricing Schedule C** on the order form for pricing information

Country Living in Any Neighborhood

■ This plan features:

— Three bedrooms

— Two full and two half baths

■ An expansive Family Room with fireplace

■ A Dining Room and Breakfast Nook lit by flowing natural light from bay windows

■ A first floor Master Suite with a double vanity bath that wraps around his-n-her closets

■ An optional basement, slab or crawl space foundation — please specify when ordering

FIRST FLOOR — 1,477 SQ. FT.
SECOND FLOOR — 704 SQ. FT.
BASEMENT — 1,374 SQ. FT.

TOTAL LIVING AREA:
2,181 SQ. FT.

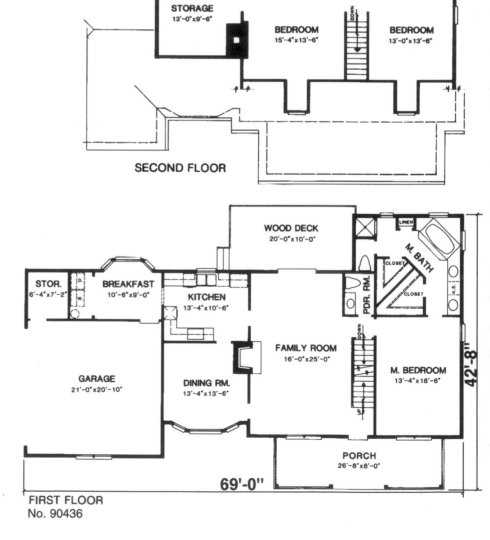

SECOND FLOOR

CLOSET
DRESS. BATH DRESS.
CLOSET

STORAGE
13'-0"x9'-6"

BEDROOM
15'-4"x13'-6"

BEDROOM
13'-0"x13'-6"

DOWN

WOOD DECK
20'-0"x10'-0"

LINEN

M. BATH

CLOSET

PDR. RM.

CLOSET

STOR.
6'-4"x7'-2"

BREAKFAST
10'-6"x9'-0"

KITCHEN
13'-4"x10'-6"

FAMILY ROOM
16'-0"x25'-0"

DOWN

M. BEDROOM
13'-4"x18'-6"

42'-8"

GARAGE
21'-0"x20'-10"

DINING RM.
13'-4"x13'-6"

UP

PORCH
26'-8"x8'-0"

69'-0"

FIRST FLOOR
No. 90436

© 1995 Donald A. Gardner Architects, Inc.

attic storage

BED RM.
10-4 x 10-0

bath

MASTER
BED RM.
13-6 x 15-8

BONUS RM.
20-0 x 14-2

cl

down

walk-in
closet

BED RM.
11-4 x 11-10

walk-in
closet

master
bath

attic
storage

SECOND FLOOR PLAN

TOTAL LIVING AREA:
1,792 SQ. FT.

Appealing Farmhouse Design

■ This plan features:

— Three bedrooms

— Two full and one half baths

■ Comfortable farmhouse features easy to build floor plan with many extras

■ Great Room which is open to the Kitchen and Breakfast bay, and expanded living space provided by the full back porch

■ For narrower lot restrictions, the Garage can be modified to open in front

■ Second floor Master Bedroom contains a walk-in closet and a private bath with a garden tub and separate shower

■ Two more bedrooms on the second floor, one with a walk-in closet, share a full bath

FIRST FLOOR — 959 SQ. F.T
SECOND FLOOR — 833 SQ. FT.
BONUS ROOM — 344 SQ. FT.
GARAGE & STORAGE — 500 SQ. FT.

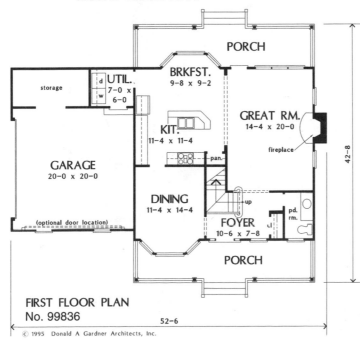

storage

UTIL.
7-0 x
6-0

d

w

BRKFST.
9-8 x 9-2

PORCH

KIT.
11-4 x 11-4

GREAT RM.
14-4 x 20-0

fireplace

GARAGE
20-0 x 20-0

pan.

DINING
11-4 x 14-4

FOYER
10-6 x 7-8

pd.
rm.

cl

42-8

(optional door location)

up

PORCH

FIRST FLOOR PLAN
No. 99836

52-6

© 1995 Donald A Gardner Architects, Inc.

Refer to **Pricing Schedule C** on the order form for pricing information

Distinctive Design

■ This plan features:

— Three bedrooms

— Two full and one half baths

■ Living Room is distinguished by warmth of bayed window and French doors leading to Family Room

■ Built-in curio cabinet adds interest to formal Dining Room

■ Well-appointed Kitchen with island cooktop and Breakfast area designed to save you steps

■ Family Room with fireplace for informal gatherings

■ Spacious Master Bedroom suite with vaulted ceiling over decorative window and plush dressing area with double walk-in closet, dual vanity and a corner whirlpool tub

■ Secondary bedrooms share a double vanity bath

SECOND FLOOR

FIRST FLOOR — 1,093 SQ. FT.
SECOND FLOOR — 905 SQ. FT.
BASEMENT — 1,093 SQ. FT.
GARAGE — 527 SQ. FT.

TOTAL LIVING AREA:
1,998 SQ. FT.

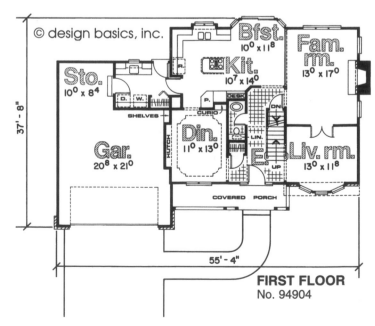

FIRST FLOOR
No. 94904

To order your Blueprints, call 1-800-235-5700

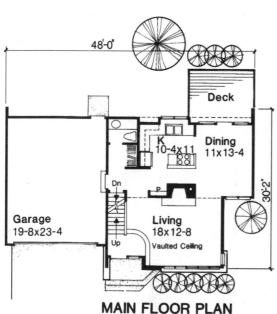

MAIN FLOOR PLAN

48'-0"

Deck

K
10-4x11

Dining
11x13-4

30'-2"

Dn

Garage
19-8x23-4

Living
18x12-8
Vaulted Ceiling

Up

P

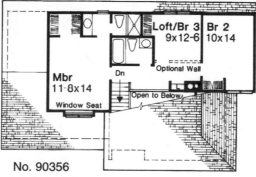

UPPER FLOOR PLAN

No. 90356

Loft/Br 3
9x12-6

Br 2
10x14

Optional Wall

Mbr
11-8x14

Dn

Window Seat

Open to Below

Balcony Overlooks Living Room Below

■ This plan features:

— Three bedrooms

— Two full and one half baths

■ A vaulted ceiling Living Room with a balcony above and a fireplace

■ An efficient, well-equipped Kitchen with stovetop island and easy flow of traffic into the Dining Room

■ A deck accessible from the Living Room

■ A luxurious Master Suite with a bay window seat, walk-in closet, dressing area, and a private shower

■ Two additional bedrooms that share a full hall bath

MAIN FLOOR — 674 SQ. FT.
UPPER FLOOR — 677 SQ. FT.

TOTAL LIVING AREA: 1,351 SQ. FT.

129

To order your Blueprints, call 1-800-235-5700

Refer to **Pricing Schedule C** on the order form for pricing information

Moderate Ranch Has Features of Much Larger Plan

■ This plan features:

— Three bedrooms

— Two full baths

■ A large Great Room with a vaulted ceiling and a stone fireplace with bookshelves on either side

■ A spacious Kitchen with ample cabinet space conveniently located next to the large Dining Room

■ A Master Suite having a large bath with a garden tub, double vanity and a walk-in closet

■ Two other large bedrooms, each with a walk-in closet and access to the full bath

■ An optional basement, slab or crawl space foundation — please specify when ordering

MAIN FLOOR — 1,811 SQ. FT.

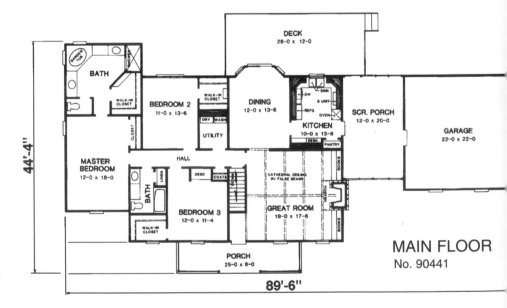

MAIN FLOOR
No. 90441

TOTAL LIVING AREA:
1,811 SQ. FT.

To order your Blueprints, call 1-800-235-5700

Refer to **Pricing Schedule C** on the order form for pricing information

© 1996 Donald A. Gardner Architects, Inc.

B. NATHAN.

DECK

8-0

TOTAL LIVING AREA: 1,689 SQ. FT.

GREAT RM.
19-0 x 16-6

fireplace

cl

pd. rm.

KIT.
11-8 x 11-6

UTIL.
d w

pan.

51-0

GARAGE
15-0 x 20-0

up

FOYER
7-4 x 8-2

DINING
11-4 x 12-0

PORCH

FIRST FLOOR PLAN

37-0

© 1996 Donald A Gardner Architects, Inc.

MASTER BED RM.
13-8 x 11-8

walk-in closet

master bath

lin.

down

BED RM.
11-4 x 10-0

cl

railing

lin.

cl

bath

BED RM.
11-4 x 11-0

SECOND FLOOR PLAN
No. 99884

Narrow Lot Home

■ This plan features:

— Three bedrooms

— Two full and one half baths

■ Deck at the rear expanding living and entertaining space from the Great Room

■ Great Room open to the center island Kitchen with pantry

■ Formal Dining Room accented by columns, located directly off the Foyer

■ Second floor Master Suite placed for utmost privacy with separate shower, garden tub and double vanity

■ Two additional bedrooms sharing a full bath

FIRST FLOOR — 875 SQ. FT.
SECOND FLOOR — 814 SQ. FT.
GARAGE & STORAGE — 317 SQ. FT.

Refer to **Pricing Schedule C** on the order form for pricing information

Executive Two-Story

■ This plan features:

— Three bedrooms

— Two full and one half baths

■ Gracefully curving staircase dominating the Foyer

■ Kitchen and Breakfast Nook separated from the Family Room by only a railing and a step down

■ Built-in entertainment center and a warming fireplace highlighting the sunken Family Room

■ Adjoining formal Living Room and Dining Room that include a fireplace in the Living Room and a built-in china cabinet area in the Dining Room

■ Master Suite boasts a sitting room and a five-piece bath

■ Bonus Room to be finished for future needs

FIRST FLOOR — 1,258 SQ. FT.
SECOND FLOOR — 858 SQ. FT.
GARAGE — 441 SQ. FT.

TOTAL LIVING AREA:
2,116 SQ. FT.

An
EXCLUSIVE DESIGN
By Weinmaster Home Design

FIRST FLOOR
No. 98800

SECOND FLOOR

To order your Blueprints, call 1-800-235-5700

Refer to **Pricing Schedule B** on the order form for pricing information

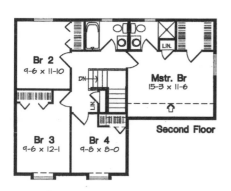

Br 2
9-6 x 11-10

Mstr. Br
15-3 x 11-6

Br 3
9-6 x 12-1

Br 4
9-8 x 8-0

Second Floor

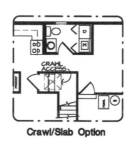

CRAWL ACCESS

Crawl/Slab Option

TOTAL LIVING AREA:
1,505 SQ. FT.

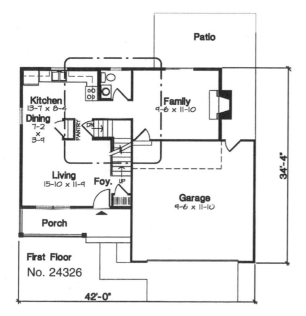

Patio

Kitchen
13-7 x 8-4

Dining
7-2 x 3-9

PANTRY

Family
9-6 x 11-10

34'-4"

Living
15-10 x 11-9

Foy.

UP

Garage
9-6 x 11-10

Porch

First Floor
No. 24326

42'-0"

Family Room With Fireplace

■ This plan features:

— Four bedrooms

— One full, one half, and one three quarter baths

■ A lovely Front Porch shading the entrance

■ A spacious Living Room that opens into the Dining Area which flows into the efficient Kitchen

■ A Family Room equipped with a cozy fireplace and sliding glass doors to a Patio

■ A Master Suite with a large walk-in closet and a private bath with a step-in shower

■ Three additional bedrooms that share a full hall bath

FIRST FLOOR — 692 SQ. FT.
SECOND FLOOR — 813 SQ. FT.
BASEMENT — 699 SQ. FT.

An EXCLUSIVE DESIGN
By Marshall Associates

Refer to **Pricing Schedule C** on the order form for pricing information

© 1991 Donald A. Gardner Architects, Inc.

Country Farmhouse

■ This plan features:

— Three bedrooms

— Two full and one half baths

■ Palladian window in clerestory dormer bathes two-story Foyer in natural light

■ Private Master Bedroom Suite offers everything: walk-in closet, whirlpool tub, shower, and dual vanity

■ Two bedrooms upstairs with dormers and storage access share a full bath

■ Skylit Bonus Room over Garage and optional basement

■ An optional basement or crawl space foundation — please specify when ordering

FIRST FLOOR — 1,356 SQ. FT.
SECOND FLOOR — 542 SQ. FT.
BONUS ROOM — 393 SQ. FT.
GARAGE & STORAGE — 543 SQ. FT.

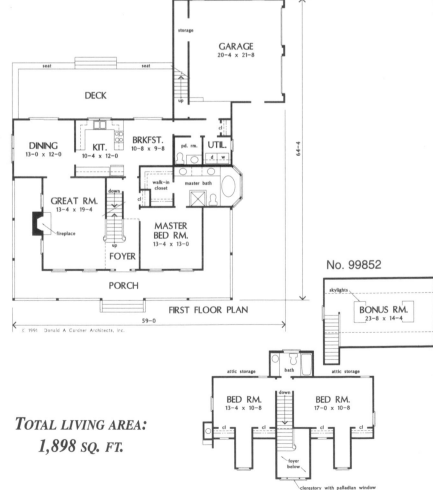

TOTAL LIVING AREA:
1,898 SQ. FT.

To order your Blueprints, call 1-800-235-5700

© 1996 Donald A Gardner Architects, Inc.

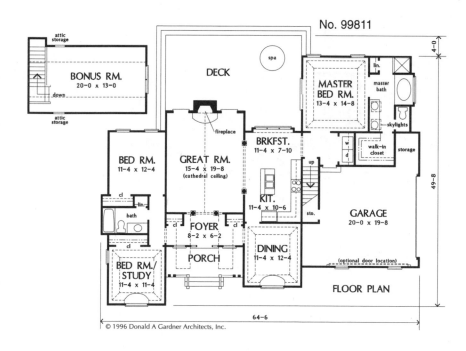

No. 99811

attic storage

BONUS RM.
20-0 x 13-0

down

attic storage

DECK

spa

MASTER BED RM.
13-4 x 14-8

lin.

master bath

skylights

BED RM.
11-4 x 12-4

GREAT RM.
15-4 x 19-8
(cathedral ceiling)

fireplace

BRKFST.
11-4 x 7-10

w
d

walk-in closet

storage

KIT.
11-4 x 10-6

up

sto.

GARAGE
20-0 x 19-8

FOYER
8-2 x 6-2

bath

BED RM./ STUDY
11-4 x 11-4

PORCH

DINING
11-4 x 12-4

(optional door location)

FLOOR PLAN

4-0

49-8

64-6

© 1996 Donald A Gardner Architects, Inc.

TOTAL LIVING AREA:
1,699 SQ. FT.

Cathedral Ceiling Enlarges Great Room

■ This plan features:

— Three bedrooms

— Two full baths

■ Two dormers add volume to the Foyer

■ Great Room, topped by a cathedral ceiling, is open to the Kitchen and Breakfast area

■ Accent columns define the Foyer, Great Room, Kitchen and Breakfast area

■ Private Master Suite crowned in a tray ceiling and highlighted by a skylit bath

■ Front bedroom topped by a tray ceiling

MAIN FLOOR — 1,699 SQ. FT.
GARAGE — 498 SQ. FT.
BONUS — 336 SQ. FT.

To order your Blueprints, call 1-800-235-5700

Refer to **Pricing Schedule B** on the order form for pricing information

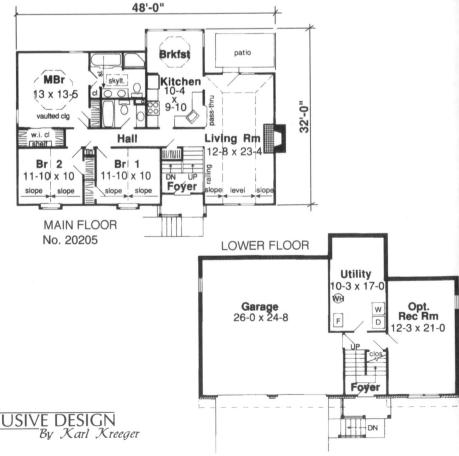

Small But Room To Grow

■ This plan features:

— Three Bedrooms

— Two full Baths

■ A Master Suite with a vaulted ceiling and its own skylit Bath

■ A fireplaced Living Room with a sloped ceiling

■ Efficient Kitchen with a Breakfast Nook

■ Options for growth on the lower level

MAIN FLOOR — 1,321 SQ. FT.
LOWER FLOOR — 286 SQ. FT.
GARAGE — 655 SQ. FT.

TOTAL LIVING AREA:
1,607 SQ. FT.

An
EXCLUSIVE DESIGN
By Karl Kreeger

48'-0"

32'-0"

Brkfst

Kitchen
10-4 x 9-10

patio

MBr
13 x 13-5
vaulted clg

skylt.

cl

st.

w.i. cl
shelf

pass-thru

Living Rm
12-8 x 23-4

Hall

Br 2
11-10 x 10
slope slope

Br 1
11-10 x 10
slope slope

DN UP
Foyer
railing
slope level slope

MAIN FLOOR
No. 20205

LOWER FLOOR

Garage
26-0 x 24-8

Utility
10-3 x 17-0
WH
F
W D

Opt. Rec Rm
12-3 x 21-0

UP
clos
Foyer
DN

To order your Blueprints, call 1-800-235-5700

TOTAL LIVING AREA:
1,170 SQ. FT.

Width 51'-10"
Depth 53'-6"

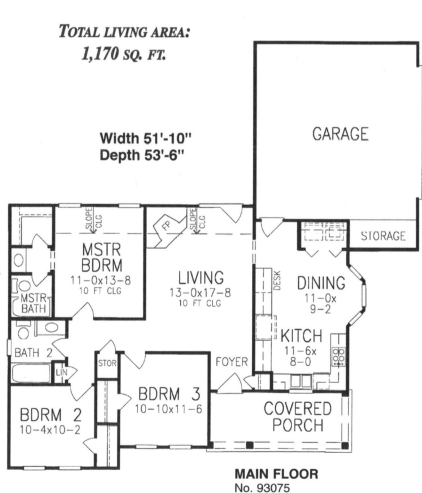

MAIN FLOOR
No. 93075

Timeless Appeal

■ This plan features:

— Three bedrooms

— Two full baths

■ Ten foot ceilings giving the living room a feeling of openness

■ Cozy corner fireplace and access to the rear yard highlight the living room

■ Dining area enhanced by a sunny bay window and is open to the kitchen

■ Bedrooms conveniently grouped and contain roomy closets

■ Master bedroom features a private bath

■ Garage located on the rear and not visible from the front

■ An optional crawl space or slab foundation — please specify when ordering

■ No materials list available

MAIN FLOOR — 1,170 SQ. FT.
GARAGE — 478 SQ. FT.

Refer to **Pricing Schedule B** on the order form for pricing information

Convenient Country

■ This plan features:

— Three bedrooms

— Two full and one half baths

■ Full front Porch provides comfortable visiting area and a sheltered entrance

■ Expansive Living Room with an inviting fireplace opens to bright Dining Room and Kitchen

■ U-shaped Kitchen with peninsula serving counter, Dining Room and nearby Pantry, Laundry and Garage entry

■ Secluded Master Bedroom with two closets and a double vanity bath

■ Two second floor bedrooms with ample closets and dormer windows, share a full bath

■ No materials list is available for this plan

FIRST FLOOR — 1,108 SQ. FT.
SECOND FLOOR — 659 SQ. FT.
BASEMENT — 875 SQ. FT.

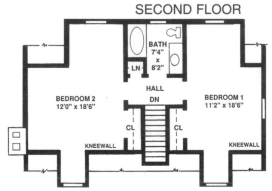

SECOND FLOOR

WIDTH 67'-0"
DEPTH 30'-0"

TOTAL LIVING AREA:
1,767 SQ. FT.

FIRST FLOOR
No. 99045

Refer to **Pricing Schedule B** on the order form for pricing information

PLAN NO. 92238

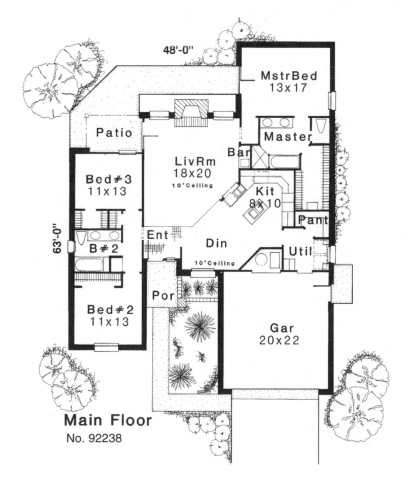

Main Floor
No. 92238

TOTAL LIVING AREA:
1,664 SQ. FT.

Easy Everyday Living

■ This plan features:

— Three bedrooms

— Two full baths

■ Front entrance accented by segmented arches, sidelight and transom windows

■ Open Living Room with focal point fireplace, wetbar and access to Patio

■ Dining area open to both the Living Room and Kitchen

■ Efficient Kitchen with a cooktop island, walk-in pantry and Utility area with a Garage entry

■ Large walk-in closet, double vanity bath and access to Patio featured in the Master Bedroom

■ Two additional bedrooms share a double vanity bath

■ No materials list is available for this plan

MAIN FLOOR — 1,664 SQ. FT.
BASEMENT — 1,600 SQ. FT.
GARAGE — 440 SQ. FT

Refer to **Pricing Schedule A** on the order form for pricing information

Lovely Second Home

■ This plan features:

— Three bedrooms

— One full and one three-quarter baths

■ Firedrum fireplace warming both entryway and Living Room

■ Dining and Living Rooms opening onto the deck, which surrounds the house on three sides

FIRST FLOOR — 808 SQ. FT.
SECOND FLOOR — 288 SQ. FT.

TOTAL LIVING AREA: 1,096 SQ. FT.

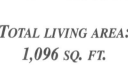

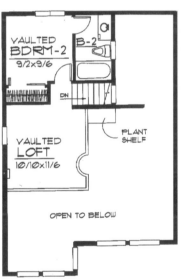

UPPER FLOOR PLAN

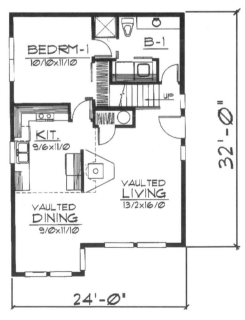

MAIN FLOOR PLAN
No. 91002

To order your Blueprints, call 1-800-235-5700

An
EXCLUSIVE DESIGN
By Westhome Planners, Ltd.

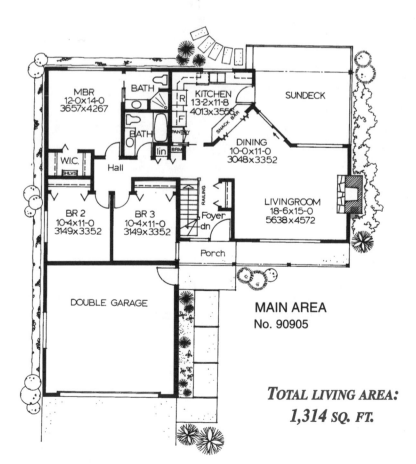

MAIN AREA
No. 90905

TOTAL LIVING AREA:
1,314 SQ. FT.

Compact Home is Surprisingly Spacious

■ This plan features:

— Three bedrooms

— One full and one three quarter baths

■ A spacious Living Room warmed by a fireplace

■ A Dining Room flowing off the Living Room, with sliding glass doors to the deck

■ An efficient, well-equipped Kitchen with a snack bar, double sink, and ample cabinet and counter space

■ A Master Suite with a walk-in closet and private full bath

■ Two additional, roomy bedrooms with ample closet space and protection from street noise from the two-car garage

MAIN AREA — 1,314 SQ. FT.
BASEMENT — 1,488 SQ. FT.
GARAGE — 484 SQ. FT.
WIDTH — 50'-0"
DEPTH — 54'-0"

PLAN NO. 10690

Gingerbread Charm

- This plan features:

— Three bedrooms

— Two and one half baths

- A wrap-around porch and rear deck adding lots of outdoor living space

- A formal Parlor and Dining Room just off the central entry

- A Family Room with a fireplace

- A Master Suite complete with a five-sided sitting nook, walk-in closets and a sunken tub

FIRST FLOOR — 1,260 SQ. FT.
SECOND FLOOR — 1,021 SQ. FT.
BASEMENT — 1,186 SQ. FT.
GARAGE — 851 SQ. FT.

TOTAL LIVING AREA:
2,281 SQ. FT.

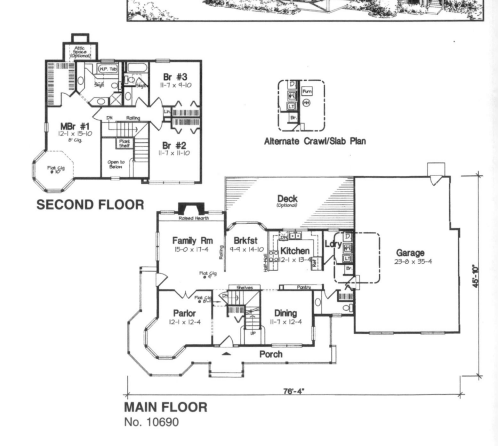

SECOND FLOOR

Alternate Crawl/Slab Plan

MAIN FLOOR
No. 10690

To order your Blueprints, call 1-800-235-5700

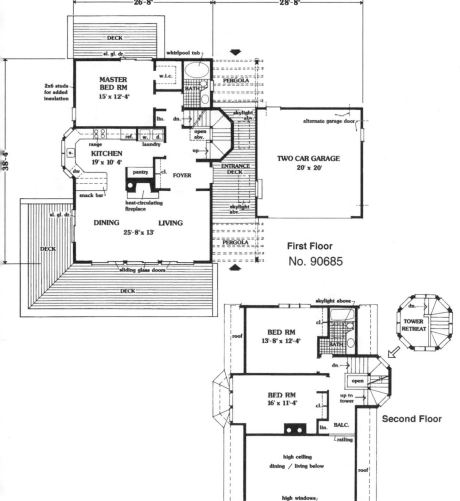

DECK

sl. gl. dr.

whirlpool tub

PERGOLA

MASTER BED RM
15' x 12'-4"

w.i.c.

BATH

2x6 studs for added insulation

skylight abv.

dn.

open abv.

alternate garage door

range

ref.

w.

d.

KITCHEN
19' x 10' 4"

laundry

up

TWO CAR GARAGE
20' x 20'

38'-4"

dw

pantry

cl.

FOYER

ENTRANCE DECK

snack bar

heat-circulating fireplace

sl. gl. dr.

DECK

DINING

LIVING
25'-8" x 13'

skylight abv.

PERGOLA

sliding glass doors

DECK

First Floor
No. 90685

26'-8"

28'-8"

skylight above

cl.

BED RM
13'-8" x 12'-4"

roof

BATH

dn.

TOWER RETREAT

dn.

open

up to tower

BED RM
16' x 11'-4"

cl.

BALC.

lin.

Second Floor

railing

high ceiling dining / living below

roof

high windows

Farmhouse Flavor

■ This plan features:

— Three bedrooms

— Two full baths

■ An octagonal stair tower

■ A Foyer opening to a Living and Dining Room combination, enhanced by a striking glass wall

■ A heat-circulating fireplace adding welcomed warmth

■ A galley-style Kitchen including a large pantry, snack bar and laundry area

■ A Master Suite with a private deck overlooking the backyard

FIRST FLOOR — 1,073 SQ. FT.
SECOND FLOOR — 604 SQ. FT.
RETREAT TOWER — 93 SQ. FT.
GARAGE — 428 SQ. FT.

TOTAL LIVING AREA: 1,770 SQ. FT.

Refer to **Pricing Schedule C** on the order form for pricing information

Family Favorite

■ This plan features:

— Five bedrooms

— Two full and one half baths

■ An efficient Kitchen with a peninsula counter opening into the Family Room

■ A cozy bay window seat in the formal Dining Room

■ A first floor Master Bedroom with an adjoining private Bath including a double vanity

■ A heat-circulating fireplace in the Living Room which has sliding glass doors to the Terrace

■ Three bedrooms located on the second floor that share a full bath

FIRST FLOOR — 1,407 SQ. FT.
SECOND FLOOR — 675 SQ. FT.

TOTAL LIVING AREA: 2,082 SQ. FT.

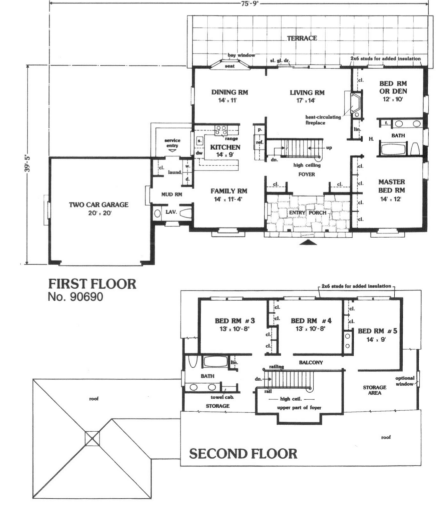

FIRST FLOOR
No. 90690

SECOND FLOOR

To order your Blueprints, call 1-800-235-5700

Refer to **Pricing Schedule A** on the order form for pricing information

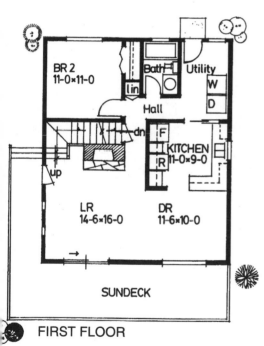

FIRST FLOOR

- BR 2 11-0×11-0
- Bath
- Utility
- W
- D
- Lin
- Hall
- dn
- F
- R
- KITCHEN 11-0×9-0
- L
- up
- LR 14-6×16-0
- DR 11-6×10-0
- SUNDECK

An EXCLUSIVE DESIGN
By Westhome Planners, Ltd.

WIDTH 27'-0"
DEPTH 32'-0"

SECOND FLOOR
No. 90847

- attic
- Ensuite
- attic
- dn
- attic
- MBR 16-0×19-6
- attic
- DECK

Versatile Chalet

■ This plan features:

— Two bedrooms

— Two full baths

■ A Sun deck entry into a spacious Living Room/Dining Room with a fieldstone fireplace, a large window and a sliding glass door

■ A well-appointed Kitchen with extended counter space and easy access to the Dining Room and the Utility area

■ A first floor bedroom adjoins a full hall bath

■ A spacious Master Bedroom, with a private Deck, a Suite bath and plenty of storage

FIRST FLOOR — 864 SQ. FT.
SECOND FLOOR — 496 SQ. FT.
BASEMENT — 864 SQ. FT.

TOTAL LIVING AREA:
1,360 SQ. FT.

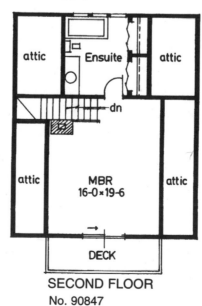

Refer to **Pricing Schedule B** on the order form for pricing information

© 1995 Donald A Gardner Architects, Inc.

Amenities of a Larger Home

■ This plan features:
— Three bedrooms
— Two full baths

■ A continuous cathedral ceiling in the Great Room, Kitchen, and Dining Room giving a spacious feel to this efficient plan

■ Skylighted Kitchen with a seven foot high wall by the Great Room and a popular plant shelf

■ Master Bedroom opens up with a cathedral ceiling and contains walk-in and linen closets and a private bath with garden tub and dual vanity

■ Cathedral ceiling as the crowing touch to the front bedrooms/study

MAIN FLOOR — 1,253 SQ. FT.
GARAGE & STORAGE — 420 SQ. FT.

TOTAL LIVING AREA: 1,253 SQ. FT.

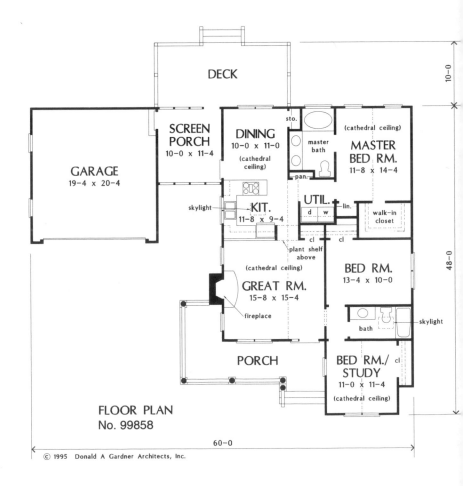

FLOOR PLAN
No. 99858

© 1995 Donald A Gardner Architects, Inc.

Refer to **Pricing Schedule A** on the order form for pricing information

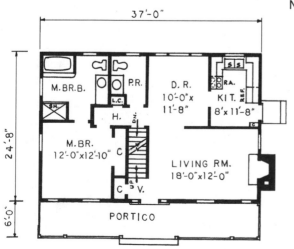

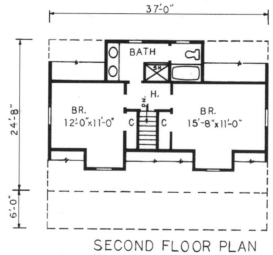

SECOND FLOOR PLAN
No. 99022

37'-0"
24'-8"
6'-0"
BATH
SH
BR. 12'-0"x11'-0"
H.
DN.
C C
BR. 15'-8"x11'-0"

FIRST FLOOR PLAN

37'-0"
24'-8"
6'-0"
M. BR. B.
P.R.
L.C.
SH
D. R. 10'-0"x 11'-8"
KIT. 8'x 11'-8"
REF.
RA.
H.
DN.
M. BR. 12'-0"x12'-10"
C
V.
C
LIVING RM. 18'-0"x12'-0"
PORTICO

Three Bedroom Traditional Country Cape

■ This plan features:

— Three bedrooms

— Two full and one half baths

■ Entry area with a coat closet

■ Ample sized Living Room with a fireplace

■ Dining Room with a view of the rear yard and located conveniently close to the Kitchen and Living Room

■ U-shaped Kitchen with a double sink, ample cabinet and counter space and a side door to the outside

■ First floor Master Suite with a private Master Bath

■ Two additional, second floor bedrooms that share a full, double vanity bath with a separate shower

FIRST FLOOR — 913 SQ. FT.
SECOND FLOOR — 581 SQ. FT.

TOTAL LIVING AREA:
1,494 SQ. FT.

Refer to **Pricing Schedule C** on the order form for pricing information

Home on a Hill

■ This plan features:

— Three bedrooms

— Two full baths

■ Window walls combining with sliders to unite active areas with a huge outdoor deck

■ Interior spaces flowing together for an open feeling, that is accentuated by the sloping ceilings and towering fireplace in the Living Room

■ An island Kitchen with easy access to the Dining Room

■ A Master Suite complete with a garden spa, abundant closet space and a balcony

FIRST FLOOR — 1,316 SQ. FT.
SECOND FLOOR — 592 SQ. FT.

TOTAL LIVING AREA: 1,908 SQ. FT.

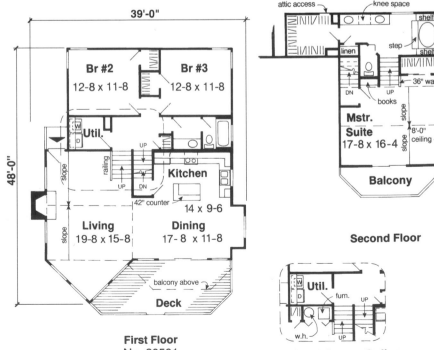

First Floor
No. 20501

39'-0"

48'-0"

Br #2
12-8 x 11-8

Br #3
12-8 x 11-8

Util.

Kitchen
14 x 9-6

42" counter

Living
19-8 x 15-8

Dining
17-8 x 11-8

balcony above

Deck

Second Floor

attic access

knee space

shelf

linen

step

shelf

36" wall

DN

UP

books

Mstr. Suite
17-8 x 16-4

8'-0" ceiling

Balcony

Pier/ Crawl Space Option

Util.

furn.

w.h.

UP

UP

Refer to **Pricing Schedule B** on the order form for pricing information

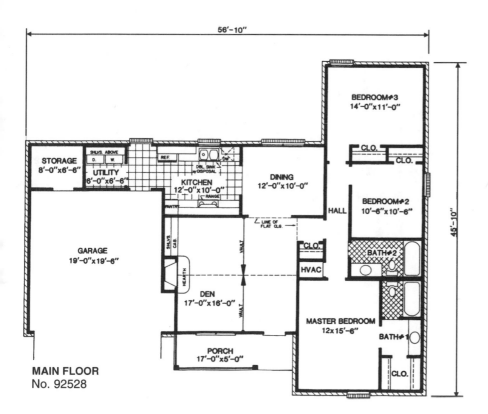

MAIN FLOOR
No. 92528

Warm and Inviting

■ This plan features:

— Three bedrooms

— Two full baths

■ A Den with a cozy fireplace and vaulted ceiling

■ A well-equipped Kitchen that contains a double sink and built-in pantry

■ A spacious Master Bedroom with a private Master Bath and walk-in closet

■ Additional bedrooms sharing full hall bath

■ An optional crawl space or slab foundation — please specify when ordering

MAIN FLOOR — 1,363 SQ. FT.
GARAGE — 434 SQ. FT.

TOTAL LIVING AREA:
1,363 SQ. FT.

Refer to **Pricing Schedule B** on the order form for pricing information

Unique Brick and Shake Siding

■ This plan features:

— Three bedrooms

— Two full baths

■ Sheltered entrance surrounded by glass

■ Windows surround a cozy fireplace in the Great Room topped by a vaulted ceiling

■ Kitchen with loads of counter and storage space, and a snackbar

■ French doors lead into the Master Bedroom Suite with a huge walk-in closet and a double vanity bath

■ Two additional bedrooms with ample closets, share a full bath

■ No materials list available for this plan

MAIN FLOOR — 1,756 SQ. FT.
BASEMENT — 1,756 SQ. FT.
GARAGE — 536 SQ. FT.

An
EXCLUSIVE DESIGN
By Ahmann Design Inc.

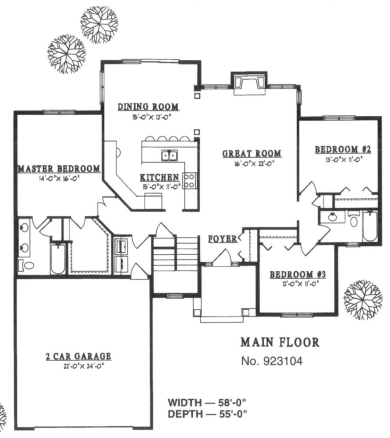

MAIN FLOOR
No. 923104

WIDTH — 58'-0"
DEPTH — 55'-0"

TOTAL LIVING AREA:
1,756 SQ. FT.

© 1996 Donald A Gardner Architects, Inc.

PLAN NO. 99812

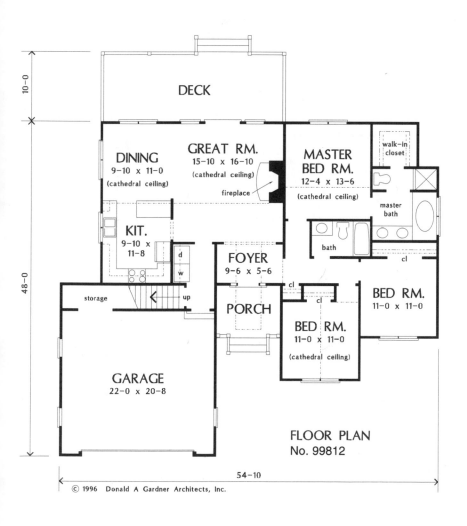

DECK

DINING
9–10 x 11–0
(cathedral ceiling)

GREAT RM.
15–10 x 16–10
(cathedral ceiling)

fireplace

MASTER
BED RM.
12–4 x 13–6
(cathedral ceiling)

walk–in
closet

master
bath

KIT.
9–10 x
11–8

d
w

FOYER
9–6 x 5–6

bath

cl

storage

up

cl

PORCH

cl

BED RM.
11–0 x 11–0

GARAGE
22–0 x 20–8

BED RM.
11–0 x 11–0
(cathedral ceiling)

FLOOR PLAN
No. 99812

10–0

48–0

54–10

© 1996   Donald A Gardner Architects, Inc.

Sunny Dormer
Brightens Foyer

■ This plan features:
—Three bedrooms
—Two full baths

■ Today's comforts with cost effective construction

■ Open Great room, Dining Room, and Kitchen topped by a cathedral ceiling emphasizing spaciousness

■ Adjoining Deck providing extra living or entertaining room

■ Front bedroom crowned in cathedral ceiling and pampered by a private bath with garden tub, dual vanity and a walk-in closet

■ Skylit Bonus Room above the garage offering flexibility and opportunity for growth

MAIN FLOOR — 1,386 SQ. FT.
GARAGE — 517 SQ. FT.
BONUS ROOM — 314 SQ. FT.

**TOTAL LIVING AREA:
1,386 SQ. FT.**

PLAN NO. 92631

Refer to **Pricing Schedule C** on the order form for pricing information

Special Details

- This plan features:

— Four bedrooms

— Two full and one half baths

- Two-story Foyer with a plant shelf and lovely railing staircase

- Great Room with corner fireplace and access to rear yard topped by two-story ceiling

- Kitchen with peninsula counter, walk-in pantry, Breakfast bay and access to Deck, Laundry, Garage entry and formal Dining Room

- Secluded Master Bedroom offers a sloped ceiling and lavish bath

- Three bedrooms on second floor share a double vanity bath

- No materials list is available for this plan

FIRST FLOOR — 1,511 SQ. FT.
SECOND FLOOR — 646 SQ. FT.
BASEMENT — 1,479 SQ. FT.
GARAGE — 475 SQ. FT.

TOTAL LIVING AREA:
2,157 SQ. FT.

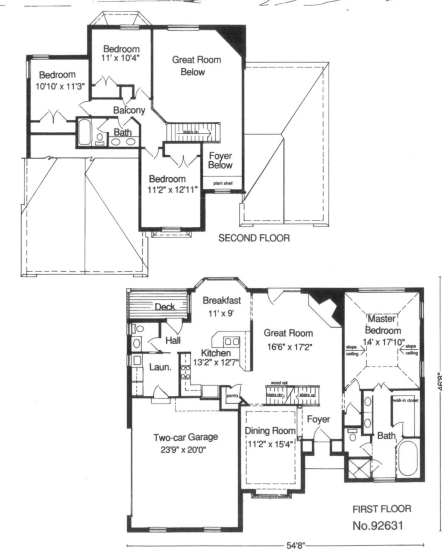

152

To order your Blueprints, call 1-800-235-5700

Refer to **Pricing Schedule B** on the order form for pricing information

Style and Convenience

■ This plan features:

— Three bedrooms

— Two full baths

■ A sheltered Porch leads into an easy-care tiled Entry

■ Spacious Living Room offers a cozy fireplace, triple window and access to Patio

■ An efficient Kitchen with a skylight, work island, Dining area, walk-in pantry and Utility/Garage entry

■ Secluded Master Bedroom highlighted by a vaulted ceiling, access to Patio and a lavish bath

■ Two additional bedrooms, one with a cathedral ceiling, share a full bath

■ No materials list available for this plan

MAIN FLOOR — 1,653 SQ. FT.
GARAGE — 420 SQ. FT.

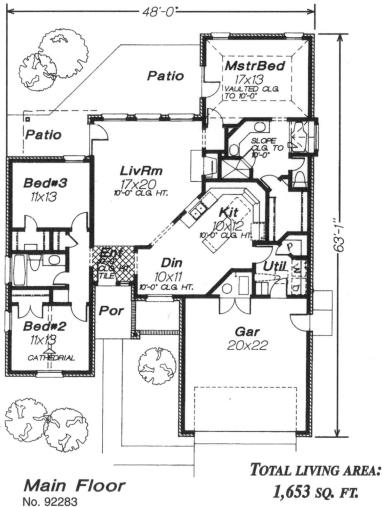

Main Floor
No. 92283

TOTAL LIVING AREA:
1,653 SQ. FT.

Refer to **Pricing Schedule A** on the order form for pricing information

Inviting Porch Adorns Affordable Home

■ This plan features:

— Three bedrooms

— Two full baths

■ A large and spacious Living Room that adjoins the Dining Room for ease in entertaining

■ A private bedroom wing offering a quiet atmosphere

■ A Master Bedroom with his-n-her closets and a private bath

■ An efficient Kitchen with a walk-in pantry

MAIN AREA — 1,160 SQ. FT.
LAUNDRY/MUDROOM — 83 SQ. FT.

TOTAL LIVING AREA: 1,243 SQ. FT.

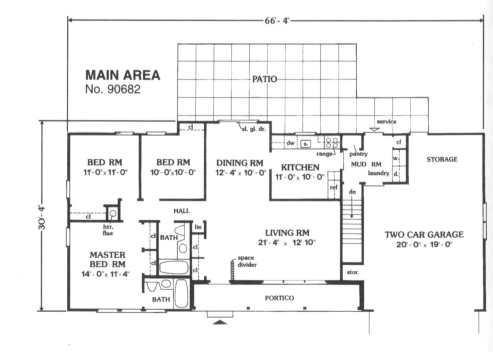

To order your Blueprints, call 1-800-235-5700

Refer to **Pricing Schedule B** on the order form for pricing information

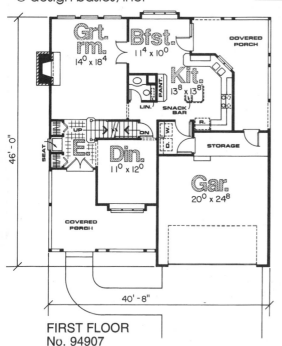

FIRST FLOOR — 905 SQ. FT.
SECOND FLOOR — 863 SQ. FT.
BASEMENT — 905 SQ. FT.
GARAGE — 487 SQ. FT.

TOTAL LIVING AREA: 1,768 SQ. FT.

© design basics, inc.

SECOND FLOOR

Mbr. 13⁰ x 14⁴
CATHEDRAL CEILING
SEAT
WHIRLPOOL
LIN.
Br. 2 10⁰ x 12⁰
10'-0" CLG.
Br. 3 11⁰ x 10⁰
SEAT
SKYLIGHT
DN

Grt. rm. 14⁰ x 18⁴
Bfst. 11⁴ x 10⁰
COVERED PORCH
Kit. 13⁸ x 13⁸
PANT.
LIN.
SNACK BAR
UP
DN
Din. 11⁰ x 12⁰
D.W.
R.
STORAGE
Gar. 20⁰ x 24⁸
SEAT
COVERED PORCH
46' - 0"
40' - 8"

FIRST FLOOR
No. 94907

Victorian Accents

■ This plan features:

— Three bedrooms

— Two full and one half baths

■ Covered Porch and double doors lead into Entry accented by a window seat and curved banister staircase

■ Decorative windows overlooking the backyard and a large fireplace highlight Great Room

■ A hub Kitchen with an island/snack bar and large pantry acesses the formal Dining Room and Breakfast area

■ Powder room, laundry area, Garage entry and storage nearby to Kitchen

■ Cathedral ceiling crowns Master Bedroom with two walk-in closets, dual vanity and a whirlpool tub

■ Two additional bedrooms, one with a vaulted ceiling above a window seat, share a full bath

Country Styled Duplex

■ This plan features(per unit):

— Two or three bedrooms

— One full and one half baths

■ Covered sitting porch, cedar shingles on gable ends, wood shutters and window boxes add to country flavor

■ Tiled entry into spacious Living area with decorative window, opens to Dining area

■ Efficient, U-shaped Kitchen with a serving counter/snackbar

■ First floor Study/Bedroom with closet and access to a half bath

■ Large second floor bedrooms offer maximum privacy with separating roof

■ Rear bedroom enhanced by two closets and private access to double vanity bath

MAIN FLOOR — 700 SQ. FT.
SECOND FLOOR — 588 SQ. FT.

TOTAL LIVING AREA PER UNIT:
1,288 SQ. FT.

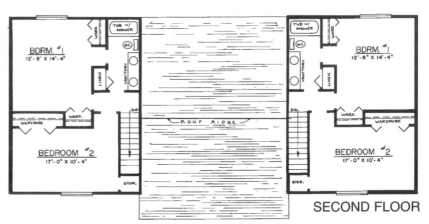

SECOND FLOOR

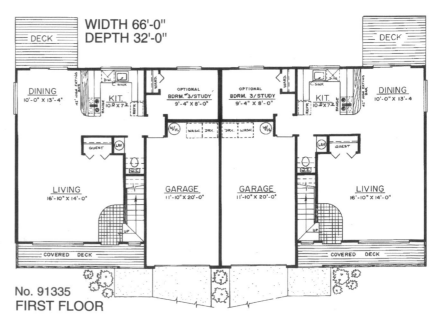

WIDTH 66'-0"
DEPTH 32'-0"

No. 91335
FIRST FLOOR

To order your Blueprints, call 1-800-235-5700

PLAN NO. 24402

Cathedral Ceiling in Living Room and Master Suite

■ This plan features:

— Three bedrooms

— Two full baths

■ A spacious Living Room with a cathedral ceiling and elegant fireplace

■ A Dining Room that adjoins both the Living Room and the Kitchen

■ An efficient Kitchen, with double sinks, ample cabinet space and peninsula counter that doubles as an eating bar

■ A convenient hallway laundry center

■ A Master Suite with a cathedral ceiling and a private Master Bath

MAIN AREA — 1,346 SQ. FT.
GARAGE — 449 SQ. FT.

TOTAL LIVING AREA:
1,346 SQ. FT.

46'-1"

53'-1"

Mstr Br
13-9 x 11-10
cathedral

Deck

Br 2
9-11 x 11-7

linen

Br 3
9-11 x 11-4

Dining
7-11 x 10-8

Kitchen
11-8 x 10-8

Living
24-1 x 14-4
cathedral

furn.   w/h

Garage
19-4 x 19-11

MAIN AREA
No. 24402

An EXCLUSIVE DESIGN *By Upright Design*

Refer to **Pricing Schedule A** on the order form for pricing information

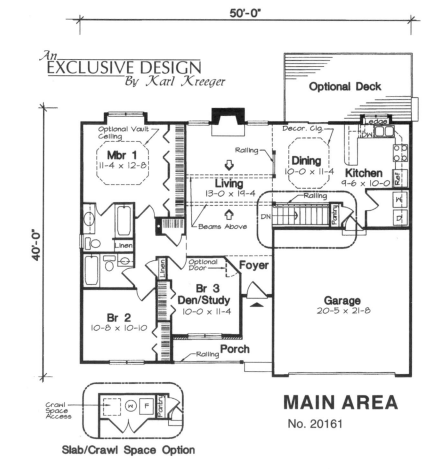

Delightful Doll House

■ This plan features:

— Three bedrooms

— Two full baths

■ A sloped ceiling in the Living Room which also has a focal point fireplace

■ An efficient Kitchen with a peninsula counter and a built-in pantry

■ A decorative ceiling and sliding glass doors to the deck in the Dining Room

■ A Master Suite with a decorative ceiling, ample closet space and a private full bath

■ Two additional bedrooms that share a full hall bath

MAIN FLOOR — 1,307 SQ. FT.
BASEMENT — 1,298 SQ. FT.
GARAGE — 462 SQ. FT.

TOTAL LIVING AREA:
1,307 SQ. FT.

An
EXCLUSIVE DESIGN
By Karl Kreeger

50'-0"

40'-0"

Optional Deck

Optional Vault Ceiling

Mbr 1
11-4 x 12-8

Railing

Decor. Clg.

Ledge
DW

Dining
10-0 x 11-4

Kitchen
9-6 x 10-0

Ref

Living
13-0 x 19-4

Railing

Beams Above

Linen

DN

Pantry

Optional Door

Foyer

Linen

Br 3
Den/Study
10-0 x 11-4

Garage
20-5 x 21-8

Br 2
10-8 x 10-10

Railing **Porch**

Crawl Space Access

Pantry

Slab/Crawl Space Option

MAIN AREA
No. 20161

Refer to **Pricing Schedule A** on the order form for pricing information

PLAN NO. 92400

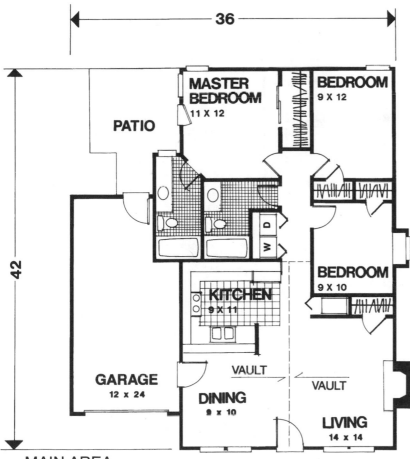

MAIN AREA
No. 92400

36

42

PATIO

MASTER BEDROOM
11 x 12

BEDROOM
9 X 12

W D

BEDROOM
9 X 10

KITCHEN
9 X 11

GARAGE
12 x 24

VAULT

VAULT

DINING
9 x 10

LIVING
14 x 14

Quaint Starter Home

- This plan features:
— Three bedrooms
— Two full baths

- A vaulted ceiling giving an airy feeling to the Dining and Living Rooms

- A streamlined Kitchen with a comfortable work area, a double sink and ample cabinet space

- A cozy fireplace in the Living Room

- A Master Suite with a large closet, French doors leading to the patio and a private bath

- Two additional bedrooms sharing a full bath

- No materials list available for this plan

MAIN AREA — 1,050 SQ. FT.

TOTAL LIVING AREA: 1,050 SQ. FT.

Refer to **Pricing Schedule C** on
the order form for pricing information

Charming Brick Home

■ This plan features:

— Three bedrooms

— Two full baths

■ Covered entrance leads to a
Living Room with fireplace

■ Island Kitchen, open to the
Dining Room, offering ample
storage and easy access to the
Laundry area and Garage

■ A Master Bedroom with a walk-
in closet, access to the Patio, and
a plush bath with a window tub,
step-in shower and double vanity

■ Two additional bedrooms, with
decorative windows, sharing a
full hall bath

■ No materials list is available for
this plan

MAIN FLOOR — 1,868 SQ. FT
BASEMENT — 1,868 SQ. FT.
GARAGE — 782 SQ. FT.

TOTAL LIVING AREA:
1,868 SQ. FT.

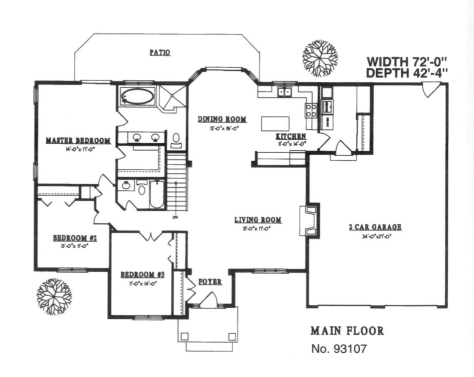

WIDTH 72'-0"
DEPTH 42'-4"

MAIN FLOOR
No. 93107

An
EXCLUSIVE DESIGN
By Ahmann Design Inc.

To order your Blueprints, call 1-800-235-5700

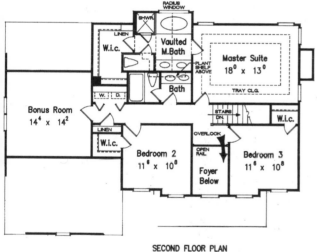

SECOND FLOOR PLAN

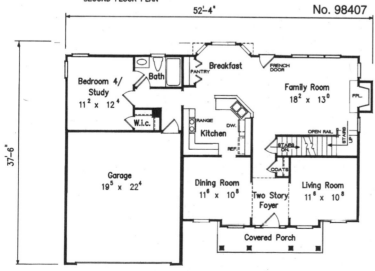

No. 98407

FIRST FLOOR PLAN

Old Fashioned With Contemporary Interior

■ This plan features:

— Four bedrooms

— Three full baths

■ A two-story Foyer is flanked by the Living and Dining Rooms

■ The Family Room features a fireplace and a French door

■ The bayed Breakfast Nook and Pantry are adjacent to the Kitchen

■ Master Suite has a trayed ceiling, an attached Bath with a vaulted ceiling and radius window

■ Two additional Bedrooms, a full Bath, a laundry closet, and Bonus room complete the upstairs floor

■ An optional basement or crawl space foundation — please specify when ordering this plan

FIRST FLOOR — 1,135 SQ. FT.
SECOND FLOOR — 917 SQ. FT.
BONUS — 216 SQ. FT.

TOTAL LIVING AREA:
2,052 SQ. FT.

© 1994 Donald A. Gardner Architects,

Mixture of Traditional and Country Charm

■ This plan features:

— Three bedrooms

— Two full and one half baths

■ Stairs to the skylit bonus room located near the Kitchen and Master Suite

■ Master Suite crowned in cathedral ceiling has a skylit bath containing a whirlpool tub and dual vanity

■ Great Room, topped by a cathedral ceiling and highlighted by a fireplace, is adjacent to the country Kitchen

■ Two additional bedrooms share a hall bath

MAIN FLOOR — 1,954 SQ. FT.
GARAGE — 649 SQ. FT.
BONUS — 436 SQ. FT.

TOTAL LIVING AREA:
1,954 SQ. FT.

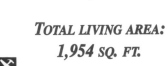

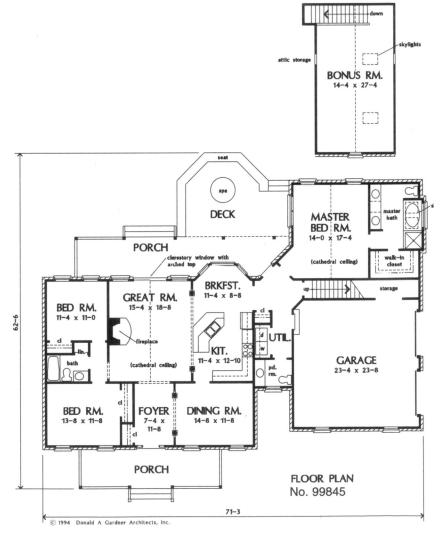

BONUS RM.
14-4 x 27-4

attic storage

skylights

down

DECK

seat

spa

PORCH

clerestory window with arched top

MASTER BED RM.
14-0 x 17-4

(cathedral ceiling)

master bath

skyligh

walk-in closet

storage

up

GREAT RM.
15-4 x 18-8

(cathedral ceiling)

fireplace

BRKFST.
11-4 x 8-8

cl

KIT.
11-4 x 12-10

d w

UTIL.

pd. rm.

GARAGE
23-4 x 23-8

BED RM.
11-4 x 11-0

cl

lin.

bath

BED RM.
13-8 x 11-8

cl

FOYER
7-4 x 11-8

cl

DINING RM.
14-8 x 11-8

PORCH

62-6

71-3

FLOOR PLAN
No. 99845

© 1994 Donald A Gardner Architects, Inc.

To order your Blueprints, call 1-800-235-5700

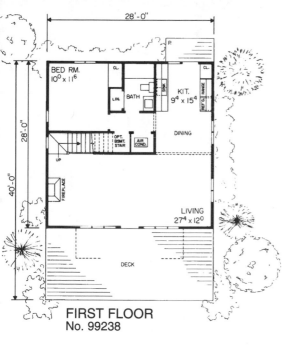

FIRST FLOOR
No. 99238

BED RM. 10⁰ x 11⁶

KIT. 9⁴ x 15⁴

DINING

LIVING 27⁴ x 12⁰

DECK

28'-0"

28'-0"

40'-0"

SECOND FLOOR

DORMITORY 17⁴ x 9⁴

MASTER BED RM. 15⁰ x 12⁰

BATH

BALCONY

ROOF

STORAGE

Economical Vacation Home

■ This plan features:

— Three bedrooms

— Two full baths

■ A large rectangular Living Room with a fireplace at one end and plenty of room for separate activities at the other end

■ A galley-style Kitchen with adjoining Dining area

■ A second-floor Master Bedroom with a children's dormitory across the hall

■ A second-floor deck outside the Master Bedroom

FIRST FLOOR — 784 SQ. FT.
SECOND FLOOR — 504 SQ. FT.

TOTAL LIVING AREA: *1,288 SQ. FT.*

Refer to **Pricing Schedule C** on the order form for pricing information

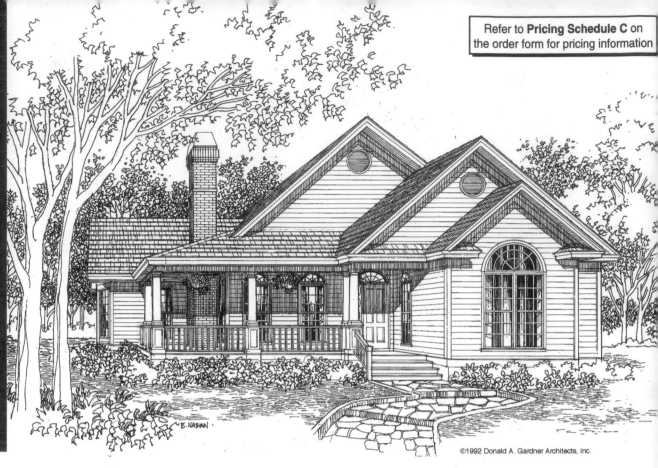

©1992 Donald A. Gardner Architects, Inc.

B. NATHAN

Perfect for Narrow Lot

■ This plan features:

— Three bedrooms

— Two full baths

■ Columns open interior for circulation and spaciousness

■ Cathedral ceilings enhance Great Room and Bedroom/Study

■ Tray ceilings dress up Dining Room, Breakfast area and Master Bedroom

■ Open Kitchen and Dining Room access Porch and Deck areas

■ Master suite features walk-in closet, dual vanity, shower and whirlpool tub

MAIN FLOOR — 1,858 SQ. FT.
GARAGE & STORAGE — 504 SQ. FT.

TOTAL LIVING AREA:
1,858 SQ. FT.

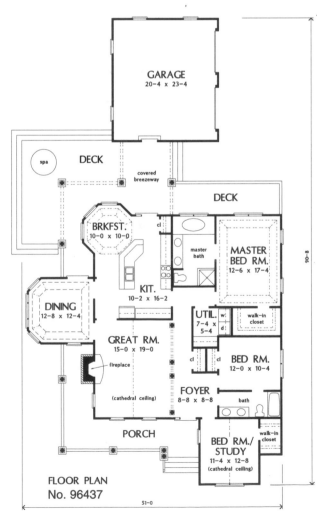

GARAGE
20-4 x 23-4

spa

DECK

covered breezeway

DECK

BRKFST.
10-0 x 10-0

cl

master bath

MASTER BED RM.
12-6 x 17-4

90-8

walk-in closet

KIT.
10-2 x 16-2

UTIL.
7-4 x 5-4

w
d

DINING
12-8 x 12-4

GREAT RM.
15-0 x 19-0

cl

cl

BED RM.
12-0 x 10-4

fireplace

FOYER
8-8 x 8-8

bath

(cathedral ceiling)

PORCH

BED RM./ STUDY
11-4 x 12-8
(cathedral ceiling)

walk-in closet

FLOOR PLAN
No. 96437

51-0

To order your Blueprints, call 1-800-235-5700

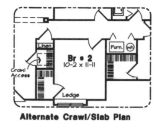

Alternate Crawl/Slab Plan

TOTAL LIVING AREA:
1,576 SQ. FT.

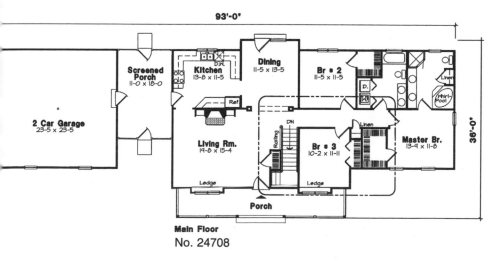

Main Floor
No. 24708

Cozy Country Ranch

■ This plan features:

— Three bedrooms

— Two full baths

■ Front Porch shelters visitors and entrance into Living Room

■ Expansive Living Room highlighted by a boxed window and hearth fireplace between built-ins

■ Efficient, U-shaped Kitchen with direct access to the Screened Porch and the Dining Room

■ Master Bedroom wing enhanced by a large walk-in closet and a double vanity bath with a whirlpool tub

■ Two additional bedrooms with large closets, share a double vanity bath with laundry center

■ No materials list available for this plan

MAIN FLOOR — 1,576 SQ. FT.
GARAGE — 576 SQ. FT.
BASEMENT — 1,454 SQ. FT.

Refer to **Pricing Schedule A** on the order form for pricing information

Formal Balance

■ This plan features:

— Three bedrooms

— Two full baths

■ A cathedral ceiling in the Living Room with a heat-circulating fireplace as the focal point

■ A bow window in the Dining Room that adds elegance as well as natural light

■ A well-equipped Kitchen that serves both the Dinette and the formal Dining Room efficiently

■ A Master Bedroom with three closets and a private Master Bath with sliding glass doors to the Master Deck with a hot tub

MAIN FLOOR — 1,476 SQ. FT.
BASEMENT — 1,361 SQ. FT.
GARAGE — 548 SQ. FT.

TOTAL LIVING AREA:
1,476 SQ. FT.

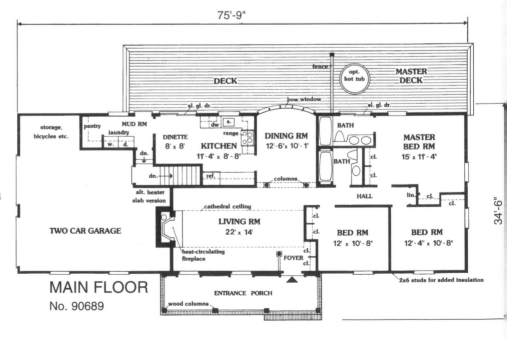

75'-9"

DECK

fence

opt. hot tub

MASTER DECK

sl. gl. dr.

bow window

sl. gl. dr.

storage, bicycles etc.

pantry

MUD RM

laundry

w. d.

dn.

DINETTE
8' x 8'

dw

s.

range

KITCHEN
11'-4" x 8'-8"

DINING RM
12'-6" x 10'-1"

BATH

BATH

MASTER BED RM
15' x 11'-4"

cl.

cl.

dn.

ref.

columns

HALL

lin.

cl.

cl.

alt. heater
slab version

cathedral ceiling

TWO CAR GARAGE

LIVING RM
22' x 14'

cl.

cl.

BED RM
12' x 10'-8"

BED RM
12'-4" x 10'-8"

cl.

heat-circulating
fireplace

cl.

FOYER

cl.

2x6 studs for added insulation

34'-6"

MAIN FLOOR

No. 90689

ENTRANCE PORCH

wood columns

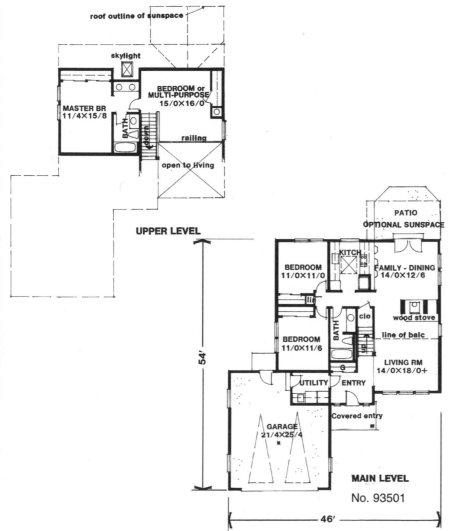

roof outline of sunspace

skylight

MASTER BR 11/4×15/8

BATH

BEDROOM or MULTI-PURPOSE 15/0×16/0

railing

open to living

UPPER LEVEL

54'

PATIO OPTIONAL SUNSPACE

BEDROOM 11/0×11/0

KITCH

FAMILY - DINING 14/0×12/6

wood stove

BEDROOM 11/0×11/6

BATH

clo

line of balc

UTILITY

ENTRY

LIVING RM 14/0×18/0+

GARAGE 21/4×25/4

Covered entry

MAIN LEVEL

No. 93501

46'

Contemporary Cape

■ This plan features:

— Four bedrooms

— Two full baths

■ Covered Entry leads into Living Room with barrel vault ceiling, arched window and cozy fireplace which divides the Family/Dining area

■ Skylight highlights compact Kitchen with open snackbar which serves Dining area and Patio/Optional Sunspace

■ Private Master Bedroom offers a wall of closets, a double vanity bath with skylight and nearby bedroom or multi-purpose room

■ Two first floor bedrooms with ample closets, share a full bath

FIRST FLOOR — 1,154 SQ. FT.
SECOND FLOOR — 585 SQ. FT.

TOTAL LIVING AREA: 1,739 SQ. FT.

167

Refer to **Pricing Schedule C** on the order form for pricing information

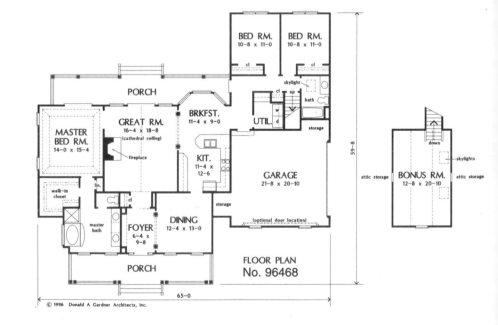

©1996 Donald A. Gardner Architects, Inc.

B. NATHAN

Easy Living Plan

■ This plan features:

— Three bedrooms

— Two full baths

■ Sunlit Foyer flows easily into the generous Great Room

■ Great Room crowned in a cathedral ceiling and accented by a fireplace

■ Accent columns define the open Kitchen and Breakfast Bay

■ Master Bedroom topped by a tray ceiling and highlighted by a well-appointed Master Bath

■ Two additional bedrooms share a skylit bath in the hall

MAIN AREA — 1,864 SQ. FT.
BONUS ROOM — 319 SQ. FT.
GARAGE — 503 SQ. FT.

> TOTAL LIVING AREA:
> 1,864 SQ. FT.

Floor plan labels:

BED RM. 10-8 x 11-0 · BED RM. 10-8 x 11-0

PORCH

BRKFST. 11-4 x 9-0 · UTIL. · skylight · cl · up · bath · storage · d w

GREAT RM. 16-4 x 18-8 (cathedral ceiling) · fireplace

MASTER BED RM. 14-0 x 15-4

KIT. 11-4 x 12-6

GARAGE 21-8 x 20-10

walk-in closet · lin.

master bath · cl

FOYER 6-4 x 9-8 · DINING 12-4 x 13-0

storage

(optional door location)

PORCH

59-8 · attic storage

65-0

FLOOR PLAN No. 96468

© 1996 Donald A Gardner Architects, Inc.

up · down · skylights

BONUS RM. 12-8 x 20-10 · attic storage

© 1992 Donald A Gardner Architects, Inc.

PLAN NO. 99800

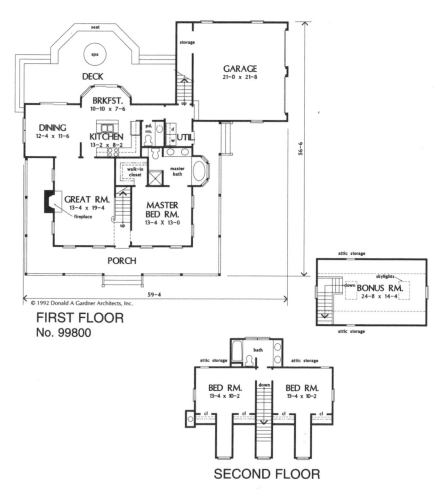

FIRST FLOOR
No. 99800

© 1992 Donald A Gardner Architects, Inc.

SECOND FLOOR

Classic Country Farmhouse

■ This plan features:

— Three bedrooms

— Two full and one half baths

■ Covered Porch gives classic country farmhouse look

■ Clerestory dormer window bathes the two-story Foyer in light

■ Great Room with fireplace opens to the Dining/Breakfast/Kitchen area, which leads to a Deck with optional spa and seating for indoor/outdoor entertaining

■ Master Bedroom offers a separate shower, whirlpool tub, and a double vanity

FIRST FLOOR — 1,145 SQ. FT.
SECOND FLOOR — 518 SQ. FT.
BONUS ROOM — 380 SQ. FT.
GARAGE & STORAGE — 509 SQ. FT.

TOTAL LIVING AREA:
1,663 SQ. FT.

Refer to **Pricing Schedule B** on the order form for pricing information

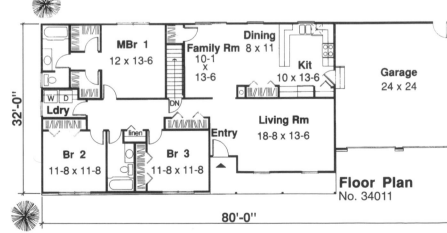

Windows Add Warmth To All Living Areas

■ This plan features:

— Three bedrooms

— Two full baths

■ A Master Suite with huge his-n-her walk-in closets and private bath

■ A second and third bedroom with ample closet space

■ A Kitchen equipped with an island counter, and flowing easily into the Dining and Family Rooms

■ A Laundry Room conveniently located near all three bedrooms

■ An optional garage

MAIN AREA— 1,672 SQ. FT.
OPTIONAL GARAGE — 566 SQ. FT.

TOTAL LIVING AREA:
1,672 SQ. FT.

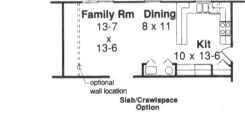

Family Rm **Dining**
13-7   8 x 11
x
13-6   **Kit**
                    10 x 13-6

optional
wall location

Slab/Crawlspace Option

MBr 1
12 x 13-6

Family Rm
10-1
x
13-6

Dining 8 x 11

Kit
10 x 13-6

Garage
24 x 24

32'-0"

W D

Ldry

DN

linen

Living Rm
18-8 x 13-6

Br 2
11-8 x 11-8

Br 3
11-8 x 11-8

Entry

Floor Plan
No. 34011

80'-0"

© 1997 Donald A Gardner Architects, Inc.

B. NATHAN

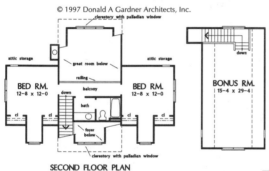

© 1997 Donald A Gardner Architects, Inc.

clerestory with palladian window

attic storage

great room below

attic storage

railing

BED RM.
12-8 x 12-0

balcony

down

BED RM.
12-8 x 12-0

bath

cl

cl

cl

cl

foyer below

BONUS RM.
15-4 x 29-4

down

clerestory with palladian window

SECOND FLOOR PLAN

TOTAL LIVING AREA:
2,188 SQ. FT.

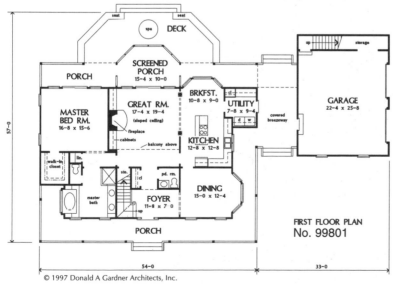

seat   seat

spa   **DECK**

SCREENED PORCH
15-4 x 10-0

PORCH

BRKFST.
10-8 x 9-0

GREAT RM.
17-4 x 19-4
(sloped ceiling)

UTILITY
7-8 x 9-4

up   storage

GARAGE
22-4 x 25-8

MASTER BED RM.
16-8 x 15-6

fireplace

cabinets

balcony above

KITCHEN
12-8 x 12-8

covered breezeway

walk-in closet

lin.

sto.

cl

pd. rm.

DINING
15-0 x 12-4

master bath

FOYER
11-8 x 7-0

up

FIRST FLOOR PLAN
No. 99801

PORCH

57-0

54-0

33-0

© 1997 Donald A Gardner Architects, Inc.

Columns Punctuate the Interior Space

■ This plan features:

— Three bedrooms

— Two full and one half baths

■ A two-story Great Room and Foyer, both with dormer windows, welcome natural light into this graceful country classic with a wrap-around porch

■ Large Kitchen, featuring a center cooking island with counter and large Breakfast area, opens to the Great Room for easy entertaining

■ Columns punctuate the interior spaces and a separate Dining Room provides a formal touch to the plan

■ Master Bedroom Suite, privately situated on the first floor, has a double vanity, garden tub, and separate shower

FIRST FLOOR — 1,618 SQ. FT.
SECOND FLOOR — 570 SQ. FT.
BONUS ROOM — 495 SQ. FT.
GARAGE & STORAGE — 649 SQ. FT.

Refer to **Pricing Schedule C** on the order form for pricing information

© 1993 Donald A. Gardner Architects, Inc.

B. NATHAN

Quaint and Cozy

■ This plan features:

— Three bedrooms

— Two full and one half bath

■ Spacious floor plan with large Great Room crowned by cathedral ceiling

■ Central kitchen with angled counter opens to the breakfast area and Great Room for easy entertaining

■ Privately located Master Bedroom has a cathedral ceiling and nearby access to the deck with an optional spa

■ Operable skylights over the tub accent the luxurious Master Bath

■ Bonus room over the garage makes expanding easy.

■ An optional crawl space or basement foundation — please specify when ordering

MAIN FLOOR — 1,864 SQ. FT.
GARAGE — 614 SQ. FT.
BONUS — 420 SQ.FT.

TOTAL LIVING AREA:
1,864 SQ. FT.

To order your Blueprints, call 1-800-235-5700

Refer to **Pricing Schedule D** on the order form for pricing information

P L A N N O . 2 4 2 6 8

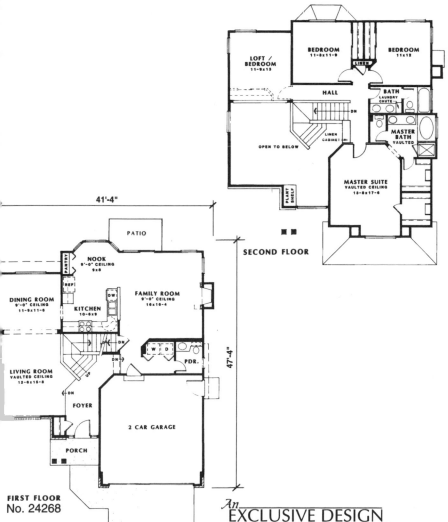

41'-4"

PATIO

PANTRY

NOOK
9'-0" CEILING
9x8

REF.

DINING ROOM
9'-0" CEILING
11-9x11-8

KITCHEN
10-6x9

DW

FAMILY ROOM
9'-0" CEILING
16x16-4

LIVING ROOM
VAULTED CEILING
12-8x16-8

UP

DN

W D

PDR.

47'-4"

DN

FOYER

2 CAR GARAGE

PORCH

FIRST FLOOR
No. 24268

LOFT / BEDROOM
11-9x13

BEDROOM
11-9x11-9

BEDROOM
11x12

LINEN

HALL

BATH
LAUNDRY CHUTE

OPEN TO BELOW

LINEN CABINET

MASTER BATH
VAULTED

PLANT SHELF

MASTER SUITE
VAULTED CEILING
13-8x17-6

SECOND FLOOR

An
EXCLUSIVE DESIGN
By Energetic Enterprises

Stately Entrance Adds to Home's Exterior

■ This plan features:

— Three or four bedrooms

— Two full and one half baths

■ A vaulted ceiling in the Living Room adding to its spaciousness

■ A formal Dining Room

■ An efficient Kitchen with double sinks, and ample storage space

■ An informal Eating Nook with a built-in pantry

■ Family Room with a fireplace

■ A plush Master Suite with a vaulted ceiling and luxurious Master Bath plus two walk-in closets

■ Two bedrooms share a full bath with a convenient laundry chute

FIRST FLOOR — 1,115 SQ. FT.
SECOND FLOOR — 1,129 SQ. FT.
BASEMENT — 1,096 SQ. FT.
GARAGE — 415 SQ. FT.

TOTAL LIVING AREA:
2,244 SQ. FT.

Refer to **Pricing Schedule A** on the order form for pricing information

A Special Kind of Coziness

■ This plan features:

— Three bedrooms

— One full and one half baths

■ An open rail staircase compliments the central Foyer

■ The Living room with it's warm fireplace combines with the Dining area

■ The Kitchen is highlighted by a desk, a pantry and a serving bar

■ Laundry conveniently located near the bedrooms

■ The Master Suite includes a private half bath

■ Two secondary bedrooms have ample closet space

MAIN FLOOR — 1,089 SQ. FT.
BASEMENT — 1,089 SQ. FT.
GARAGE — 462 SQ. FT.

TOTAL LIVING AREA:
1,089 SQ. FT.

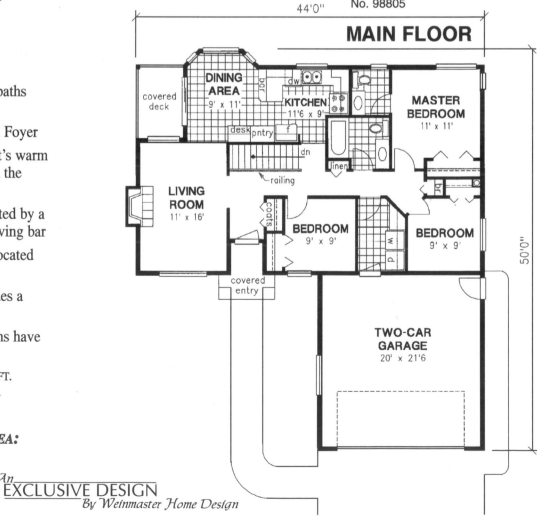

No. 98805

MAIN FLOOR

44'0"

50'0"

covered deck

DINING AREA
9' x 11'

bar

dw

KITCHEN
11'6 x 9'

desk

pntry

f

dn

linen

railing

MASTER BEDROOM
11' x 11'

LIVING ROOM
11' x 16'

coats

BEDROOM
9' x 9'

w

BEDROOM
9' x 9'

covered entry

TWO-CAR GARAGE
20' x 21'6

An
EXCLUSIVE DESIGN
By Weinmaster Home Design

To order your Blueprints, call 1-800-235-5700

PLAN NO. 98430

No. 98430

Main floor

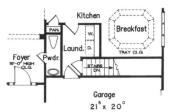

OPT. BASEMENT STAIRS LOCATION

MAIN FLOOR — 1,884 SQ. FT.
BASEMENT — 1,908 SQ. FT.
GARAGE — 495 SQ. FT.

TOTAL LIVING AREA:
1,884 SQ. FT.

With All the Amenities

■ This plan features:
— Three bedrooms
— Two full and one half baths

■ Sixteen foot high ceiling over the Foyer

■ Arched openings highlight the hallway accessing the fireplaced Great Room

■ French door to the rear yard and decorative columns at its arched entrance

■ Vaulted ceiling in Dining Room

■ Expansive Kitchen features a center work island, a built-in pantry and a breakfast area defined by a tray ceiling

■ Master Suite has tray ceiling treatment, lavish private bath and huge walk-in closet

■ Secondary bedrooms have private access to a full bath

■ An optional basement, slab or crawl space foundation — please specify when ordering

Enhanced by a Columned Porch

■ This plan features:

— Three bedrooms

— Two full baths

■ A Great Room with a fireplace and decorative ceiling

■ A large efficient Kitchen with Breakfast area

■ A Master Bedroom with a private Master Bath and walk-in closet

■ A formal Dining Room located near the Kitchen

■ Two additional bedrooms with walk-in closets and use of full hall bath

■ An optional crawl space or slab foundation — please specify when ordering

MAIN FLOOR — 1,754 SQ. FT.
GARAGE — 552 SQ. FT.

TOTAL LIVING AREA:
1,754 SQ. FT.

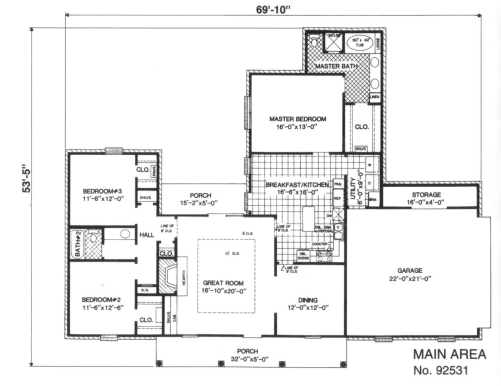

MAIN AREA
No. 92531

To order your Blueprints, call 1-800-235-5700

© 1993 Donald A Gardner Architects, Inc.

TOTAL LIVING AREA:
1,576 SQ. FT.

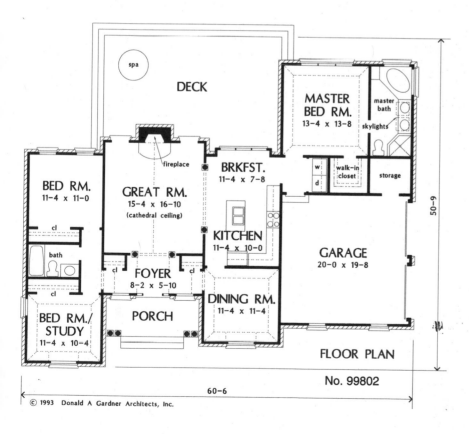

FLOOR PLAN

No. 99802

60-6

© 1993 Donald A Gardner Architects, Inc.

Traditional Beauty

- This plan features:
- — Three bedrooms
- — Two full baths
- Traditional beauty with large arched windows, round columns, covered porch, brick veneer and an open floor plan
- Clerestory dormers above covered porch lighting the Foyer
- Cathedral ceiling and fireplace enhancing the Great Room
- Island Kitchen with Breakfast area accessing the large Deck with an optional spa
- Columns defining spaces
- Tray ceiling over the Master Bedroom, Dining Room and Bedroom/Study
- Dual vanity, separate shower, and whirlpool tub in the Master Bath

MAIN FLOOR — 1,576 SQ. FT.
GARAGE — 465 SQ. FT.

Compact and Convenient Colonial

■ This plan features:

— Three bedrooms

— Two full and one half baths

■ Traditional Entry with landing staircase, closet and powder room

■ Living Room with focal point fireplace opens to formal Dining Room for ease in entertaining

■ Efficient, L-shaped Kitchen with built-in pantry, eating Nook and Garage entry

■ Corner Master Bedroom with private bath and attic access

■ Two additional bedrooms with ample closets share a double vanity bath

FIRST FLOOR — 624 SQ. FT.
SECOND FLOOR — 624 SQ. FT.
GARAGE — 510 SQ. FT.

TOTAL LIVING AREA:
1,248 SQ. FT.

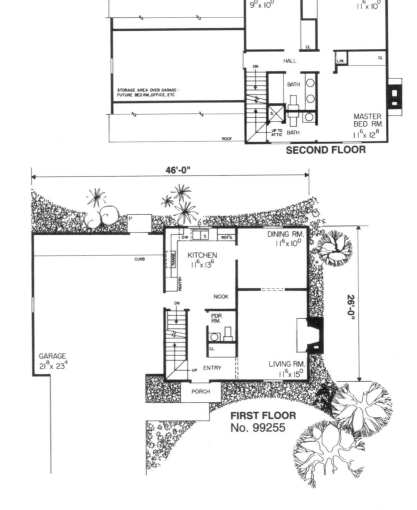

SECOND FLOOR

FIRST FLOOR
No. 99255

PLAN NO. 93133

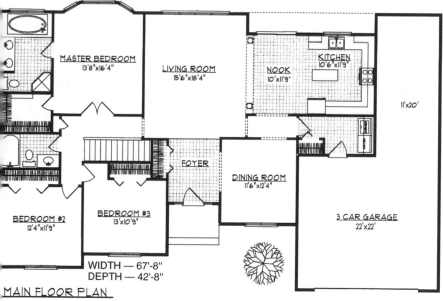

TOTAL LIVING AREA:
1,761 SQ. FT.

MASTER BEDROOM
13'8"x16'4"

LIVING ROOM
15'6"x18'4"

NOOK
10'x11'9"

KITCHEN
10'6"x11'9"

11'x20'

FOYER

DINING ROOM
11'6"x12'4"

3 CAR GARAGE
22'x22'

BEDROOM #2
12'4"x11'9"

BEDROOM #3
13'x10'9"

WIDTH — 67'-8"
DEPTH — 42'-8"

MAIN FLOOR PLAN
No. 93133

An
EXCLUSIVE DESIGN
By Ahmann Design Inc.

Triple Tandem Garage

■ This plan features:

— Three bedrooms

— Two full baths

■ A large Foyer leading to the bright and spacious Living Room

■ A large open Kitchen with a central work island

■ A handy Laundry Room with a pantry and garage access

■ A Master Suite with a bay windowed sitting area and French doors, as well as a private Master Bath with a oversized tub, corner shower and room-sized walk-in closet

■ Two additional front bedrooms that share a full bath

■ A triple tandem garage with space for a third car, boat or just extra work and storage space

■ No materials list available for this plan

MAIN FLOOR — 1,761 SQ. FT.
BASEMENT — 1,761 SQ. FT.
GARAGE — 658 SQ. FT.

Refer to **Pricing Schedule C** on the order form for pricing information

A Modern Look At Colonial Styling

■ This plan features:

— Three bedrooms

— Two full and one half baths

■ Brick detailing and keystones highlight elevation

■ Two-story Foyer opens to formal Living and Dining rooms

■ Expansive Family Room with a hearth fireplace between built-in shelves and Deck access

■ U-shaped Kitchen with serving counter, Breakfast alcove, and nearby Garage entry

■ Elegant Master Bedroom with a decorative ceiling, large walk-in closet and a double vanity bath

■ Two additional bedrooms share a full bath, laundry and Bonus area

FIRST FLOOR — 987 SQ. FT.
SECOND FLOOR — 965 SQ. FT.
FINISHED STAIRCASE — 72 SQ. FT.
BONUS — 272 SQ. FT.

TOTAL LIVING AREA:
2,024 SQ. FT.

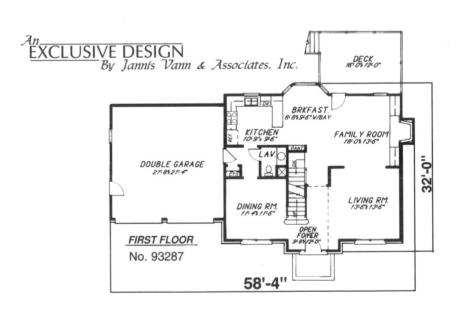

An
EXCLUSIVE DESIGN
By Jannis Vann & Associates, Inc.

FIRST FLOOR
No. 93287

58'-4"

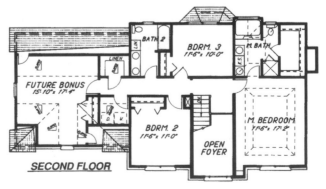

SECOND FLOOR

180

Refer to **Pricing Schedule C** on the order form for pricing information

FIRST FLOOR — 1,405 SQ. FT.
SECOND FLOOR — 453 SQ. FT.
BONUS ROOM — 300 SQ. FT.
BASEMENT — 1,405 SQ. FT.
GARAGE — 490 SQ. FT.

TOTAL LIVING AREA:
1,858 SQ. FT.

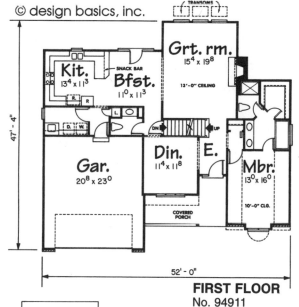

© design basics, inc.

FIRST FLOOR
No. 94911

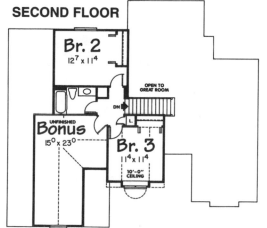

SECOND FLOOR

Fieldstone Facade and Arched Windows

■ This plan features:
— Three bedrooms
— Two full and one half baths

■ Inviting Covered Porch shelters entrance

■ Expansive Great Room enhanced by warm fireplace and three transom windows

■ Breakfast area adjoins Great Room giving a feeling of more space

■ An efficient Kitchen with counter snack bar and nearby laundry and Garage entry

■ A first floor Master Bedroom suite with an arched window below a sloped ceiling and a double vanity bath

■ Two additional bedrooms share a Bonus area and a full bath on the second floor

Refer to **Pricing Schedule B** on the order form for pricing information

A-Frame for Year-Round Living

- **■** This plan features:
- — Three bedrooms
- — One full and one three quarter baths
- **■** A vaulted ceiling in the Living Room with a massive fireplace
- **■** A wrap-around sun deck that gives you a lot of outdoor living space
- **■** A luxurious Master Suite complete with a walk-in closet, full bath and private Deck
- **■** Two additional bedrooms that share a full hall bath

MAIN FLOOR — 1,238 SQ. FT.
LOFT — 464 SQ. FT.
BASEMENT — 1,175 SQ. FT.
WIDTH — 34'-0"
DEPTH — 56'-0"

An
EXCLUSIVE DESIGN
By Westhome Planners, Ltd.

TOTAL LIVING AREA:
1,702 SQ. FT.

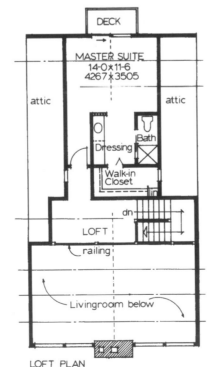

DECK

MASTER SUITE
14-0 x 11-6
4267 x 3505

attic   attic

Dressing   Bath

Walk-in Closet

lin

dn

LOFT

railing

Livingroom below

LOFT PLAN

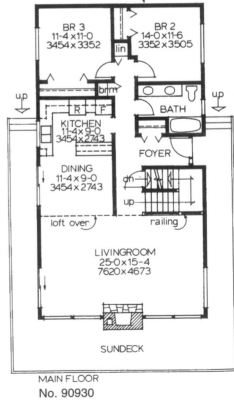

Full Basement under

BR 3
11-4 x 11-0
3454 x 3352

BR 2
14-0 x 11-6
3352 x 3505

lin

up   up

R   F   BATH

KITCHEN
11-4 x 9-0
3454 x 2743

DINING
11-4 x 9-0
3454 x 2743

FOYER

dn

up

loft over   railing

LIVINGROOM
25-0 x 15-4
7620 x 4673

SUNDECK

MAIN FLOOR
No. 90930

To order your Blueprints, call 1-800-235-5700

Refer to **Pricing Schedule C** on the order form for pricing information

© 1996 Donald A. Gardner Architects, Inc.

Traditional Two-Story

- This plan features:
  — Three bedrooms
  — Two full and one half baths
- Great Room crowned in a cathedral ceiling and highlighted by a fireplace and colonnaded opening
- A pass-through above the Kitchen sink making both serving and cleaning up a snap
- Traffic flows easily into the Dining Room topped by a tray ceiling and spilling out onto the deck when needed
- Secluded Master Suite highlighted by a generous walk-in closet and private bath with separate shower, enclosed toilet, and corner garden tub
- Two secondary bedrooms upstairs share a full bath

FIRST FLOOR — 1,116 SQ. FT.
SECOND FLOOR — 442 SQ. FT.
GARAGE & STORAGE — 313 SQ. FT.

First Floor Plan

master bath
MASTER BED RM.
13-2 x 13-0
walk-in closet
DECK
w d
UTIL.
lin.
KITCHEN
9-0 x 11-8
pd. rm.
cl
GARAGE
14-4 X 20-8
DINING
11-4 x 12-0
GREAT RM.
14-8 x 16-0
(cathedral ceiling)
fireplace
FOYER
7-0 x 6-9
up
PORCH
52-0
49-0

FIRST FLOOR PLAN

© 1996 Donald A Gardner Architects, Inc.

Second Floor Plan

BED RM.
11-0 x 10-8
attic storage
attic storage
cl
cl
BED RM.
10-10 x 11-8
bath
down
great room below

SECOND FLOOR PLAN
No. 99883

TOTAL LIVING AREA:
1,558 SQ. FT.

To order your Blueprints, call 1-800-235-5700

B. NATHAN

© 1990 Donald A. Gardner Architects, Inc.

Compact Three Bedroom

■ This plan features:

—Three bedrooms

—Two full baths

■ Contemporary interior punctuated by elegant columns

■ Dormers above the covered porch light the foyer leading to the dramatic Great Room crowned in a cathedral ceiling and enhanced by a fireplace

■ Great Room opens to the island Kitchen with Breakfast area and access to a spacious rear deck

■ Tray ceilings adding interest to the Bedroom/Study, Dining Room and the Master Bedroom

■ Luxurious Master Bedroom suite highlighted by a walk-in closet and a bath with dual vanity, separate shower and a pampering whirlpool tub

MAIN FLOOR — 1,452 SQ. FT.
GARAGE AND STORAGE — 427 SQ. FT.

TOTAL LIVING AREA: 1,452 SQ. FT.

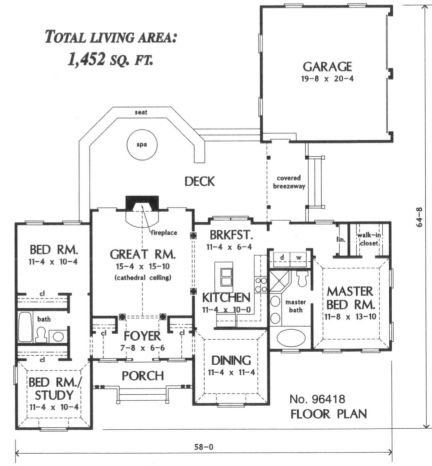

seat

spa

DECK

GARAGE
19-8 x 20-4

covered breezeway

fireplace

BED RM.
11-4 x 10-4

GREAT RM.
15-4 x 15-10
(cathedral ceiling)

BRKFST.
11-4 x 6-4

lin.

walk-in closet

cl

bath

cl

KITCHEN
11-4 x 10-0

master bath

MASTER BED RM.
11-8 x 13-10

cl

FOYER
7-8 x 6-6

cl

BED RM./
STUDY
11-4 x 10-4

PORCH

DINING
11-4 x 11-4

No. 96418
FLOOR PLAN

64-8

58-0

© 1990 Donald A. Gardner Architects, Inc.

To order your Blueprints, call 1-800-235-5700

Refer to **Pricing Schedule B** on
the order form for pricing information

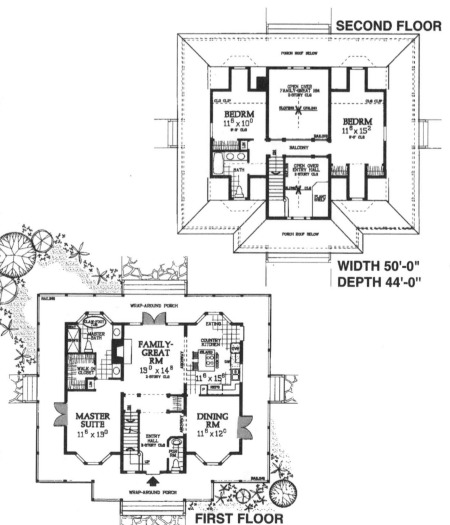

SECOND FLOOR

WIDTH 50'-0"
DEPTH 44'-0"

FIRST FLOOR
No. 99285

Southern Hospitality

■ This plan features:

— Three bedrooms

— Two full and one half baths

■ Porch surrounding and shading entire home

■ Two-story Entry Hall with a landing staircase and arched window

■ Double doors access to Porch from Family-Great Room, Dining Room and Master Suite

■ Country Kitchen with cooktop island/snackbar, Eating alcove and archway to Family Room with cozy fireplace

■ Master Suite with bay window, walk-in closet and private bath

■ Upstairs, two double dormer bedrooms share a full bath

FIRST FLOOR — 1171 SQ. FT.
SECOND FLOOR — 600 SQ. FT.

TOTAL LIVING AREA:
1,771 SQ. FT.

Refer to **Pricing Schedule D** on the order form for pricing information

European Styling with a Georgian Flair

■ This plan features:

— Four bedrooms

— Two full baths

■ Elegant European styling spiced up with Georgian Styling

■ Arched windows, quoins and shutters on the exterior, a columned covered front and a rear porch

■ Formal foyer gives access to the dining room to the left and spacious Den straight ahead

■ Kitchen flows into the informal eating area and is separated from the den by an angled extended counter eating bar

■ Split bedroom plan, master suite privately place to the rear

■ Three additional bedrooms share a full bath in the hall

■ An optional crawl space or slab foundation — please specify when ordering

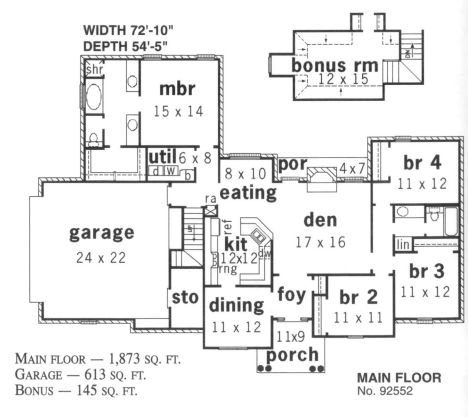

WIDTH 72'-10"
DEPTH 54'-5"

MAIN FLOOR — 1,873 SQ. FT.
GARAGE — 613 SQ. FT.
BONUS — 145 SQ. FT.

MAIN FLOOR
No. 92552

TOTAL LIVING AREA:
1,873 SQ. FT.

To order your Blueprints, call 1-800-235-5700

Refer to **Pricing Schedule B** on the order form for pricing information

An
EXCLUSIVE DESIGN
By Greg Stafford

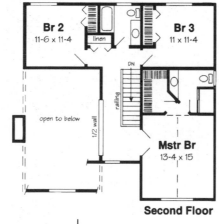

Br 2
11-6 x 11-4

linen

Br 3
11 x 11-4

DN

open to below

railing

1/2 wall

Mstr Br
13-4 x 15

Second Floor

46'-8"

Dining
12-1 x 11-4

Kitchen
13 x 11-4

W D

DN

pantry

Great Rm
14 x 21-8

open to above

UP

Garage
22 x 23-4

35'-8"

First Floor
No. 24610

Second Floor Balcony Overlooks Great Room

■ This plan features:

— Three bedrooms

— Two full and one half baths

■ A Great Room with a focal point fireplace and a two-story ceiling

■ Kitchen has an island, double sinks, built-in pantry and ample storage and counter space

■ A first floor Laundry Room

■ A Dining Room with easy access to the Kitchen and the outside

■ A Master Suite with a private master Bath and a walk-in closet

■ Two additional bedrooms with ample closet space that share a full hall bath

FIRST FLOOR — 891 SQ. FT.
SECOND FLOOR — 894 SQ. FT.
GARAGE — 534 SQ. FT.
BASEMENT — 891 SQ. FT.

TOTAL LIVING AREA:
1,785 SQ. FT.

To order your Blueprints, call 1-800-235-5700

Refer to **Pricing Schedule B** on the order form for pricing information

Easy Living Plan

■ This plan features:

— Three bedrooms

— Two full and one half baths

■ Kitchen, Breakfast Bay, and Family Room blend into a spacious open living area

■ Convenient Laundry Center is tucked into the rear of the Kitchen

■ Luxurious Master Suite is topped by a tray ceiling while a vaulted ceiling is in the bath

■ Two roomy secondary bedrooms share the full bath in the hall

■ Please specify a basement, crawl space or slab foundation when ordering

FIRST FLOOR — 828 SQ. FT.
SECOND FLOOR — 772 SQ. FT.
BASEMENT — 828 SQ. FT.
GARAGE — 473 SQ. FT.

TOTAL LIVING AREA:
1,600 SQ. FT.

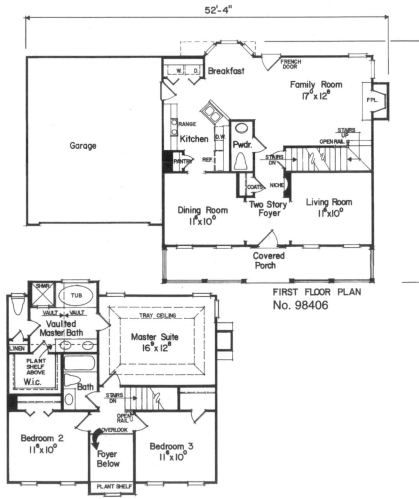

FIRST FLOOR PLAN
No. 98406

SECOND FLOOR PLAN

To order your Blueprints, call 1-800-235-5700

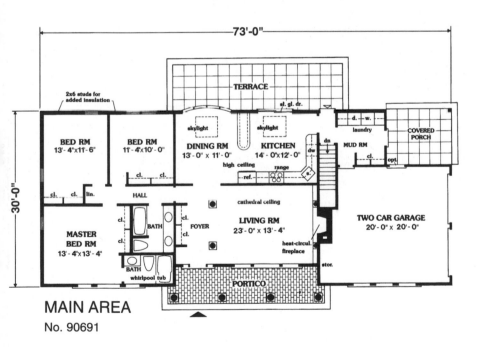

MAIN AREA

No. 90691

Classic Features

■ This plan features:

— Three bedrooms

— Two full baths

■ A cathedral ceiling in the Living Room with a heat-circulating fireplace

■ A spectacular bow window and skylight in the Dining Room

■ A sliding glass door and skylight in the Kitchen

■ A Master Bedroom including a private Master Bath with a whirlpool tub

■ Two additional bedrooms that share a full, double vanity hall bath

MAIN AREA— 1,530 SQ. FT.
BASEMENT — 1,434 SQ. FT.

TOTAL LIVING AREA:
1,530 SQ. FT.

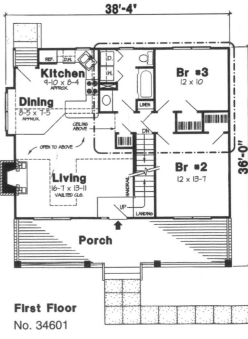

Large Front Porch Adds a Country Touch

■ This plan features:

— Three bedrooms

— Two full baths

■ A country-styled Front Porch

■ Vaulted ceiling in the Living Room which includes a fireplace

■ An efficient Kitchen with double sinks and peninsula counter that may double as an eating bar

■ Two first floor bedrooms with ample closet space

■ A second floor Master Suite with sloped ceiling, walk-in closet and private Master Bath

FIRST FLOOR — 1,007 SQ. FT.
SECOND FLOOR — 408 SQ. FT.
BASEMENT — 1,007 SQ. FT.

TOTAL LIVING AREA: 1,415 SQ. FT.

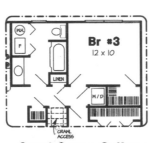

Crawl Space Option

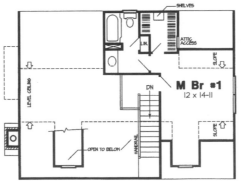

Second Floor

First Floor
No. 34601

To order your Blueprints, call 1-800-235-5700

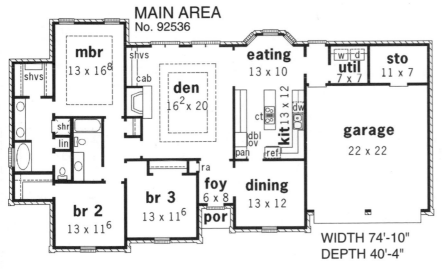

MAIN AREA
No. 92536

mbr
13 x 16⁸

shvs

shvs

cab

den
16²x 20

eating
13 x 10

w d
util
7 x 7

sto
11 x 7

shr
lin

ct
kit 13 x 12

dw

dbl
ov

garage
22 x 22

pan

ref

br 2
13 x 11⁶

br 3
13 x 11⁶

ra

foy
6 x 8

por

dining
13 x 12

WIDTH 74'-10"
DEPTH 40'-4"

MAIN AREA — 1,869 SQ. FT.
GARAGE — 561 SQ. FT.

TOTAL LIVING AREA:
1,869 SQ. FT.

Traditional Brick with Detailing

■ This plan features:

—Three bedrooms

—Two full baths

■ Covered entry leads into the Foyer, the formal Dining Room and the Den

■ Expansive Den with a decorative ceiling over a hearth fireplace and sliding glass doors to the rear yard

■ Country Kitchen with a built-in pantry, double ovens and a cooktop island easily serves the Breakfast area and Dining Room

■ Private Master Bedroom suite with a decorative ceiling, a walk-in closet, a double vanity and a whirlpool tub

■ Two additional bedrooms share a full bath

■ An optional crawl space or slab foundation — please specify when ordering

Refer to **Pricing Schedule B** on the order form for pricing information

A Modern Slant On A Country Theme

■ This plan features:

—Three bedrooms

—Two full and one half baths

■ Country styled front porch highlighting exterior enhanced by dormer windows

■ Modern open floor plan for a more spacious feeling

■ Great Room accented by a quaint, corner fireplace and a ceiling fan

■ Dining Room flowing from the Great Room for easy entertaining

■ Kitchen graced by natural light from near by bay window and a convenient snackbar for meals on the go

■ Master suite secluded in separate wing for total privacy

■ Two additional bedrooms sharing full bath in the hall

FIRST FLOOR — 1,648 SQ. FT.
GARAGE — 479 SQ. FT.

TOTAL LIVING AREA:
1,648 SQ. FT.

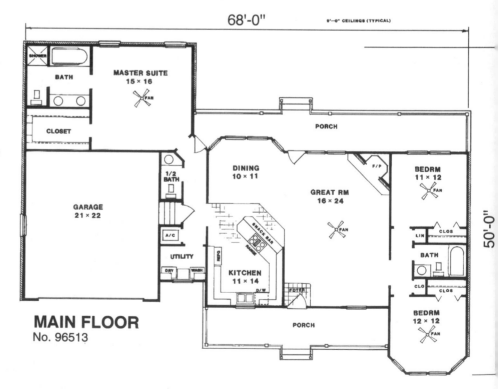

MAIN FLOOR
No. 96513

To order your Blueprints, call 1-800-235-5700

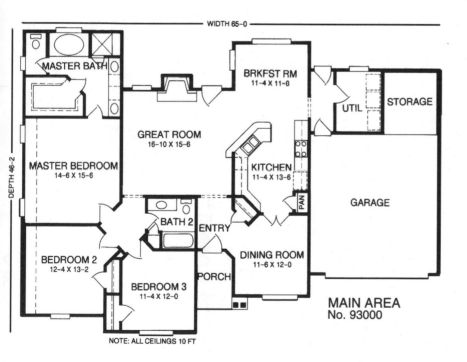

WIDTH 65-0

DEPTH 46-2

MASTER BATH

BRKFST RM
11-4 X 11-8

UTIL

STORAGE

GREAT ROOM
16-10 X 15-6

KITCHEN
11-4 X 13-6

MASTER BEDROOM
14-6 X 15-6

PAN

GARAGE

BATH 2

ENTRY

BEDROOM 2
12-4 X 13-2

DINING ROOM
11-6 X 12-0

PORCH

BEDROOM 3
11-4 X 12-0

MAIN AREA
No. 93000

NOTE: ALL CEILINGS 10 FT

Cozy Traditional

■ This plan features:

— Three bedrooms

— Two full baths

■ An angled eating bar separating the Kitchen, Breakfast Room and Great Room, while leaving these areas open for easy entertaining

■ An efficient, well-appointed Kitchen that is convenient to both the formal Dining Room and the sunny Breakfast Room

■ A spacious Master Suite with oval tub, step-in shower, double vanity and walk-in closet

■ Two additional bedrooms with ample closet space that share a full hall bath

■ No materials list is available for this plan

FIRST FLOOR — 1,862 SQ. FT.
GARAGE — 520 SQ. FT.

TOTAL LIVING AREA:
1,862 SQ. FT.

Refer to **Pricing Schedule B** on the order form for pricing information

Modern Design Highlighted by Split Roofline

■ This plan features:

— Three bedrooms

— Two baths

■ An energy efficient solar hot water system with solar flat-plate collector panels and double glazed windows

■ A Living/Dining area accentuated by massive stonefaced, heat-circulating fireplace

■ Two upstairs bedrooms sharing a skylit full bath

FIRST FLOOR — 960 SQ. FT.
SECOND FLOOR — 580 SQ. FT.
WOOD DECK — 460 SQ. FT.

TOTAL LIVING AREA:
1,540 SQ. FT.

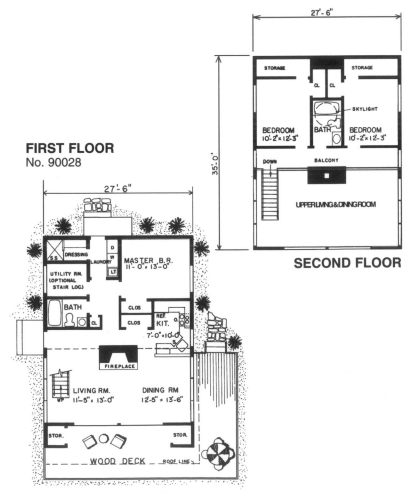

FIRST FLOOR
No. 90028

27'-6"

DRESSING
LAUNDRY
UTILITY RM. (OPTIONAL STAIR LOC.)
MASTER B.R. 11'-0" x 13'-0"
BATH
CLOS
CLOS
REF. KIT. 7'-0" x 10'-0"
FIREPLACE
LIVING RM. 11'-5" x 13'-0"
DINING RM 12'-5" x 13'-6"
STOR.
STOR.
WOOD DECK
ROOF LINE

27'-6"

35'-0"

STORAGE
STORAGE
CL CL
BEDROOM 10'-2" x 12'-3"
BATH
SKYLIGHT
BEDROOM 10'-2" x 12'-3"
DOWN
BALCONY
UPPER LIVING & DINING ROOM

SECOND FLOOR

An
EXCLUSIVE DESIGN
By Westhome Planners, Ltd.

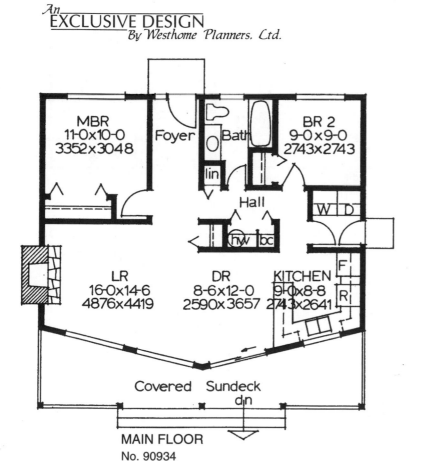

MAIN FLOOR
No. 90934

A Nest for Empty-Nesters

■ This plan features:

— Two bedrooms

— One full bath

■ An economical design

■ A covered sun deck adding outdoor living space

■ A mudroom/laundry area inside the side door, trapping dirt before it can enter the house

■ An open layout between the Living Room with fireplace, Dining Room and Kitchen

MAIN FLOOR — 884 SQ. FT.
WIDTH — 34'-0"
DEPTH — 28'-0"

TOTAL LIVING AREA:
884 SQ. FT.

Refer to **Pricing Schedule B** on the order form for pricing information

Secluded Master Suite

■ This plan features:

— Three bedrooms

— Two full and one half baths

■ Great Room with a vaulted ceiling, sunburst window and hearth fireplace

■ Columns frame entrance to formal Dining Room with decorative ceiling

■ Kitchen with breakfast bar, and Breakfast area

■ Master Bedroom offers an angled ceiling, private Deck, a large walk-in closet and plush bath

■ Two additional bedrooms with ample closets, share a full bath

■ No materials list is available for this plan

FIRST FLOOR — 900 SQ. FT.
SECOND FLOOR — 841 SQ. FT.
GARAGE — 609 SQ. FT.

TOTAL LIVING AREA:
1,741 SQ. FT.

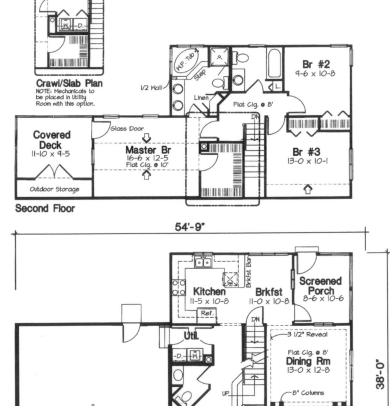

Crawl/Slab Plan
NOTE: Mechanicals to be placed in Utility Room with this option.

Second Floor

Br #2
9-6 x 10-8

Flat Clg. @ 8'

Br #3
13-0 x 10-1

Covered Deck
11-10 x 9-5

Glass Door

Master Br
16-6 x 12-5
Flat Clg. @ 10'

Outdoor Storage

1/2 Wall

W.P. Tub

Stop

Linen

First Floor
No. 24720

54'-9"

38'-0"

Kitchen
11-5 x 10-8

Brkfst
11-0 x 10-8

Screened Porch
8-6 x 10-6

Ref.

Util.

3 1/2" Reveal

Flat Clg. @ 8'
Dining Rm
13-0 x 12-8

8" Columns

Flat Clg. @ 8'
Foyer

UP.

Garage
24-0 x 24-5

Great Rm
16-5 x 12-8

Porch

196

TOTAL LIVING AREA:
1,654 SQ. FT.

MAIN FLOOR
No. 96506

Attractive Ceiling Treatments and Open Layout

■ This plan features:

— Three bedrooms

— Two full and one half baths

■ Great Room and Master Suite with step-up ceiling treatments

■ A cozy fireplace providing warm focal point in the Great Room

■ Open layout between Kitchen, Dining and Great Room lending a more spacious feeling

■ Five-piece, private bath and walk-in closet in the pampering Master Suite

■ Two additional bedrooms located at opposite end of home

MAIN FLOOR — 1,654 SQ. FT.
GARAGE — 480 SQ. FT.

Refer to **Pricing Schedule B** on the order form for pricing information

Perfect Plan for Busy Family

■ This plan features:

— Three bedrooms

— Two full baths

■ Covered Entry opens to vaulted Foyer

■ Spacious Family Room with another vaulted ceiling, a central fireplace and expansive backyard views

■ Angular and efficient Kitchen with an eating bar, built-in desk, Dining area with outdoor access, and nearby laundry and Garage entry

■ Secluded Master Bedroom with a large walk-in closet and double vanity bath

■ Two additional bedrooms with ample closets and easy access to a full bath

■ No materials list is available for this plan

MAIN FLOOR — 1,756 SQ. FT.
BASEMENT — 1,756 SQ. FT.

An
EXCLUSIVE DESIGN
By Ahmann Design Inc.

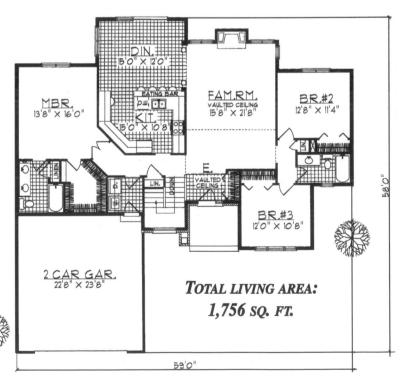

TOTAL LIVING AREA:
1,756 SQ. FT.

MAIN FLOOR PLAN
No. 93191

To order your Blueprints, call 1-800-235-5700

R. NATHAN

First Floor Plan

seat

DECK

spa

arched window above door

GREAT RM.
15-4 x 16-4
(cathedral ceiling)

KIT./BRKFST.
13-3 x 15-0

fireplace

MASTER
BED RM.
12-0 x 13-6

walk-in closet

cl

pd. rm.

master bath

UTIL.
7-4 x 7-4

w
d

sto.

up

DINING
12-4 x 12-4

up

storage

FOYER
8-3 x 5-0

cl

PORCH

GARAGE
20-0 x 20-0

FIRST FLOOR PLAN
No. 99877

56-7

64-0

TOTAL LIVING AREA:
1,698 SQ. FT.

Second Floor Plan

BED RM.
10-7 x 11-7

cl

down

attic storage

cl

bath

BED RM.
12-4 x 10-8

down

BONUS RM.
11-4 x 20-0

SECOND FLOOR PLAN

Touch of Class

- This plan features:
- — Three bedrooms
- — Two full and one half baths

- Round columns, an arched entrance, and arched windows brining elegance to this elevation

- Interior columns adding a touch of class and separating the Dining Room from the Foyer

- A cathedral ceiling in the large Great Room with arched window

- Conveniently located Kitchen with island counter adjacent to the Dining Room, the Great Room and the Breakfast Bay

- Master Bedroom with private bath and lavish amenities plus ample closet space

- Two additional bedrooms and a full bath on the second floor

FIRST FLOOR — 1,288 SQ. FT.
SECOND FLOOR — 410 SQ. FT.
GARAGE & STORAGE — 494 SQ. FT.
BONUS ROOM — 289 SQ. FT.

Family Get-Away

■ This plan features:

— Three bedrooms

— Two and one half baths

■ A Wrap-around Porch for views and visiting provides access into the Great Room and Dining area

■ A spacious Great Room with a two-story ceiling and dormer window above a massive fireplace

■ A combination Dining/Kitchen with an island work area and breakfast bar opening to a Great Room and adjacent to the laundry/storage and half-bath area

■ A private two-story Master Bedroom with a dormer window, walk-in closet, double vanity bath and optional deck with hot tub

■ Two second floor bedrooms sharing a full bath

FIRST FLOOR — 1,061 SQ. FT.
SECOND FLOOR — 499 SQ. FT.
BASEMENT — 1,061 SQ. FT.

TOTAL LIVING AREA: 1,560 SQ. FT.

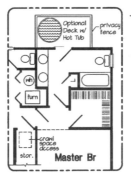

Alternate Foundation Plan

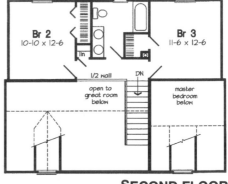

SECOND FLOOR

Br 2 10-10 x 12-6
Br 3 11-6 x 12-6
1/2 wall
DN
open to great room below
master bedroom below

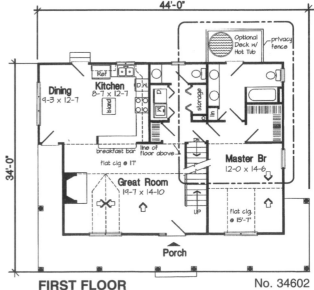

44'-0"

34'-0"

Optional Deck w/ Hot Tub
privacy fence

Dining 9-3 x 12-7
Kitchen 8-7 x 12-7
island
Ref
breakfast bar
flat clg @ 17'
line of floor above

storage

Great Room 19-7 x 14-10
UP
flat clg. @ 15'-7'

Master Br 12-0 x 14-6

Porch

FIRST FLOOR   No. 34602

Refer to **Pricing Schedule B** on the order form for pricing information

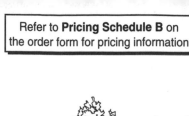

An EXCLUSIVE DESIGN
By Independent Designs

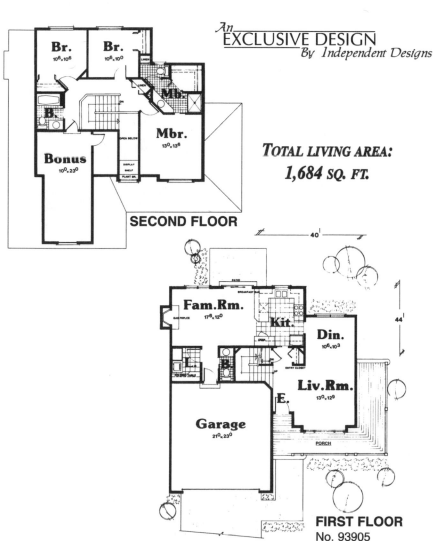

SECOND FLOOR

TOTAL LIVING AREA: **1,684 SQ. FT.**

Br. 10⁶ x 10⁶

Br. 10⁶ x 10⁰

Mb.

B

Mbr. 13⁰ x 13⁶

Bonus 10⁰ x 23⁰

Fam. Rm. 17⁶ x 12⁰

Kit.

Din. 10⁶ x 10³

Liv. Rm. 13⁰ x 12⁹

Garage 21⁰ x 23⁰

FIRST FLOOR
No. 93905

Country Elegance

■ This plan features:

— Three bedrooms

— Two full and one half baths

■ Welcoming front Porch leads into open Entry with landing staircase

■ Expansive Living Room/Dining area highlighted by multiple windows front and back

■ Family Room with gas fireplace, and a sliding glass door to Patio

■ Efficient U-shaped Kitchen with built-in desk and eating bar

■ Private Master Bedroom with an arched window, plush bath and walk-in closet

■ Two additional bedrooms with large closets share a full bath

■ Bonus Room with another arched window and storage space

■ No materials list is available for this plan

FIRST FLOOR — 913 SQ. FT.
SECOND FLOOR — 771 SQ. FT.
GARAGE — 483 SQ. FT.

Refer to **Pricing Schedule B** on the order form for pricing information

© 1994 Donald A. Gardner Architects, Inc.

Perfect for Family Gatherings

■ This plan features:
— Three bedrooms
— Two full baths

■ An open layout between the Great Room, Kitchen, and Breakfast Bay sharing a cathedral ceiling and a fireplace

■ Master Bedroom with a soaring cathedral ceiling, direct access to the deck and a well appointed bath with a large walk-in closet

■ Additional bedrooms sharing a full bath in the hall

■ Centrally located utility and storage spaces

MAIN FLOOR — 1,346 SQ. FT.

GARAGE AND STORAGE — 462 SQ. FT.

TOTAL LIVING AREA:
1,346 SQ. FT.

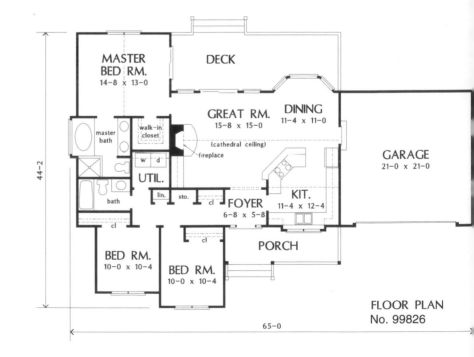

©1994 Donald A. Gardner Architects, Inc.

B. NATHAN

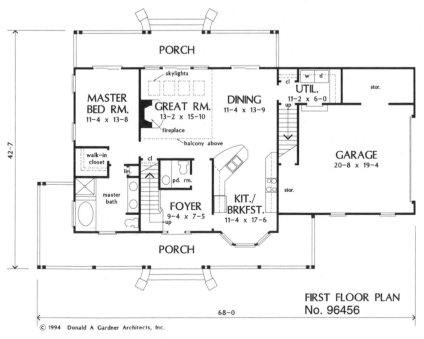

SECOND FLOOR PLAN

attic storage

great room below

railing

BED RM.
11-4 x 10-0

down

bath

BED RM.
11-4 x 10-0

attic storage

skylights

BONUS RM.
20-8 x 15-4

down

cl   cl   cl   cl

foyer below

PORCH

skylights

MASTER
BED RM.
11-4 x 13-8

GREAT RM.
13-2 x 15-10

fireplace

balcony above

DINING
11-4 x 13-9

w   d

cl

UTIL.
11-2 x 6-0

up

stor.

walk-in closet

lin.

cl

pd. rm.

master bath

FOYER
9-4 x 7-5

up

KIT./
BRKFST.
11-4 x 17-6

stor.

GARAGE
20-8 x 19-4

PORCH

42-7

68-0

FIRST FLOOR PLAN
No. 96456

© 1994 Donald A Gardner Architects, Inc.

Sense of Spaciousness

■ This plan features:

— Three bedrooms

— Two full and one half baths

■ Creative use of natural lighting gives a feeling of spaciousness to this country home

■ Traffic flows easily from the bright Foyer into the Great Room which has a vaulted ceiling and skylights

■ The open floor plan is efficient for Kitchen/Breakfast area and the Dining Room

■ Master Bedroom suite features a walk-in closet and a private bath with whirlpool tub

■ Two second floor bedrooms with storage access, share a full bath

FIRST FLOOR — 1,180 SQ. FT.
SECOND FLOOR — 459 SQ. FT.
BONUS ROOM — 385 SQ. FT.
GARAGE & STORAGE — 533 SQ. FT.

TOTAL LIVING AREA:
1,639 SQ. FT.

Refer to **Pricing Schedule C** on the order form for pricing information

Plush Master Bedroom Wing

■ This plan features:

— Three bedrooms

— Two full baths

■ A raised, tiled Foyer with decorative window leading into an expansive Living Room, accented by a tiled fireplace and framed by French doors

■ An efficient Kitchen with a walk-in pantry and serving bar adjoining the Breakfast and Utility areas

■ A private Master Bedroom, crowned by a stepped ceiling, offering an atrium door to outside, a huge, walk-in closet and a luxurious bath

■ Two additional bedrooms with walk-in closets, share a full hall bath

■ No materials list is available for this plan

MAIN FLOOR — 1,849 SQ. FT.
GARAGE — 437 SQ. FT.

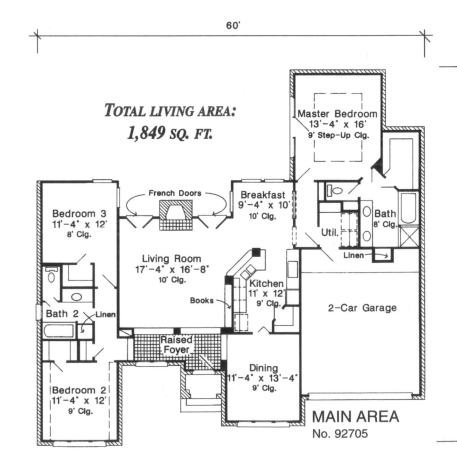

TOTAL LIVING AREA: 1,849 SQ. FT.

Master Bedroom
13'-4" x 16'
9' Step-Up Clg.

Bath
8' Clg.

Util.

Linen

Breakfast
9'-4" x 10'
10' Clg.

French Doors

Bedroom 3
11'-4" x 12'
8' Clg.

Living Room
17'-4" x 16'-8"
10' Clg.

Kitchen
11' x 12'
9' Clg.

Books

2-Car Garage

Bath 2   Linen

Raised Foyer

Dining
11'-4" x 13'-4"
9' Clg.

Bedroom 2
11'-4" x 12'
9' Clg.

MAIN AREA
No. 92705

60'

To order your Blueprints, call 1-800-235-5700

TOTAL LIVING AREA:
1,554 SQ. FT.

An **EXCLUSIVE DESIGN**
By *Plan One Homes, Inc.*

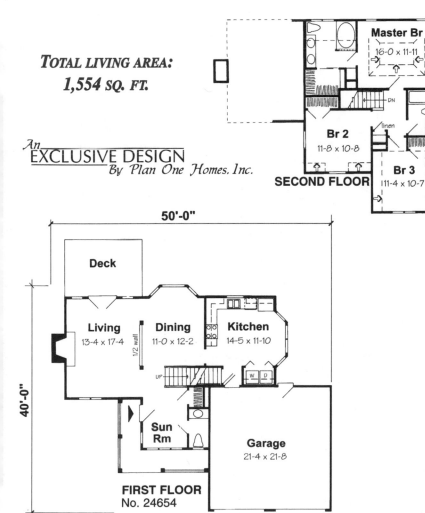

SECOND FLOOR

Master Br
16-0 x 11-11

Br 2
11-8 x 10-8

linen

Br 3
11-4 x 10-7

50'-0"

Deck

Living
13-4 x 17-4

Dining
11-0 x 12-2

Kitchen
14-5 x 11-10

1/2 wall

UP

W D

40'-0"

Sun
Rm

Garage
21-4 x 21-8

FIRST FLOOR
No. 24654

Country Influence

■ This plan features:

— Three bedrooms

— Two full and one half baths

■ Front Porch entry into unique
Sun Room with half bath and
coat closet

■ Open Living Room enhanced by
palladium window, focal point
fireplace and atrium door to Deck

■ Bay window brightens formal
Dining Room

■ Efficient L-shaped Kitchen with
bay window eating area, laundry
closet and handy Garage entrance

■ Plush Master Bedroom offers
another bay window crowned by
tray ceiling and private bath with
double vanity

■ Two additional bedrooms with
arched window and ample closets
share full bath

FIRST FLOOR — 806 SQ. FT.
SECOND FLOOR — 748 SQ. FT.
GARAGE — 467 SQ. FT.

Refer to **Pricing Schedule C** on the order form for pricing information

Master Suite with Private Sun Deck

■ This plan features:

— Four bedrooms

— Two full and one half baths

■ A sunken Living Room, formal Dining Room, and island Kitchen enjoying an expansive view of the patio and backyard

■ A fireplaced Living Room keeping the house toasty after the sun goes down

■ Skylights brightening the balcony and Master Bath

■ An optional basement, slab or crawl space foundation — please specify when ordering.

MAIN LEVEL — 1,249 SQ. FT.
UPPER LEVEL — 890 SQ. FT.
GARAGE — 462 SQ. FT.

TOTAL LIVING AREA:
2,139 SQ. FT.

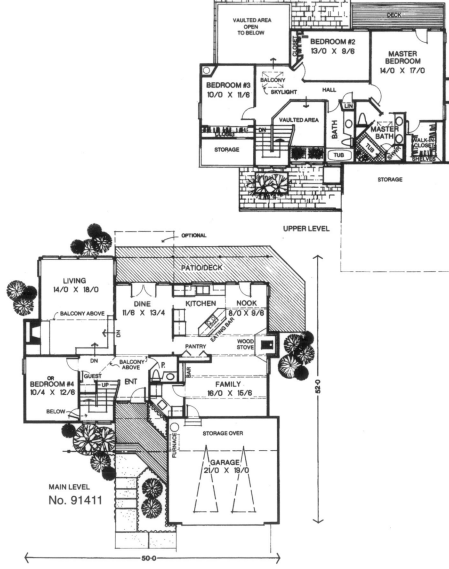

UPPER LEVEL

MAIN LEVEL
No. 91411

Refer to **Pricing Schedule B** on the order form for pricing information

An EXCLUSIVE DESIGN
By Westhome Planners, Ltd.

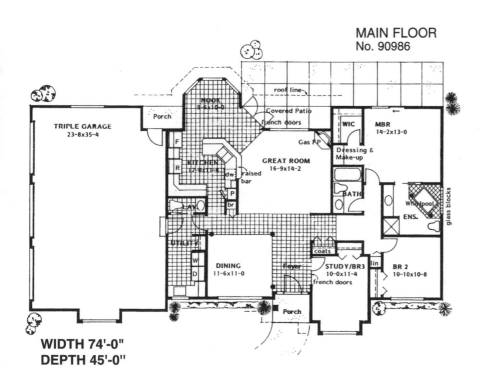

MAIN FLOOR
No. 90986

WIDTH 74'-0"
DEPTH 45'-0"

TOTAL LIVING AREA:
1,731 SQ. FT.

Surrounded with Sunshine

■ This plan features:
— Three bedrooms
— Two full and one half baths

■ An Italianate style, featuring columns and tile originally designed to sit on the edge of a golf course

■ Tile used from the Foyer, into the Kitchen and Nook, as well as in the Utility Room

■ A whirlpool tub in the elaborate and spacious Master Bedroom suite

■ A Great Room with a corner gas fireplace

■ A turreted Breakfast Nook and an efficient Kitchen with peninsula counter

■ Two family bedrooms that share a full hall bath

MAIN AREA — 1,731 SQ. FT.
GARAGE — 888 SQ. FT.
BASEMENT — 1,715 SQ. FT.

Refer to **Pricing Schedule B** on the order form for pricing information

Attractive Gables and Arches

- This plan features:
— Three bedrooms
— Two full baths

- Entry opens to formal Dining Room with arched window

- Angles and transom windows add interest to the Great Room

- Bright Hearth area expands Breakfast/Kitchen area and shares three-sided fireplace

- Efficient Kitchen offers an angled snack bar, a large pantry and nearby laundry/Garage entry

- Secluded Master Bedroom suite crowned by decorative ceiling, a large walk-in closet and a plush bath with a whirlpool tub

- Secondary bedrooms located separately from master suite

MAIN FLOOR — 1,782 SQ. FT.
BASEMENT — 1,782 SQ. FT.
GARAGE — 466 SQ. FT.

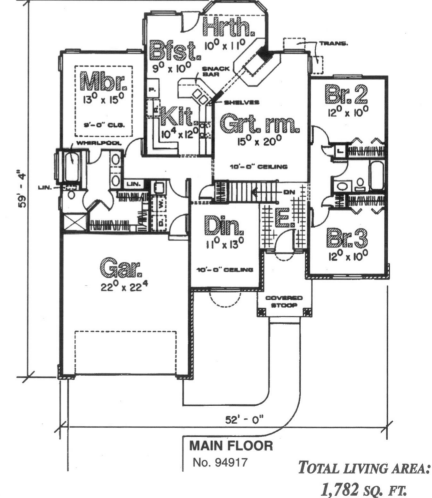

© design basics, inc.

Hrth. 10⁰ x 11⁰

Bfst. 9⁰ x 10⁰   SNACK BAR

Mbr. 13⁰ x 15⁰   9'-0" CLG.

WHIRLPOOL

Kit. 10⁴ x 12⁰   SHELVES

Grt. rm. 15⁰ x 20⁰   10'-0" CEILING

Br. 2 12⁰ x 10⁰

TRANS.

LIN.   LIN.   D.W.

59' - 4"

Gar. 22⁰ x 22⁴

Din. 11⁰ x 13⁰   10'-0" CEILING

Br. 3 12⁰ x 10⁰

COVERED STOOP

52' - 0"

MAIN FLOOR
No. 94917

TOTAL LIVING AREA: 1,782 SQ. FT.

© 1992 Donald A. Gardner Architects, Inc.

First Floor Plan

No. 99875

© 1992 Donald A Gardner Architects, Inc.

GARAGE
23-4 x 21-4

DECK

spa

seat

storage

up

covered breezeway

SCREEN PORCH
12-0 x 14-8

skylights

master bath

walk-in closet

GREAT RM.
16-0 x 19-2

fireplace

balcony above

BRKFST.
12-4 x 10-2

UTIL.

w d

KITCHEN
12-0 x 14-8

MASTER BED RM.
12-4 x 16-0

sto.

cl

pd. rm.

DINING
14-4 x 12-4

FOYER
12-6 x 7-10

up

PORCH

74-2

57-6   18-10

attic storage

skylights

down

BONUS RM.
27-0 x 12-0

attic storage

FIRST FLOOR PLAN

Second Floor Plan

clerestory window with arched top

great room below

attic storage

attic storage

railing

BED RM.
12-4 x 10-4

BED RM.
12-4 x 11-9

down

LOFT/STUDY
9-0 x 10-0

shelves

lin.

bath

attic storage

foyer below

attic storage

SECOND FLOOR PLAN

TOTAL LIVING AREA:
2,161 SQ. FT.

Wrapping Front Porch

■ This plan features:

— Three bedrooms

— Two full and one half baths

■ Two-story Foyer enjoys natural light from window above

■ Elegant bay window highlights the Dining Room

■ Kitchen directly accesses the formal Dining Room and the informal Breakfast Bay for ease in serving

■ Great Room accesses the skylit screened porch

■ Lavish Master Suite with garden tub, separate shower, double vanity and a walk-in closet

■ Two additional bedrooms on the second floor sharing a full double vanity bath in the hall

FIRST FLOOR — 1,526 SQ. FT.
SECOND FLOOR — 635 SQ. FT.
BONUS ROOM — 355 SQ. FT.
GARAGE — 610 SQ. FT.

To order your Blueprints, call 1-800-235-5700

Refer to **Pricing Schedule C** on the order form for pricing information

Enchanting Entry

■ This plan features:

— Three bedrooms

— Two full and one half baths

■ Split Entry leads down to Family Room, Utility Room, Den, half bath and two-car Garage

■ Up a half-flight of stairs leads to the large Living Room highlighted by a double window

■ Dining Room convenient to Living Room and Kitchen

■ Efficient Kitchen with rear yard access and room for eating

■ Corner Master Bedroom offers an over-sized closet and private bath

■ Two additional bedrooms with double windows, share a full bath

UPPER FLOOR — 1,331 SQ. FT.
LOWER FLOOR — 663 SQ. FT.
GARAGE — 584 SQ. FT.

TOTAL LIVING AREA:
1,994 SQ. FT.

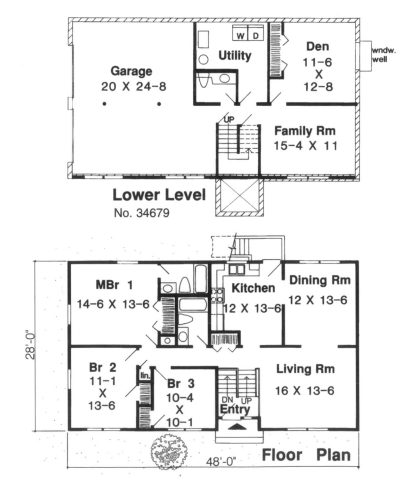

To order your Blueprints, call 1-800-235-5700

TOTAL LIVING AREA:
1,660 SQ. FT.

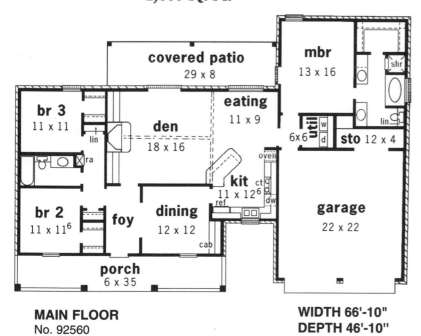

MAIN FLOOR
No. 92560

WIDTH 66'-10"
DEPTH 46'-10"

Covered Front and Rear Porches

■ This plan features:

—Three bedrooms

—Two full baths

■ Traditional country styling with front and rear covered porches

■ Peninsula counter/eating bar in Kitchen for meals on the go

■ Informal Breakfast area and formal Dining room with built-in cabinet

■ Vaulted ceiling and cozy fireplace highlighting Den

■ Master Bedroom in private corner pampered by five-piece bath

■ Split bedroom plan with additional bedrooms at the opposite of home sharing full bath

■ An optional slab or crawl space foundation — please specify when ordering

MAIN FLOOR — 1,660 SQ. FT.
GARAGE — 544 SQ. FT.

Refer to **Pricing Schedule A** on the order form for pricing information

Three Porches Offer Outdoor Charm

■ This plan features:

— Three bedrooms

— Two full baths

■ An oversized log burning fireplace in the spacious Living/Dining area which is two stories high with sliding glass doors

■ Three Porches offering the maximum in outdoor living space

■ A private bedroom located on the second floor

■ An efficient Kitchen including an eating bar and access to the covered Dining Porch

FIRST FLOOR — 974 SQ. FT.
SECOND FLOOR — 300 SQ. FT.

TOTAL LIVING AREA: 1,274 SQ. FT.

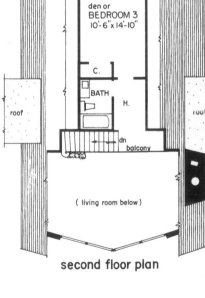

second floor plan

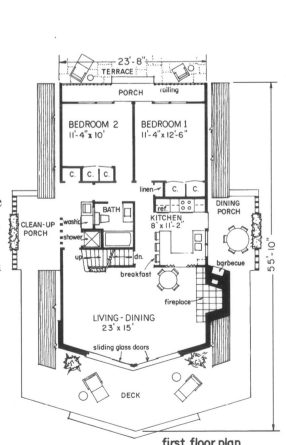

first floor plan
No. 90048

© 1996 Donald A. Gardner Architects, Inc.

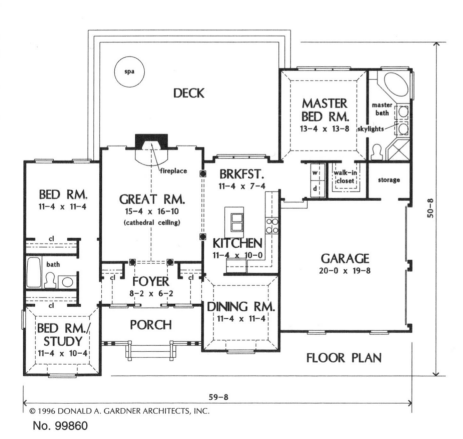

spa

DECK

MASTER BED RM.
13-4 x 13-8

master bath

skylights

fireplace

BRKFST.
11-4 x 7-4

w d

walk-in closet

storage

BED RM.
11-4 x 11-4

GREAT RM.
15-4 x 16-10
(cathedral ceiling)

KITCHEN
11-4 x 10-0

GARAGE
20-0 x 19-8

cl

bath

FOYER
8-2 x 6-2

cl cl

50-8

cl

BED RM./ STUDY
11-4 x 10-4

PORCH

DINING RM.
11-4 x 11-4

FLOOR PLAN

59-8

© 1996 DONALD A. GARDNER ARCHITECTS, INC.

No. 99860

TOTAL LIVING AREA:
1,498 SQ. FT

Home Builders on a Budget

■ This plan features:

— Three bedrooms

— Two full baths

■ Down-sized country plan for home builder on a budget

■ Columns punctuate open, one-level floor plan and connect Foyer with clerestory window dormers

■ Front Porch and large, rear Deck extend living space outdoors

■ Tray ceilings decorate Master Bedroom, Dining Room and Bedroom/Study

■ Private Master Bath features garden tub, double vanity, separate shower and skylights

MAIN FLOOR — 1,498 SQ. FT.
GARAGE & STORAGE — 427 SQ. FT.

Refer to **Pricing Schedule C** on the order form for pricing information

© 1996 Donald A Gardner Architects, Inc.

Designed For Easy Building And Easy Living

■ This plan features:

— Three Bedrooms

— Two full baths

■ Refined, traditional exterior created by brick, double dormers, and a hip roof

■ Foyer opens to a generous Great Room with cathedral ceiling and fireplace

■ Columns define entrance to Kitchen with a center island

■ Master Bedroom, Dining Room, and front Bedroom/Study receive distinction from tray ceilings

MAIN FLOOR — 1,800 SQ. FT.
GARAGE — 477 SQ. FT.

TOTAL LIVING AREA:
1,800 SQ. FT.

PATIO

MASTER BED RM.
13-4 x 14-8

skylight

master bath

lin.

BED RM.
11-4 x 12-0

GREAT RM.
15-4 x 18-6
(cathedral ceiling)

fireplace

BRKFST.
11-4 x 9-4

w
d

walk-in closet

storage

cl

lin.

bath

KIT.
11-4 x 11-8

GARAGE
20-0 x 19-8

cl

FOYER
8-2 x 6-2

cl

BED RM./
STUDY
11-4 x 11-4

PORCH

DINING
11-4 x 12-6

storage

FLOOR PLAN
No. 99814

53-5

62-2

© 1996 Donald A Gardner Architects, Inc.

214

To order your Blueprints, call 1-800-235-5700

PLAN NO. 94041

An **EXCLUSIVE DESIGN** By **CRANE DESIGN** inc.

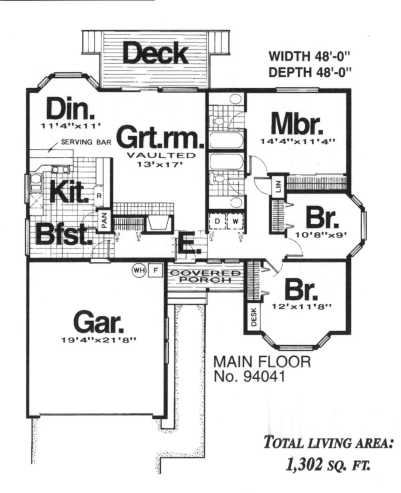

Deck

WIDTH 48'-0"
DEPTH 48'-0"

Din. 11'4"x11'

SERVING BAR

Grt.rm. VAULTED 13'x17'

Mbr. 14'4"x11'4"

Kit.

Bfst.

PAN

R

LIN

Br. 10'8"x9'

D W

E.

WH F

COVERED PORCH

DESK

Br. 12'x11'8"

Gar. 19'4"x21'8"

MAIN FLOOR
No. 94041

TOTAL LIVING AREA:
1,302 SQ. FT.

Terrific Great Room

■ This plan features:

— Three bedrooms

— Two full baths

■ Vaulted ceiling and fireplace in the Great Room

■ Built-in pantry, breakfast area and peninsula counter in the Kitchen

■ A private bath in the Master Bedroom

■ Two secondary bedrooms accented by bay windows

■ Front bedroom contains a built-in desk

■ Bay window adding elegance to the formal Dining Room which adjoins with the Great Room

■ No materials list is available for this plan

MAIN FLOOR — 1,302 SQ. FT.
GARAGE — 440 SQ. FT.

Refer to **Pricing Schedule B** on the order form for pricing information

Back Yard Views

- This plan features:
  — Three bedrooms
  — Two full baths
- Front Porch accesses open Foyer, and spacious Dining Room and Great Room with sloped ceilings
- Corner fireplace, windows and atrium door to Patio enhance Great Room
- Convenient Kitchen with a pantry, peninsula serving counter for bright Breakfast area and nearby Laundry/Garage entry
- Luxurious bath, walk-in closet and back yard view offered in Master Bedroom
- Two additional bedrooms, one with an arched window, share full bath
- No materials list available for this plan

MAIN FLOOR — 1,746 SQ. FT.
GARAGE — 480 SQ. FT.
BASEMENT — 1,697 SQ. FT.

TOTAL LIVING AREA:
1,746 SQ. FT.

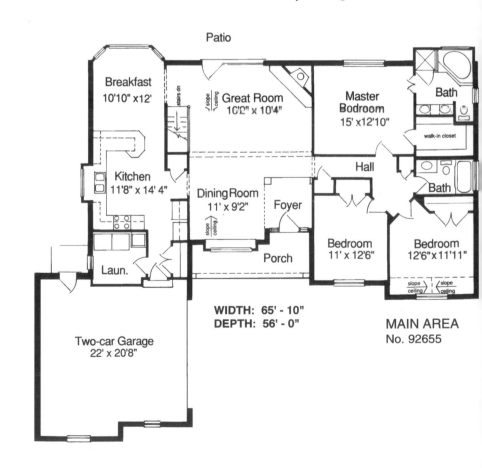

WIDTH: 65' - 10"
DEPTH: 56' - 0"

MAIN AREA
No. 92655

To order your Blueprints, call 1-800-235-5700

© 1992 Donald A. Gardner Architects, Inc.

Charming Country Ranch

■ This plan features:

—Three bedrooms

—Two full baths

■ A cathedral ceiling in the Great Room and bay windows maximizing light and space

■ Foyer opening to the Dining Room, Great Room and leading to the two family bedrooms and a full bath

■ Open central Kitchen with cook top island servicing the Great Room, Breakfast area, Dining Room and deck with seating and optional spa area

■ Master bedroom, located at the rear for privacy, opening to the deck with a walk-in closet and bath with a separate shower, garden tub, and double vanity

MAIN FLOOR — 1,445 SQ. FT.
GARAGE & STORAGE — 506 SQ. FT.

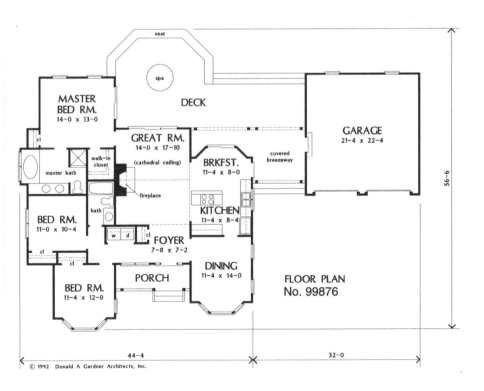

© 1992 Donald A Gardner Architects, Inc.

TOTAL LIVING AREA:
1,445 SQ. FT.

To order your Blueprints, call 1-800-235-5700

Refer to **Pricing Schedule B** on the order form for pricing information

Hip Roof Ranch

■ This plan features:

— Three bedrooms

— Two full baths

■ Cozy front Porch leads into Entry with vaulted ceiling and sidelights

■ Open Living Room enhanced by a cathedral ceiling, a wall of windows and corner fireplace

■ Large and efficient Kitchen with an extended counter and a bright Dining area with access to Screen Porch

■ Convenient Utility area with access to Garage and Storage area

■ Spacious Master Bedroom with a walk-in closet and private bath

■ Two additional bedrooms with ample closets, share a full bath

■ No materials list available for this plan

MAIN FLOOR — 1,540 SQ. FT.
BASEMENT — 1,540 SQ. FT.

An
EXCLUSIVE DESIGN
By Ahmann Design Inc.

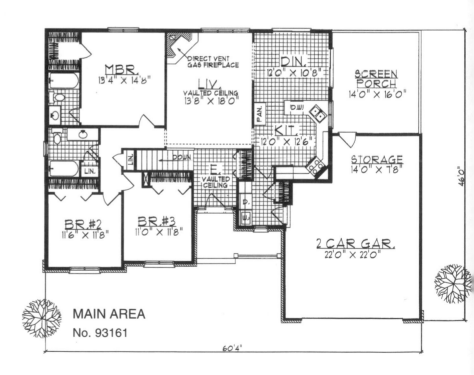

MAIN AREA
No. 93161

TOTAL LIVING AREA:
1,540 SQ. FT.

To order your Blueprints, call 1-800-235-5700

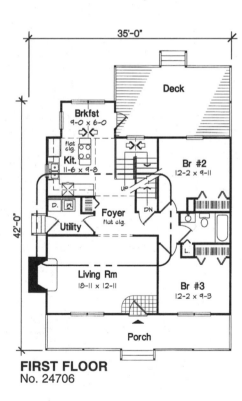

Country Porch Topped by Dormer

■ This plan features:

— Three bedrooms

— Two full baths

■ Front Porch leads into tiled entry

■ Side entrance leads into Utility Room and central Foyer with a landing staircase

■ Country-size Kitchen with cook-top island, bright Breakfast area

■ Second floor Master Bedroom offers lovely dormer window, vaulted ceiling, walk-in closet and double vanity bath

■ Two additional bedrooms with ample closets, share a full bath

■ No materials list is available for this plan

FIRST FLOOR — 1,035 SQ. FT.
SECOND FLOOR — 435 SQ. FT.
BASEMENT — 1,018 SQ. FT.

TOTAL LIVING AREA:
1,470 SQ. FT.

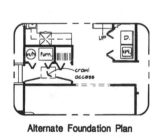

Alternate Foundation Plan

FIRST FLOOR
No. 24706

35'-0"
42'-0"

Deck
Brkfst 9-0 x 6-0
Kit. 11-6 x 9-8
Br #2 12-2 x 9-11
Foyer flat clg.
Utility
UP
DN
Living Rm 18-11 x 12-11
Br #3 12-2 x 9-3
Porch

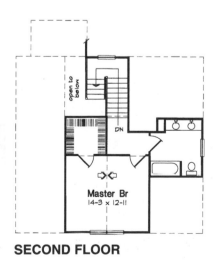

open to below
DN
Master Br 14-3 x 12-11

SECOND FLOOR

Refer to **Pricing Schedule B** on the order form for pricing information

Beckoning Country Porch

■ This plan features:

— Three bedrooms

— Two full and one half baths

■ Country styled exterior with dormer windows above friendly front Porch

■ Vaulted ceiling and central fireplace accent the spacious Great Room

■ L-shaped Kitchen/Dining Room with work island and atrium door to back yard

■ First floor Master Suite with vaulted ceiling, walk-in closet, private bath and optional private Deck with hot tub

■ Two additional bedrooms on the second floor with easy access to full bath

Br 2
10-10 x 12-6

Br 3
11-6 x 12-6

railing   DN

open to great room below

open to master bedroom below

SECOND FLOOR

FIRST FLOOR — 1,061 SQ. FT.
SECOND FLOOR — 499 SQ. FT.
BASEMENT — 1,061 SQ. FT.

TOTAL LIVING AREA:
1,560 SQ. FT.

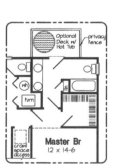

Optional Deck w/ Hot Tub   privacy fence

Master Br
12 x 14-6

crawl space access

Alternate Foundation Plan

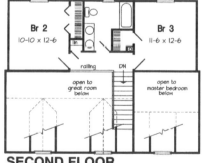

FIRST FLOOR
No. 34603

Optional Deck w/ Hot Tub   privacy fence

Kitchen
8-1 x 12-7

Dining
9-8 x 12-7
8' clg

Master Br
12 x 14-6
vault clg

Great Room
19-7 x 14-10
vault clg

UP

Porch

34'-0"

40'-0"

Refer to **Pricing Schedule C** on the order form for pricing information

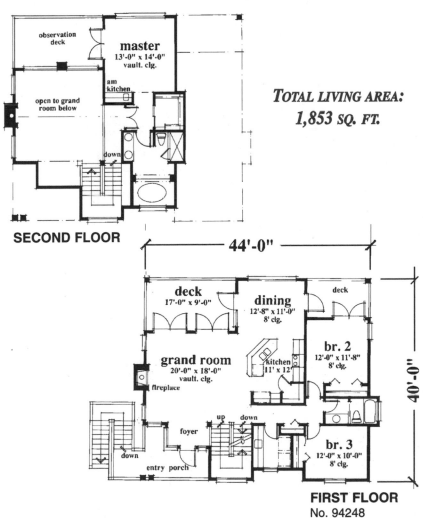

observation deck

master
13'-0" x 14'-0"
vault. clg.

am kitchen

open to grand room below

down

SECOND FLOOR

TOTAL LIVING AREA:
1,853 SQ. FT.

44'-0"

40'-0"

deck
17'-0" x 9'-0"

dining
12'-8" x 11'-0"
8' clg.

deck

grand room
20'-0" x 18'-0"
vault. clg.

kitchen
11' x 12'

br. 2
12'-0" x 11'-8"
8' clg.

fireplace

up   down

foyer

down

br. 3
12'-0" x 10'-0"
8' clg.

entry porch

FIRST FLOOR
No. 94248

Delightful Home

■ This plan features:

— Three bedrooms

— Two full baths

■ Grand Room with a fireplace, vaulted ceiling and double French doors to the rear deck

■ Kitchen and Dining Room open to continue the overall feel of spaciousness

■ Kitchen has a large walk-in pantry, island with a sink and dishwasher creating a perfect triangular workspace

■ Dining Room with doors to both decks, has expanses of glass looking out to the rear yard

■ Master Bedroom features a double door entry, private bath, and a morning kitchen

■ No materials list is available for this plan

FIRST FLOOR — 1,342 SQ. FT.
SECOND FLOOR — 511 SQ. FT.
GARAGE — 1,740 SQ. FT.

Refer to **Pricing Schedule C** on the order form for pricing information

© 1997 Donald A Gardner Architects, Inc.

Country Style Home With Corner Porch

■ This plan features:

— Three bedrooms

— Two full baths

■ Dining Room has four floor to ceiling windows that overlook front porch

■ Great Room topped by a cathedral ceiling, enhanced by a fireplace and sliding doors to the back porch

■ Utility Room located near Kitchen and Breakfast Nook

■ Master Bedroom has a walk in closet and private bath

■ Two additional bedrooms with ample closet space share a full bath

■ A skylight Bonus Room over the two-car garage

MAIN FLOOR — 1,815 SQ. FT.
GARAGE — 522 SQ, FT.
BONUS — 336 SQ. FT.

TOTAL LIVING AREA:
1,815 SQ. FT.

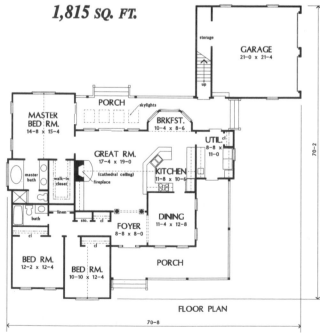

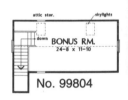

No. 99804

To order your Blueprints, call 1-800-235-5700

Refer to **Pricing Schedule B** on the order form for pricing information

TOTAL LIVING AREA:
1,778 SQ. FT.

An EXCLUSIVE DESIGN
By Jannis Vann & Associates, Inc.

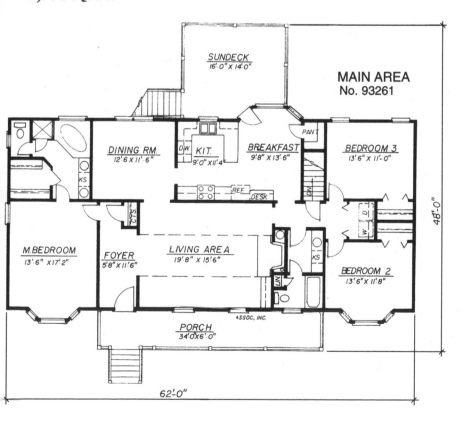

SUNDECK
16'-0" X 14'-0"

MAIN AREA
No. 93261

DINING RM.
12'-6" X 11'-6"

KIT.
9'-0" X 11'-4"

BREAKFAST
9'-8" X 13'-6"

PANT

BEDROOM 3
13'-6" X 11'-0"

DW.

REF. DESK

M. BEDROOM
13'-6" X 17'-2"

FOYER
5'-8" X 11'-6"

LIVING AREA
19'-8" X 15'-6"

W D

BEDROOM 2
13'-6" X 11'-8"

KS

UN

ASSOC., INC.

PORCH
34'-0" X 6'-0"

48'-0"

62'-0"

Bay Windows and a Terrific Front Porch

■ This plan features:

— Three bedrooms

— Two full baths

■ A Country style front porch

■ An expansive Living Area that includes a fireplace

■ A Master Suite with a private Master Bath and a walk-in closet, as well as a bay window view of the front yard

■ An efficient Kitchen that serves the sunny Breakfast Area and the Dining Room with equal ease

■ A built-in pantry and a desk add to the conveniences in the Breakfast Area

■ Two additional bedrooms that share the full hall bath

■ A convenient main floor Laundry Room

MAIN AREA — 1,778 SQ. FT.
BASEMENT — 1,008 SQ. FT.
GARAGE — 728 SQ. FT.

Refer to **Pricing Schedule C** on the order form for pricing information

Enticing Two-Story Traditional

■ This plan features:

— Four bedrooms

— Two and one half baths

■ A porch serving as a wonderful, relaxing area to enjoy the outdoors

■ A Dining Room including a decorative ceiling and easy access to the Kitchen

■ A Kitchen/Utility area with access to the Garage

■ A Living Room with double doors into the Family Room which features a fireplace and access to the patio

■ A Master Bedroom with two enormous walk-in closets, as a dressing area and private bath

FIRST FLOOR — 955 SQ. FT.
SECOND FLOOR — 1,005 SQ. FT.
BASEMENT — 930 SQ. FT.
GARAGE — 484 SQ. FT.

TOTAL LIVING AREA:
1,960 SQ. FT.

226

An EXCLUSIVE DESIGN
By Karl Kreeger

SECOND FLOOR

BATH

BEDROOM 4
9'-10" x 13'-0"

BEDROOM 3
10'-10" x 13'-0"

DRESSING AREA

C.

LINEN

HALL

B.

V.

VAULTED CEILING
MASTER BEDROOM
14'-4" x 13'-4"

BEDROOM 2
10'-10 x 10'-0"

SLOPED CEILING

Slab/Crawlspace Option

FIRST FLOOR
No. 34027

OPT. PATIO

STEP

GARAGE
21'-8" x 21'-4"

KITCHEN
14'-4" x 9'-6"

FAMILY ROOM
14'-4" x 15'-4"

PAN.

UTIL

W D

P.R.

C.

DINING ROOM
10'-10"x13'-4"

FOYER

LIVING ROOM
10'-10" x 13'-4"

PORCH

52'-0"

31'-0"

To order your Blueprints, call 1-800-235-5700

An
EXCLUSIVE DESIGN
By Westhome Planners, Ltd.

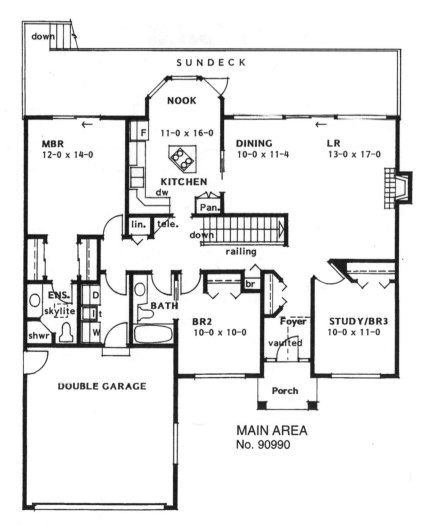

MAIN AREA
No. 90990

Comfort and Style

■ This plan features:

— Two bedrooms with possible
third bedroom/den

— One full and one three quarter
baths

■ An unfinished daylight basement,
providing possible space for
family recreation

■ A Master Suite complete with
private bath and skylight

■ A large Kitchen including an
eating nook

■ A sundeck that is easily
accessible from the Master Suite,
Nook and the Living/Dining area

MAIN AREA — 1,423 SQ. FT.
BASEMENT — 1,423 SQ. FT.
GARAGE — 399 SQ. FT.
WIDTH — 46'-0"
DEPTH — 52'-0"

TOTAL LIVING AREA:
1,423 SQ. FT.

Refer to **Pricing Schedule C** on the order form for pricing information

Covered Porch with Columns

■ This plan features:

— Three bedrooms

— Two full baths

■ The Foyer with 12′ ceiling leads past decorative columns into the Family Room with a center fireplace

■ The Living Room and Dining Room are linked by the Foyer and have windows overlooking the front porch

■ The Kitchen has a serving bar and is adjacent to the Breakfast Nook which has a French door that opens to the backyard

■ The private Master Suite has a tray ceiling, a vaulted bath with a double vanity, and a walk in closet

■ The two other bedrooms share a full bath

■ Please specify a basement, slab or a crawl space foundation when ordering this plan

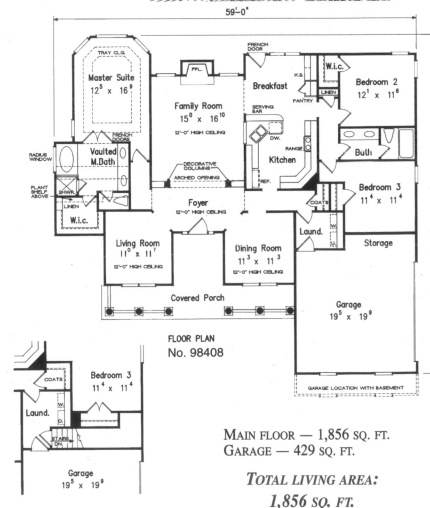

FLOOR PLAN
No. 98408

OPT. BASEMENT STAIR LOCATION

MAIN FLOOR — 1,856 SQ. FT.
GARAGE — 429 SQ. FT.

TOTAL LIVING AREA:
1,856 SQ. FT.

To order your Blueprints, call 1-800-235-5700

© 1992 Donald A. Gardner Architects, Inc. E. NATHAN

The Deck Dominates this Home

■ This plan features:

— Three bedrooms

— Two full baths

■ The front Porch and back Deck give this home additional living space

■ The cathedral ceiling in the Great room and Dining Room make this home appear more spacious

■ The Master Suite includes skylights, a cathedral ceiling and a walk-in closet

■ Two additional bedrooms have access to a hallway bathroom

■ The built-in seats on the back Deck give visual access to the living area fireplace

■ An optional basement or a slab foundation — please specify when ordering

MAIN FLOOR — 1,287 SQ. FT.
GARAGE — 427 SQ. FT.

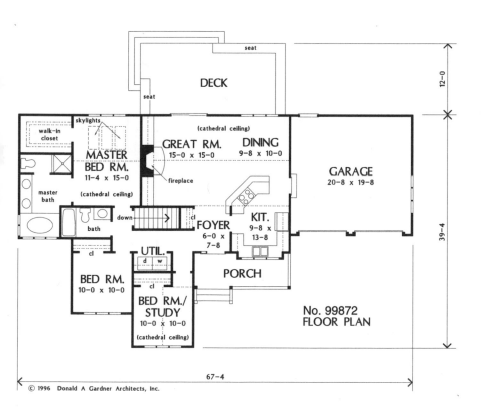

seat

DECK

seat

12-0

skylights

walk-in closet

MASTER BED RM.
11-4 x 15-0

(cathedral ceiling)

GREAT RM.
15-0 x 15-0

(cathedral ceiling)

DINING
9-8 x 10-0

GARAGE
20-8 x 19-8

master bath

fireplace

bath

down

cl

FOYER
6-0 x 7-8

KIT.
9-8 x 13-8

39-4

cl

cl

BED RM.
10-0 x 10-0

UTIL.
d | w

cl

PORCH

BED RM./ STUDY
10-0 x 10-0

(cathedral ceiling)

No. 99872
FLOOR PLAN

67-4

© 1996 Donald A Gardner Architects, Inc.

TOTAL LIVING AREA:
1,287 SQ. FT.

229

To order your Blueprints, call 1-800-235-5700

Refer to **Pricing Schedule A** on the order form for pricing information

For an Established Neighborhood

■ This plan features:

— Three bedrooms

— Two full baths

■ A covered entrance sheltering and welcoming visitors

■ A Living Room enhanced by natural light streaming in from the large front window

■ A bayed formal Dining Room with direct access to the Sun Deck and the Living Room

■ An efficient, galley Kitchen

■ An informal Breakfast Room with direct access to the Sun Deck

■ A large Master Suite equipped with a walk-in closet and a full private Bath

■ Two additional bedrooms that share a full hall bath

MAIN AREA — 1,276 SQ. FT.
FINISHED STAIRCASE — 16 SQ. FT.
BASEMENT — 392 SQ. FT.
GARAGE — 728 SQ. FT.

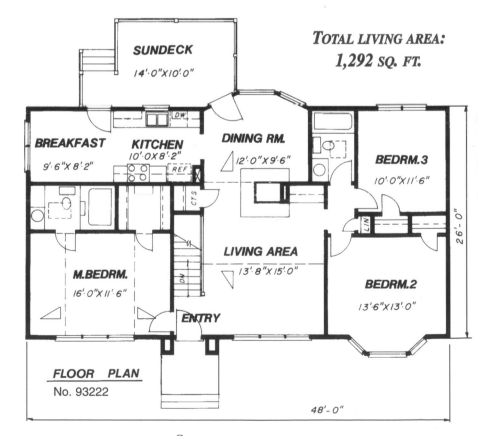

SUNDECK
14'.0"X10'.0"

TOTAL LIVING AREA:
1,292 SQ. FT.

BREAKFAST
9'.6"X8'.2"

KITCHEN
10'.0X8'.2"

DINING RM.
12'.0"X9'.6"

BEDRM.3
10'.0"X11'.6"

LIVING AREA
13'.8"X15'.0"

M.BEDRM.
16'.0"X11'.6"

BEDRM.2
13'.6"X13'.0"

ENTRY

FLOOR PLAN
No. 93222

26'-0"

48'-0"

An
EXCLUSIVE DESIGN
By Jannis Vann & Associates. Inc.

To order your Blueprints, call 1-800-235-5700

One Floor Convenience

- ■ This plan features:
- — Three bedrooms
- — Two full baths
- ■ Vaulted Foyer blending with the vaulted Great Room giving a larger feeling to the home
- ■ Formal Dining Room opening into the Great Room allowing for a terrific living area in which to entertain
- ■ Kitchen including a serving bar and easy flow into the Breakfast Room
- ■ Master Suite topped by a decorative tray ceiling and a vaulted ceiling in the Master Bath
- ■ Two additional bedrooms sharing the full bath in the hall
- ■ An optional crawl space or slab foundation — please specify when ordering
- ■ No materials list is available for this plan

MAIN FLOOR — 1,359 SQ. FT.
GARAGE — 439 SQ. FT.

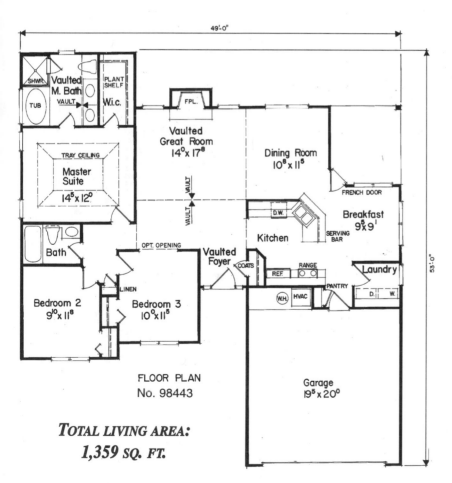

FLOOR PLAN
No. 98443

TOTAL LIVING AREA:
1,359 SQ. FT.

Refer to **Pricing Schedule C** on the order form for pricing information

Brick and Wood Highlighted by Sunbursts

■ This plan features:

— Three bedrooms

— Two full and one half baths

■ Sheltered Porch entrance leads into two-story Foyer

■ Beautiful bay window brightens Living Room which opens into the formal Dining Room

■ Efficient, L-shaped Kitchen has a built-in pantry and Dining area

■ Comfortable Family Room with focal point fireplace topped by cathedral ceiling

■ Master Bedroom offers two closets and a private bath

■ Two additional bedrooms with large closets share a full bath

■ No materials list is available for this plan

FIRST FLOOR — 1,094 SQ. FT.
SECOND FLOOR — 719 SQ. FT.
GARAGE — 432 SQ. FT.

TOTAL LIVING AREA:
1,813 SQ. FT.

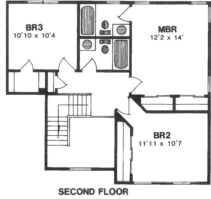

SECOND FLOOR
No. 94104

BR3
10'10 x 10'4

MBR
12'2 x 14'

BR2
11'11 x 10'7

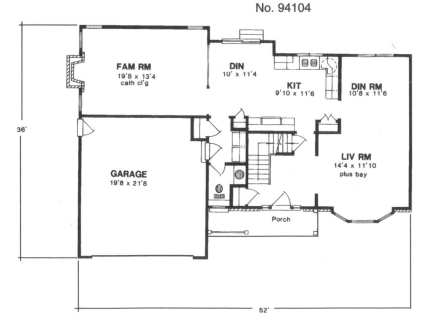

FAM RM
19'8 x 13'4
cath cl'g

DIN
10' x 11'4

KIT
9'10 x 11'6

DIN RM
10'8 x 11'6

GARAGE
19'8 x 21'8

LIV RM
14'4 x 11'10
plus bay

Porch

36'

52'

FIRST FLOOR

To order your Blueprints, call 1-800-235-5700

PLAN NO. 90288

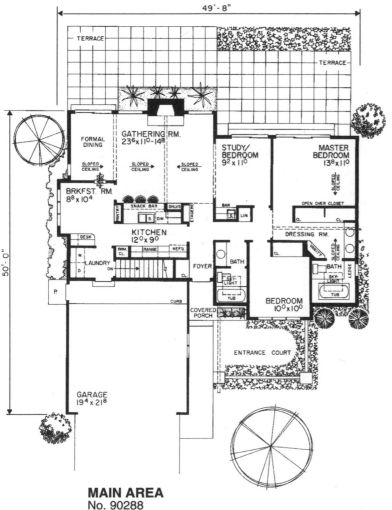

49'-8"

TERRACE

TERRACE

FORMAL DINING

SLOPED CEILING

GATHERING RM. 23⁶ x 11⁰ - 14⁸

SLOPED CEILING

SLOPED CEILING

STUDY/ BEDROOM 9² x 11⁰

MASTER BEDROOM 13⁸ x 11⁰

SLOPED CEILING

OPEN OVER CLOSET

BRKFST. RM. 8⁸ x 10⁴

SNACK BAR

SHLVS

BAR

CL.

CL.

DESK

KITCHEN 12⁰ x 9⁰

RANGE

REFG.

FOYER

BATH

DRESSING RM.

VANITY

SLOPED CEILING

LEDGE

W.

LAURY.

DN

SKY- LIGHT

TUB

BEDROOM 10⁰ x 10⁰

BATH

SKY- LIGHT

TUB

D.

CURB

COVERED PORCH

ENTRANCE COURT

GARAGE 19⁴ x 21⁸

50'-0"

MAIN AREA
No. 90288

Soaring Ceilings Add Space and Drama

■ This plan features:

— Two bedrooms (with optional third bedroom)

— Two full baths

■ A sunny Master Suite with a sloping ceiling, private terrace entry, and luxurious garden bath with an adjoining Dressing Room

■ A Gathering Room with a fireplace, study and formal Dining Room, flowing together for a more spacious feeling

■ A convenient pass-through that adds to the efficiency of the galley Kitchen and adjoining Breakfast Room

MAIN AREA — 1,387 SQ. FT.
GARAGE — 440 SQ. FT.

TOTAL LIVING AREA:
1,387 SQ. FT.

No. 35001
Today's Family Living Made Easy

- This plan features:
— Three bedrooms
— Two full and one half baths
- A welcoming country porch sheltering the entrance
- A large Living Room that flows into the Dining Room creating a great area for entertaining
- An efficient U-shaped Kitchen that includes an informal Breakfast area and a laundry center
- A convenient entrance from the Garage into the Kitchen
- A private Master Suite with a full Bath and two closets
- A Den/Office with ample closet space, enabling it to double as a Guest Room
- Two additional bedrooms on the second floor that share a full hall bath
- An optional Deck/Patio that will increase your living space in the warmer weather

FIRST FLOOR — 1,081 SQ. FT.
SECOND FLOOR — 528 SQ. FT.

TOTAL LIVING AREA:
1,609 SQ. FT.

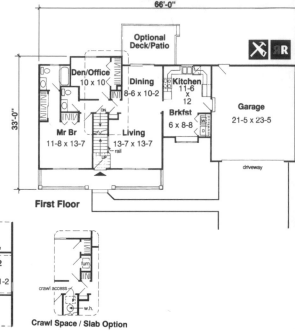

First Floor

Second Floor
No. 35001

Crawl Space / Slab Option

No. 94944
Spectacular Sophistication

- This plan features:
— Four bedrooms
— Two full and one half baths
- Open Foyer with circular window and a plant shelf leads into the Dining Room
- Great Room with an inviting fireplace and windows front and back
- Open Kitchen has a work island and accesses the Breakfast area
- Master Bedroom features a nine-foot boxed ceiling, a walk-in closet and whirlpool bath
- Three additional bedrooms share a full bath with a double vanity

FIRST FLOOR — 941 SQ. FT.
SECOND FLOOR — 992 SQ. FT.
BASEMENT — 941 SQ. FT.
GARAGE — 480 SQ. FT.

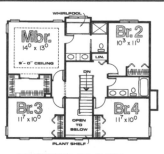

SECOND FLOOR
No. 94944

TOTAL LIVING AREA:
1,933 SQ. FT.

© design basics, inc.

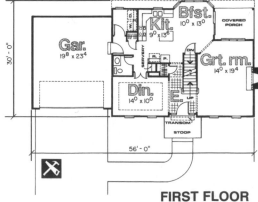

FIRST FLOOR

234

No. 90440
Rustic Warmth

- This plan features:
  - Three bedrooms
  - Two full baths
- A fireplaced Living Room with built-in bookshelves
- A fully-equipped Kitchen with an island
- A sunny Dining Room with glass sliders to a wood deck
- A first floor Master Suite with walk-in closet and lavish Master Bath
- An optional basement or crawl space foundation — please specify when ordering

FIRST FLOOR — 1,100 SQ. FT.

SECOND FLOOR — 664 SQ. FT.

BASEMENT — 1,100 SQ. FT.

TOTAL LIVING AREA:
1,764 SQ. FT.

No. 90440

WOOD DECK
14-0 x 10-0

DINING
10-6 x 14-2
(INCL BAY)

KITCHEN
10-0 x 12-2

UTILITY

WALK-IN CLOSET

M. BEDROOM
13-6 x 13-8

FOYER

LIVING ROOM
17-2 x 14-10

MAIN FLOOR

PORCH
26-0 x 6-0

34-0

40-0

WALK-IN CLOSET

ATTIC STORAGE

SLOPED CEILING

HALL

BEDROOM 2
13-6 x 13-4

BEDROOM 3
12-8 x 15-4

FOYER (BELOW)

STORAGE

WALK-IN CLOSET

SLOPED CEILING

ATTIC STORAGE

SECOND FLOOR

No. 93202
Compact and Comfortable

■ This plan features:
— Three bedrooms
— Two full baths

■ Arched window highlights front entrance, Foyer and staircase

■ Spacious Living Area with focal point fireplace and Deck access

■ Efficient, U-shaped Kitchen easily serves bright Dining Room and Deck

■ Private Master Bedroom with walk-in closet and double vanity bath with a raised tub

■ Two additional bedrooms with ample closets, share a full bath

■ Lower level with Garage, Storage and future Playroom

MAIN FLOOR — 1,447 SQ. FT.
BASEMENT — 950 SQ. FT.
GARAGE — 400 SQ. FT.

TOTAL LIVING AREA:
1,447 SQ. FT.

SECOND FLOOR

FIRST FLOOR
No. 93202

An
EXCLUSIVE DESIGN
By Jannis Vann & Associate

No. 98423
Easy One Floor Living

■ This plan features:
— Three bedrooms
— Two full baths

■ A spacious Family Room topped by a vaulted ceiling and highlighted by a large fireplace and a French door to the rear yard

■ A serving bar open to the Family Room and the Dining Room, a pantry and a peninsula counter adding more efficiency to the Kitchen

■ A crowning tray ceiling over the Master Bedroom and a vaulted ceiling over the Master Bath

■ A vaulted ceiling over the cozy Sitting Room in the Master Suite

■ Two additional bedrooms, roomy in size sharing the full bath in the hall

■ An optional basement, crawl space or slab foundation — please specify when ordering

MAIN FLOOR — 1,671 SQ. FT.
BASEMENT — 1,685 SQ. FT.
GARAGE — 400 SQ. FT.

TOTAL LIVING AREA:
1,671 SQ. FT.

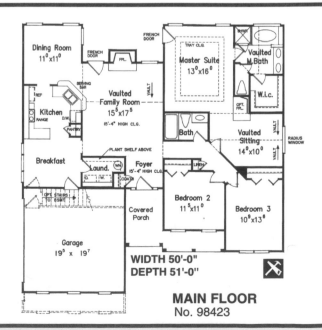

WIDTH 50'-0"
DEPTH 51'-0"

MAIN FLOOR
No. 98423

No. 96409
Impressive Great Room

■ This plan features:

– Three bedrooms

– Two full and one half baths

■ Gabled dormers and a palladian window over a country style front porch

■ Impressive Great Room separated from the Dining Room by columns

■ U-shaped Kitchen dividing the two eating areas, each with access to the rear deck through French doors

■ First floor Master Suite having a private skylit bath with a walk-in closet

■ Two secondary bedrooms sharing a full bath

■ Bonus room accessed by its own back stairs for future expansion

FIRST FLOOR — 1,330 SQ. FT.

SECOND FLOOR — 634 SQ. FT.

GARAGE & STORAGE — 501 SQ. FT.

BONUS ROOM — 436 SQ. FT.

TOTAL LIVING AREA:
1,964 SQ. FT.

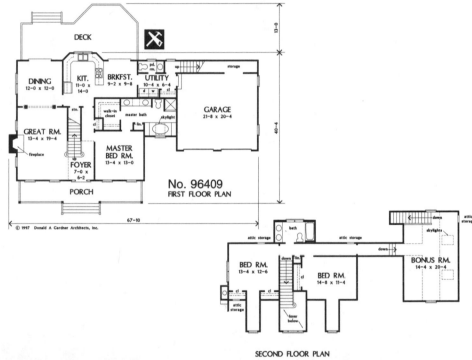

No. 96409
FIRST FLOOR PLAN

© 1997 Donald A Gardner Architects, Inc.

SECOND FLOOR PLAN

No. 98427
Split Bedroom Plan

- This plan features:
— Three bedrooms
— Two full baths
- Dining room is crowned by a tray ceiling
- Living Room/Den privatized by double doors at entrance, and is enhanced by a bay window
- The Kitchen includes a walk-in pantry and a corner double sink
- The vaulted Breakfast Room flows naturally from the Kitchen
- The Master Suite is topped by a tray ceiling, and contains a compartmental bath and two walk-in closets
- Two roomy additional bedrooms share a full bath in the hall
- Please specify a basement or crawl space foundation when ordering

MAIN FLOOR — 2,051 SQ. FT.
BASEMENT — 2,051 SQ. FT.
GARAGE — 441 SQ. FT.

TOTAL LIVING AREA:
2,051 SQ. FT.

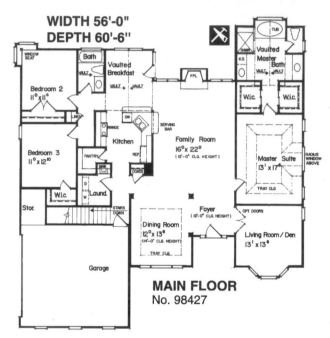

WIDTH 56'-0"
DEPTH 60'-6"

MAIN FLOOR
No. 98427

No. 96428
Dignity and Grace

- This plan features:
— Three bedrooms
— Two full baths
- A brick and stucco exterior with a hip roof and columns
- Formal Dining Room distinguished by a tray ceiling and a box bay window opens to the kitchen for easy meal service and clean up
- Kitchen with ample counter and storage space including an extended counter/cooktop
- Great Room crowned in a cathedral ceiling for a feeling of spaciousness
- Master Bedroom, generous in size, with an extravagant private bath and a large walk-in closet
- Two additional bedrooms sharing the full bath in the hall

MAIN FLOOR — 1,538 SQ. FT.
GARAGE & STORAGE — 513 SQ. FT.

TOTAL LIVING AREA:
1,538 SQ. FT.

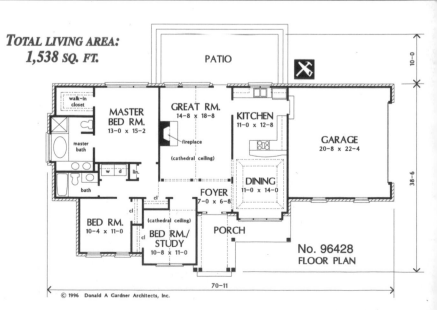

No. 96428
FLOOR PLAN

© 1996 Donald A Gardner Architects, Inc.

PRICE CODE C

No. 93904
Country Porch Shelters Entry

■ This plan features:
 – Three bedrooms
 – Two full and one half baths
■ A two-story Foyer illuminated by an arched window above
■ A formal Living Room adjoined to the Dining Room by an arched opening
■ A second arched opening into the Family Room highlighted by a gas fireplace
■ An efficient Kitchen equipped with an island and a bayed breakfast area
■ A lavish Master Bath with a garden tub and a walk-in closet adding pampering features to the Master Suite
■ Two additional bedrooms that share the full hall bath
■ A bonus room for future expansion
■ No materials list is available for this plan

FIRST FLOOR — 1,121 SQ. FT.
SECOND FLOOR — 748 SQ. FT.

An
EXCLUSIVE DESIGN
By Independent Designs

WIDTH 61'-0"
DEPTH 32'-0"

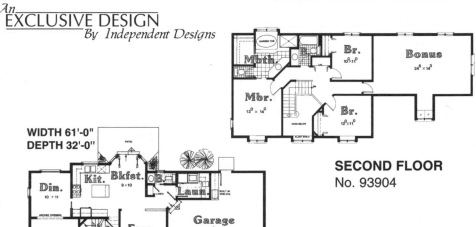

FIRST FLOOR

SECOND FLOOR
No. 93904

TOTAL LIVING AREA:
1,869 SQ. FT.

PRICE CODE C

© 1996 Donald A. Gardner Architects, Inc.

No. 96485
Cozy Cottage with Character

■ This plan features:
— Three bedrooms
— Two full baths

■ Dormer, gables, and a wrapping front porch giving character to this narrow and cozy cottage

■ A fireplace as the focal point of the vaulted Great room

■ Kitchen opens to the Dining Room and has a pantry and deck access

■ Master Suite boasting an optional door to the deck, walk-in closet, and a fully equipped bath

■ Two secondary bedrooms share a full bath with dual vanity

■ Bonus space for future expansion

MAIN FLOOR — 1,454 SQ. FT.
GARAGE & STORAGE — 321 SQ. FT.
BONUS ROOM — 424 SQ. FT.

TOTAL LIVING AREA:
1,454 SQ. FT.

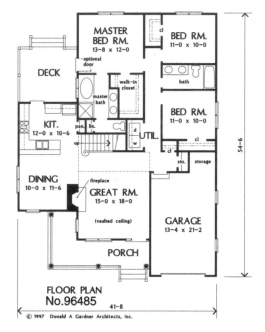

FLOOR PLAN
No.96485

© 1997 Donald A Gardner Architects, Inc.

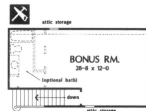

BONUS RM.
28–8 x 12–0

(optional bath)

No. 96410
For a Sloping Lot

■ This plan features:
— Three bedrooms
— Two full baths

■ Cathedral ceilings gracing the Great Room, Dining Room, Kitchen and Screened Porch

■ Exposed wood beams adding rustic charm to the spacious Great Room

■ Master Suite with rear deck access, a generous walk-in closet and a private bath with dual vanity, separate tub and shower and an enclosed toilet

■ Two additional bedrooms, at opposite end of home from Master Suite, sharing a full bath

MAIN FLOOR — 1,680 SQ. FT.
GARAGE & STORAGE — 514 SQ. FT.
BASEMENT — 1,653 SQ. FT.

TOTAL LIVING AREA:
1,680 SQ. FT.

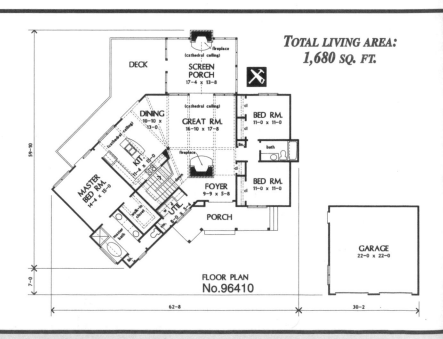

FLOOR PLAN
No.96410

240

No. 93073
Pleasing to the Eye

■ This plan features:
— Three bedrooms
— Two full baths

■ A large covered front porch opening to a foyer with nine foot ceilings

■ Kitchen with a dining area with a bay window, built-in desk and a sunny window over the sink

■ Living room including a corner fireplace and ten foot ceilings

■ Bedrooms grouped for homeowner convenience

■ Master suite topped by a sloped ceiling pampered by a private bath and walk-in closet

■ Two-car garage with optional door locations located at the rear of the home

■ An optional crawl space or slab foundation — please specify when ordering

■ No materials list is available for this plan

MAIN FLOOR — 1,202 SQ. FT.
GARAGE — 482 SQ. FT.

TOTAL LIVING AREA:
1,202 SQ. FT.

OPTIONAL GARAGE DOOR LOCATION

SLOPE CLG

MSTR BDRM
11-0x13-8
10 FT CLG

FP SLOPE CLG

LIVING
13-0x17-8
10 FT CLG

GARAGE

MSTR BATH

BATH 2

STOR

BDRM 3
10-10x11-6

FOYER
9 FT CLG

STORAGE

LIN

BDRM 2
10-4x10-2

DESK

DINING
11-0x9-2
9 FT CLG

Width 51'-10"
Depth 43'-10"

COVERED PORCH

KITCH
11-6x
8-0
9 FT CLG

MAIN FLOOR
No. 93073

No. 96408
Four Bedroom Country Classic

■ This plan features:
— Four bedrooms
— Two full and one half baths
■ Foyer open to the Dining Room creating a hall with a balcony over the vaulted Great Room
■ Great Room opens to the deck and to the island Kitchen with convenient pantry
■ Nine foot ceilings on the first floor expand volume
■ Master Suite pampered by a whirlpool tub, double vanity, separate shower, and access to the deck
■ Bonus room to be finished now or later

FIRST FLOOR — 1,499 SQ. FT.
SECOND FLOOR — 665 SQ. FT.
GARAGE & STORAGE — 567 SQ. FT.
BONUS ROOM — 380 SQ. FT.

**TOTAL LIVING AREA:
2,164 SQ. FT.**

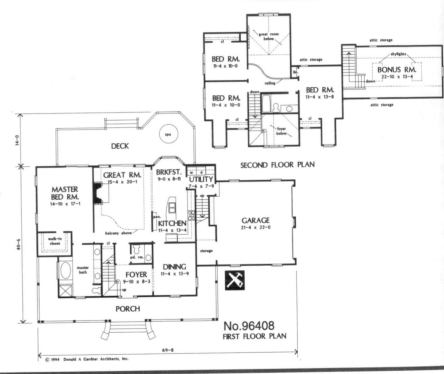

SECOND FLOOR PLAN

No.96408
FIRST FLOOR PLAN

© 1994 Donald A Gardner Architects, Inc.

No. 94138
Friendly Front Porch

■ This plan features:
— Three bedrooms
— Two full and one half baths
■ Country, homey feeling with wrap-around Porch
■ Adjoining Living Room and Dining Room creates spacious feeling
■ Efficient Kitchen easily serves Dining area with extended counter and a built-in pantry
■ Spacious Family Room with optional fireplace and access to Laundry/Garage entry
■ Large Master Bedroom with a walk-in closet and access to a full bath, offers a private bath option
■ Two additional bedrooms with ample closets and full bath access
■ No materials list is available for this plan

FIRST FLOOR — 900 SQ. FT.
SECOND FLOOR — 676 SQ. FT.
GARAGE — 448 SQ. FT.

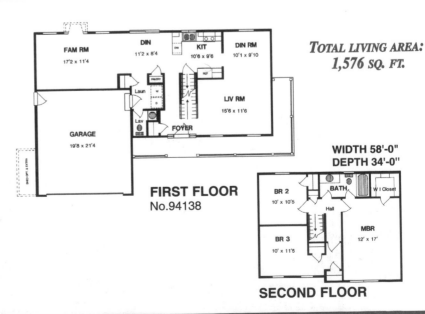

**TOTAL LIVING AREA:
1,576 SQ. FT.**

FIRST FLOOR
No.94138

**WIDTH 58'-0"
DEPTH 34'-0"**

SECOND FLOOR

242

No. 98411
Style and Convenience

■ This plan features:
— Three bedrooms
— Two full baths

■ Large front windows, dormers and an old-fashioned porch giving a pleasing style to the home

■ A vaulted ceiling topping the Foyer flowing into the Family Room which is highlighted by a fireplace

■ A Formal Dining Room flowing from the Family Room crowned in an elegant vaulted ceiling

■ An efficient Kitchen enhanced by a pantry, a pass through to the Family Room and direct access to the Dining Room and Breakfast Room

■ A decorative tray ceiling, a five-piece private bath and a walk-in closet in the Master Suite

■ Two additional bedrooms, roomy in size, sharing the full bath in the hall

■ An optional basement or crawl space foundation — please specify when ordering

MAIN FLOOR — 1,373 SQ. FT.
BASEMENT — 1,386 SQ. FT.

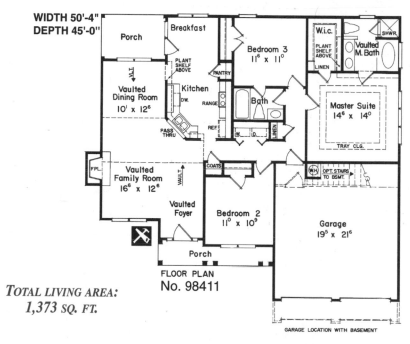

WIDTH 50'-4"
DEPTH 45'-0"

TOTAL LIVING AREA:
1,373 SQ. FT.

FLOOR PLAN
No. 98411

GARAGE LOCATION WITH BASEMENT

PRICE CODE B

No. 90671
Adapt this Colonial to Your Lifestyle

■ This plan features:

— Four bedrooms

— Two full baths

■ A Living Room with a beam ceiling and a fireplace

■ An eat-in Kitchen efficiently serving the formal Dining Room

■ A Master Bedroom with his-n-her closets

■ Two upstairs bedrooms sharing a split bath

FIRST FLOOR — 1,056 SQ. FT.

SECOND FLOOR — 531 SQ. FT.

TOTAL LIVING AREA:
1,587 SQ. FT.

FIRST FLOOR

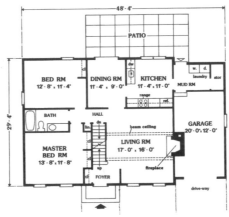

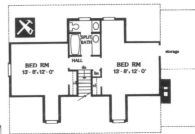

SECOND FLOOR
No.90671

No. 35009
Simple and Practical

■ This plan features:

— One bedroom

— One full bath

■ A front Deck area to relax on

■ A U-shaped Kitchen with an efficient layout, double sink and ample workspace

■ A Dining area that views the front deck and yard

■ A Living Room with a built-in entertainment center and view of the front deck and yard

■ A large Bedroom that includes a double closet

■ A Loft overlooking the Dining and Living rooms, that can be expanded as future needs arrive

FIRST FLOOR — 763 SQ. FT.

SECOND FLOOR — 240 SQ. FT.

TOTAL LIVING AREA:
1,003 SQ. FT.

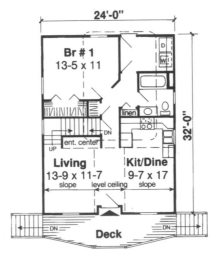

FIRST FLOOR

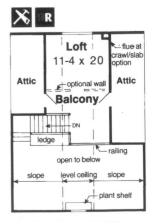

SECOND FLOOR
No. 35009

No. 96460

Open Spaces Compliment Flowing Design

■ This plan features:

— Three bedrooms

— Two full and one half baths

■ Dormers and a cathedral ceiling amplify the volume in the integrated Foyer and Great Room

■ Kitchen, Dining Room, Breakfast Bay, and the Great Room access the back Porches

■ Downstairs Master Bedroom accented by a tray ceiling with his-n-her walk-in closets

■ Two additional bedrooms highlighted by a versatile nook for sitting or studying

■ A full bath and a flexible skylit Bonus Room round out the plan

FIRST FLOOR — 1,458 SQ. FT.
SECOND FLOOR — 484 SQ. FT.
GARAGE & STORAGE — 497 SQ. FT.
BONUS ROOM — 257 SQ. FT.

TOTAL LIVING AREA:
1,942 SQ. FT.

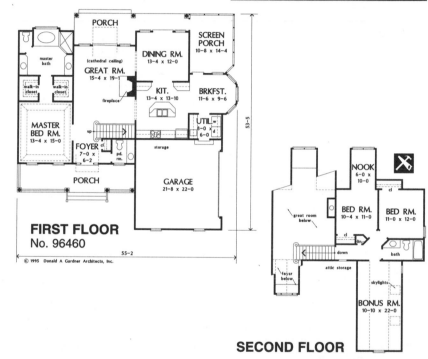

FIRST FLOOR
No. 96460

© 1995 Donald A Gardner Architects, Inc.

SECOND FLOOR

Everything You Need...
...to Make Your Dream Come True!

You pay only a fraction of the original cost for home designs by respected professionals.

You've Picked Your Dream Home!

You can already see it standing on your lot... you can see yourselves in your new home... enjoying family, entertaining guests, celebrating holidays. All that remains ahead are the details. That's where we can help. Whether you plan to build-it-yourself, be your own contractor, or hand your plans over to an outside contractor, your Garlinghouse blueprints provide the perfect beginning for putting yourself in your dream home right away.

We even make it simple for you to make professional design modifications. We can also provide a materials list for greater economy.

My grandfather, L.F. Garlinghouse, started a tradition of quality when he founded this company in 1907. For over 90 years, homeowners and builders have relied on us for accurate, complete, professional blueprints. Our plans help you get results fast... and save money, too! These pages will give you all the information you need to order. So get started now... I know you'll love your new Garlinghouse home!

Sincerely,

EXTERIOR ELEVATIONS

Elevations are scaled drawings of the front, rear, left and right sides of a home. All of the necessary information pertaining to the exterior finish materials, roof pitches and exterior height dimensions of your home are defined.

CABINET PLANS

These plans, or in some cases elevations, will detail the layout of the kitchen and bathroom cabinets at a larger scale. This gives you an accurate layout for your cabinets or an ideal starting point for a modified custom cabinet design. Available for most plans in our collection.

TYPICAL WALL SECTION

This section is provided to help your builder understand the structural components and materials used to construct the exterior walls of your home. This section will address insulation, roof components, and interior and exterior wall finishes. Your plans will be designed with either 2x4 or 2x6 exterior walls, but most professional contractors can easily adapt the plans to the wall thickness you require. Available for most plans in our collection.

FIREPLACE DETAILS

If the home you have chosen includes a fireplace, the fireplace detail will show typical methods to construct the firebox, hearth and flue chase for masonry units, or a wood frame chase for a zero-clearance unit. Available for most plans in our collection.

FOUNDATION PLAN

These plans will accurately dimension the footprint of your home including load bearing points and beam placement if applicable. The foundation style will vary from plan to plan. Your local climatic conditions will dictate whether a basement, slab or crawlspace is best suited for your area. In most cases, if your plan comes with one foundation style, a professional contractor can easily adapt the foundation plan to an alternate style.

ROOF PLAN

The information necessary to construct the roof will be included with your home plans. Some plans will reference roof trusses, while many others contain schematic framing plans. These framing plans will indicate the lumber sizes necessary for the rafters and ridgeboards based on the designated roof loads.

TYPICAL CROSS SECTION

A cut-away cross-section through the entire home shows your building contractor the exact correlation of construction components at all levels of the house. It will help to clarify the load bearing points from the roof all the way down to the basement.

DETAILED FLOOR PLANS

The floor plans of your home accurately dimension the positioning of all walls, doors, windows, stairs and permanent fixtures. They will show you the relationship and dimensions of rooms, closets and traffic patterns. Included is the schematic of the electrical layout. This layout is clearly represented and does not hinder the clarity of other pertinent information shown. All these details will help your builder properly construct your new home.

STAIR DETAILS

If stairs are an element of the design you have chosen, then a cross-section of the stairs will be included in your home plans. This gives your builders the essential reference points that they need for headroom clearance, and riser and tread dimensions. Available for most plans in our collection.

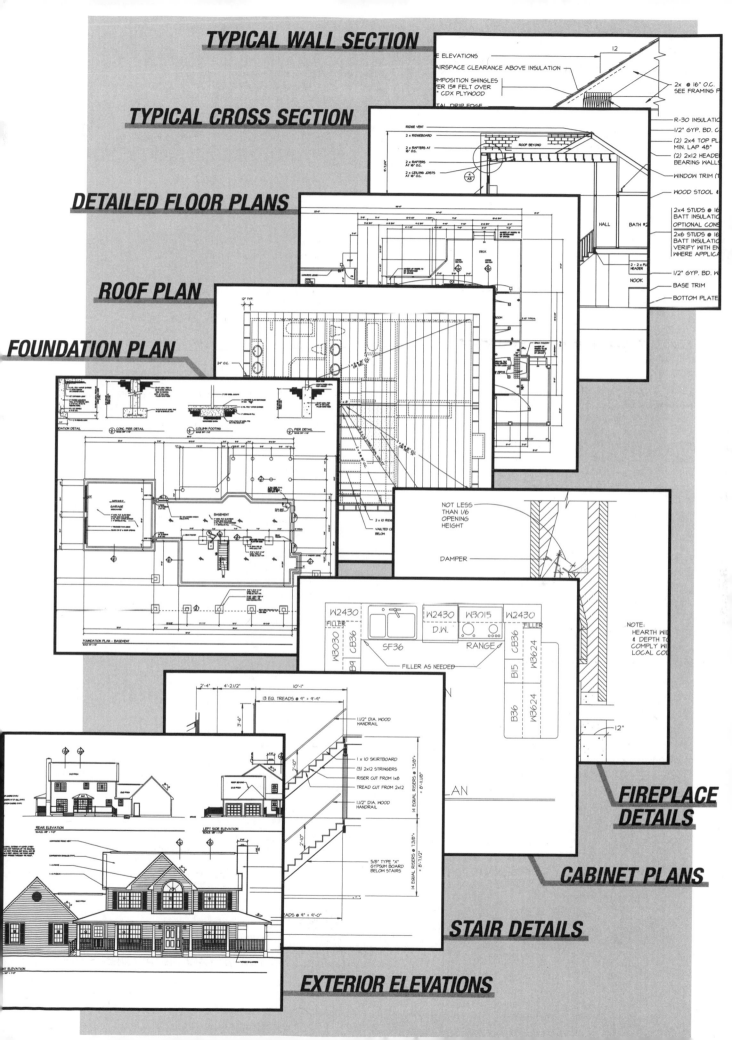

TYPICAL WALL SECTION

TYPICAL CROSS SECTION

DETAILED FLOOR PLANS

ROOF PLAN

FOUNDATION PLAN

FIREPLACE DETAILS

CABINET PLANS

STAIR DETAILS

EXTERIOR ELEVATIONS

Garlinghouse Options & Extras ...Make Your Dream A Home

Reversed Plans Can Make Your Dream Home Just Right!

"That's our dream home...if only the garage were on the other side!"
You could have exactly the home you want by flipping it end-for-end. Check it out by holding your dream home page of this book up to a mirror. Then simply order your plans "reversed." We'll send you one full set of mirror-image plans (with the writing backwards) as a master guide for you and your builder.

The remaining sets of your order will come as shown in this book so the dimensions and specifications are easily read on the job site...but most plans in our collection come stamped "REVERSED" so there is no construction confusion.

As Shown   Reversed

We can only send reversed plans with multiple-set orders. There is a $50 charge for this service.

Some plans in our collection are available in Right Reading Reverse. Right Reading Reverse plans will show your home in reverse, with the writing on the plan being readable. This easy-to-read format will save you valuable time and money. Please contact our Customer Service Department at (860) 343-5977 to check for Right Reading Reverse availability. (There is a $125 charge for this service.)

Specifications & Contract Form

We send this form to you free of charge with your home plan order. The form is designed to be filled in by you or your contractor with the exact materials to use in the construction of your new home. Once signed by you and your contractor it will provide you with peace of mind throughout the construction process.

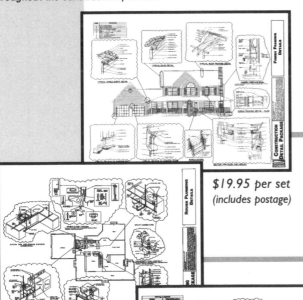

$19.95 per set
(includes postage)

Remember To Order Your Materials List

It'll help you save money. Available at a modest additional charge, the Materials List gives the quantity, dimensions, and specifications for the major materials needed to build your home. You will get faster, more accurate bids from your contractors and building suppliers — and avoid paying for unused materials and waste. Materials Lists are available for all home plans except as otherwise indicated, but can only be ordered with a set of home plans. Due to differences in regional requirements and homeowner or builder preferences... electrical, plumbing and heating/air conditioning equipment specifications are not designed specifically for each plan. However, non-plan specific detailed typical prints of residential electrical, plumbing and construction guidelines can be provided. Please see below for additional information. If you need a detailed materials cost you might need to purchase a Zip Quote. (Details follow)

Detail Plans Provide Valuable Information About Construction Techniques

Because local codes and requirements vary greatly, we recommend that you obtain drawings and bids from licensed contractors to do your mechanical plans. However, if you want to know more about techniques — and deal more confidently with subcontractors — we offer these remarkably useful detail sheets. These detail sheets will aid in your understanding of these technical subjects. **The detail sheets are not specific to any one home plan and should be used only as a general reference guide.**

RESIDENTIAL CONSTRUCTION DETAILS

Ten sheets that cover the essentials of stick-built residential home construction. Details foundation options — poured concrete basement, concrete block, or monolithic concrete slab. Shows all aspects of floor, wall and roof framing. Provides details for roof dormers, overhangs, chimneys and skylights. Conforms to requirements of Uniform Building code or BOCA code. Includes a quick index and a glossary of terms.

RESIDENTIAL PLUMBING DETAILS

Eight sheets packed with information detailing pipe installation methods, fittings, and sized. Details plumbing hook-ups for toilets, sinks, washers, sump pumps, and septic system construction. Conforms to requirements of National Plumbing code. Color coded with a glossary of terms and quick index.

RESIDENTIAL ELECTRICAL DETAILS

Eight sheets that cover all aspects of residential wiring, from simple switch wiring to service entrance connections. Details distribution panel layout with outlet and switch schematics, circuit breaker and wiring installation methods, and ground fault interrupter specifications. Conforms to requirements of National Electrical Code. Color coded with a glossary of terms.

Modifying Your Favorite Design, Made *EASY!*

OPTION #1

Modifying Your Garlinghouse Home Plan

Simple modifications to your dream home, including minor non-structural changes and material substitutions, can be made between you and your builder by marking the changes directly on your blueprints. However, if you are considering making significant changes to your chosen design, we recommend that you use the services of The Garlinghouse Co. Design Staff. We will help take your ideas and turn them into a reality, just the way you want. Here's our procedure!

When you place your Vellum order, you may also request a free Garlinghouse Modification Kit. In this kit, you will receive a red marking pencil, furniture cut-out sheet, ruler, a self addressed mailing label and a form for specifying any additional notes or drawings that will help us understand your design ideas. Mark your desired changes directly on the Vellum drawings. NOTE: Please use only a **red pencil** to mark your desired changes on the Vellum. Then, return the redlined Vellum set in the original box to The Garlinghouse Company at, 282 Main Street Extension, Middletown, CT 06457. **IMPORTANT:** Please **roll** the Vellums for shipping, **do not fold** the Vellums for shipping.

We also offer modification estimates. We will provide you with an estimate to draft your changes based on your specific modifications before you purchase the vellums, for a $50 fee. After you receive your estimate, if you decide to have The Garlinghouse Company Design Staff do the changes, the $50 estimate fee will be deducted from the cost of your modifications. If, however, you choose to use a different service, the $50 estimate fee is non-refundable.

Within 5 days of receipt of your plans, you will be contacted by a member of The Garlinghouse Co. Design Staff with an estimate for the design services to draw those changes. A 50% deposit is required before we begin making the actual modifications to your plans.

Once the preliminary design changes have been made to the floor plans and elevations, copies will be sent to you to make sure we have made the exact changes you want. We will wait for your approval before continuing with any structural revisions. The Garlinghouse Co. Design Staff will call again to inform you that your modified Vellum plan is complete and will be shipped as soon as the final payment has been made. For additional information call us at 1-860-343-5977. Please refer to the Modification Pricing Guide for estimated modification costs. Please call for Vellum modification availability for plan numbers 85,000 and above.

OPTION #2

Reproducible Vellums for Local Modification Ease

If you decide not to use the Garlinghouse Co. Design Staff for your modifications, we recommend that you follow our same procedure of purchasing our Vellums. You then have the option of using the services of the original designer of the plan, a local professional designer, or architect to make the modifications to your plan. With a Vellum copy of our plans, a design professional can alter the drawings just the way you want, then you can print as many copies of the modified plans as you need to build your house. And, since you have already started with our complete detailed plans, the cost of those expensive professional services will be significantly less than starting from scratch. Refer to the price schedule for Vellum costs. Again, please call for Vellum availability for plan numbers 85,000 and above.

IMPORTANT RETURN POLICY: Upon receipt of your Vellums, if for some reason you decide you do not want modified plan, then simply return the Kit and the unopened Vellums. Reproducible Vellum copies of our home plans are copyright protected and only sold under the terms of a license agreement that you will receive with your order. Should you not agree to the terms, then the Vellums may be returned, **unopened,** for a full refund less the shipping and handling charges, plus a 15% restocking fee. For any additional information, please call us at 1-860-343-5977.

MODIFICATION PRICING GUIDE

CATEGORIES	ESTIMATED COST
KITCHEN LAYOUT — PLAN AND ELEVATION	$175.00
BATHROOM LAYOUT — PLAN AND ELEVATION	$175.00
FIREPLACE PLAN AND DETAILS	$200.00
INTERIOR ELEVATION	$125.00
EXTERIOR ELEVATION — MATERIAL CHANGE	$140.00
EXTERIOR ELEVATION — ADD BRICK OR STONE	$400.00
EXTERIOR ELEVATION — STYLE CHANGE	$450.00
NON BEARING WALLS (INTERIOR)	$200.00
BEARING AND/OR EXTERIOR WALLS	$325.00
WALL FRAMING CHANGE — 2X4 TO 2X6 OR 2X6 TO 2X4	$240.00
ADD/REDUCE LIVING SPACE — SQUARE FOOTAGE	QUOTE REQUIRED
NEW MATERIALS LIST	$.20 SQUARE FOOT
CHANGE TRUSSES TO RAFTERS OR CHANGE ROOF PITCH	$300.00
FRAMING PLAN CHANGES	$325.00
GARAGE CHANGES	$325.00
ADD A FOUNDATION OPTION	$300.00
FOUNDATION CHANGES	$250.00
RIGHT READING PLAN REVERSE	$575.00
ARCHITECTS SEAL (Available for most states)	$300.00
ENERGY CERTIFICATE	$150.00
LIGHT AND VENTILATION SCHEDULE	$150.00

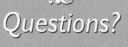

Questions?

Call our customer service department at *1-860-343-5977*

"How to obtain a construction cost calculation based on labor rates and building material costs in your Zip Code area!"

ZIP-QUOTE!
HOME COST CALCULATOR

ZIP QUOTE
HOME COST CALCULATOR
see order pages for details

WHY?

Do you wish you could quickly find out the building cost for your new home without waiting for a contractor to compile hundreds of bids? Would you like to have a benchmark to compare your contractor(s) bids against? **Well, Now You Can!!,** with **Zip-Quote** Home Cost Calculator. Zip-Quote is only available for zip code areas within the United States.

HOW?

Our new **Zip-Quote** Home Cost Calculator will enable you to obtain the calculated building cost to construct your new home, based on labor rates and building material costs within your zip code area, without the normal delays or hassles usually associated with the bidding process. Zip-Quote can be purchased in two separate formats, an itemized or a bottom line format.

"How does **Zip-Quote** actually work?" When we receive your **Zip-Quote** order, we process your specific home plan building materials list through our Home Cost Calculator which contains up-to-date rates for all residential labor trades and building material costs in your zip code area. "The result?" A calculated cost to build your dream home in your zip code area. This calculation will help you (as a consumer or a builder) evaluate your building budget. This is a valuable tool for anyone considering building a new home.

All database information for our calculations is furnished by Marshall & Swift, L.P. For over 60 years, Marshall & Swift L.P. has been a leading provider of cost data to professionals in all aspects of the construction and remodeling industries.

OPTION 1

The **Itemized Zip-Quote** is a detailed building material list. Each building material list line item will separately state the labor cost, material cost and equipment cost (if applicable) for the use of that building material in the construction process. Each category within the building material list will be subtotaled and the entire Itemized cost calculation totaled at the end. This building materials list will be summarized by the individual building categories and will have additional columns where you can enter data from your contractor's estimates for a cost comparison between the different suppliers and contractors who will actually quote you their products and services.

OPTION 2

The **Bottom Line Zip-Quote** is a one line summarized total cost for the home plan of your choice. This cost calculation is also based on the labor cost, material cost and equipment cost (if applicable) within your local zip code area.

COST

The price of your **Itemized Zip-Quote** is based upon the pricing schedule of the plan you have selected, in addition to the price of the materials list. Please refer to the pricing schedule on our order form. The price of your initial **Bottom Line Zip-Quote** is $29.95. Each additional **Bottom Line Zip-Quote** ordered in conjunction with the initial order is only $14.95. **Bottom Line Zip-Quote** may be purchased separately and does NOT have to be purchased in conjunction with a home plan order.

FYI

An **Itemized Zip-Quote** Home Cost Calculation can ONLY be purchased in conjunction with a Home Plan order. The **Itemized Zip-Quote** can not be purchased separately. The **Bottom Line Zip-Quote** can be purchased seperately and doesn't have to be purchased in conjunction with a home plan order. Please consult with a sales representative for current availability. If you find within 60 days of your order date that you will be unable to build this home, then you may exchange the plans and the materials list towards the price of a new set of plans (see order info pages for plan exchange policy). The **Itemized Zip-Quote** and the **Bottom Line Zip-Quote** are NOT returnable. The price of the initial **Bottom Line Zip-Quote** order can be credited towards the purchase of an **Itemized Zip-Quote** order only. Additional **Bottom Line Zip-Quote** orders, within the same order can not be credited. Please call our Customer Service Department for more information.

Zip-Quote is available for plans where you see this symbol in the index. ⚡ Plans 90,000 and above are not available until September 1998.

SOME MORE INFORMATION

The Itemized and Bottom Line Zip-Quotes give you approximate costs for constructing the particular house in your area. These costs are not exact and are only intended to be used as a preliminary estimate to help determine the affordability of a new home and/or a guide to evaluate the general competitiveness of actual price quotes obtained through local suppliers and contractors. However, Zip-Quote cost figures should never be relied upon as the only source of information in either case. The Garlinghouse Company and Marshall & Swift L.P. can not guarantee any level of data accuracy or correctness in a Zip-Quote and disclaim all liability for loss with respect to the same, in excess of the original purchase price of the Zip-Quote product. All Zip-Quote calculations are based upon the actual blueprint materials list with options as selected by customer and do not reflect any differences that may be shown on the published house renderings, floor plans, or photographs.

Order Code No. H8SM8

Order Form

Plan prices guaranteed until 3/6/99 — After this date call for updated pricing

____ set(s) of blueprints for plan #_____ $_____

____ Vellum & Modification kit for plan #_____ $_____

____ Additional set(s) @ $30 each for plan #_____ $_____

____ Mirror Image Reverse @ $50 each $_____

____ Right Reading Reverse @ $125 each $_____

____ Materials list for plan #_____ $_____

____ Detail Plans @ $19.95 each

      ❏ Construction ❏ Plumbing ❏ Electrical $_____

____ Bottom line ZIP Quote@$29.95 for plan #_____ $_____

____ Additional Bottom Line Zip Quote

      @ $14.95 for plan(s) #_____

_____ $_____

____ Itemized ZIP Quote for plan(s) #_____ $_____

Shipping (see charts on opposite page) $_____

Subtotal $_____

Sales Tax (CT residents add 6% sales tax, KS residents add 6.15% sales tax) (Not required for all states) $_____

TOTAL AMOUNT ENCLOSED $_____

Send your check, money order or credit card information to:
(No C.O.D.'s Please)
Please submit all <u>United States</u> & <u>Other Nations</u> orders to:

Garlinghouse Company
P.O. Box 1717
Middletown, CT. 06457

Please Submit all <u>Canadian</u> plan orders to:

Garlinghouse Company
60 Baffin Place, Unit #5
Waterloo, Ontario N2V 1Z7

ADDRESS INFORMATION:

NAME:_____

STREET:_____

CITY:_____

STATE:_____ **ZIP:**_____

DAYTIME PHONE:_____

Credit Card Information

Charge To: ❏ Visa   ❏ Mastercard

Card # ⌷⌷⌷⌷⌷⌷⌷⌷⌷⌷⌷⌷⌷⌷⌷⌷

Signature _____ Exp. ____/____

IMPORTANT INFORMATION TO READ BEFORE YOU PLACE YOUR ORDER

How Many Sets Of Plans Will You Need?

The Standard 8-Set Construction Package

Our experience shows that you'll speed every step of construction and avoid costly building errors by ordering enough sets to go around. Each tradesperson wants a set — the general contractor and all subcontractors; foundation, electrical, plumbing, heating/air conditioning and framers. Don't forget your lending institution, building department and, of course, a set for yourself.

The Minimum 4-Set Construction Package

If you're comfortable with arduous follow-up, this package can save you few dollars by giving you the option of passing down plan sets as work progresses. You might have enough copies to go around if work goes exactly as scheduled and no plans are lost or damaged by subcontractors. But for only $50 more, the 8-set package eliminates these worries.

The Single Study Set

We offer this set so you can study the blueprints to plan your dream home in detail. As with all of our plans, they are stamped with a copyright warning. Remember, one set is never enough to build your home. In pursuant to copyright laws, it is <u>illegal</u> to reproduce any blueprint.

Our Reorder and Exchange Policies:

If you find after your initial purchase that you require additional sets of plans you may purchase them from us at special reorder prices (please call for pricing details) provided that you reorder within 6 months of your original order date. There is a $28 reorder processing fee that is charged on all reorders. For more information on reordering plans please contact our Customer Service Department at (860) 343-5977.

We want you to find your dream home from our wide selection of home plans. However, if for some reason you find that the plan you have purchased from us does not meet your needs, then you may exchange that plan for any other plan in our collection. We allow you sixty days from your original invoice date to make an exchange. At the time of the exchange you will be charged a processing fee of 15% of the total amount of your original order plus the difference in price between the plans (if applicable) plus the cost to ship the new plans to you. Call our Customer Service Department at (860) 343-5977 for more information. Please Note: Reproducible vellums can only be exchanged if they are unopened.

Important Shipping Information

Please refer to the shipping charts on the order form for service availability for your specific plan number. Our delivery service must have a street address or Rural Route Box number — never a post office box. (PLEASE NOTE: Supplying a P.O. Box number <u>only</u> will delay the shipping of your order.) Use a work address if no one is home during the day.

Orders being shipped to APO or FPO must go via First Class Mail. Please include the proper postage.

For our International Customers, only Certified bank checks and money orders are accepted and must be payable in U.S. currency. For speed, we ship international orders Air Parcel Post. Please refer to the chart for the correct shipping cost.

Important Canadian Shipping Information

To our friends in Canada, we have a plan design affiliate in Kitchener, Ontario. This relationship will help you avoid the delays and charges associated with shipments from the United States. Moreover, our affiliate is familiar with the building requirements in your community and country. We prefer payments in U.S. Currency. If you, however, are sending Canadian funds please add 40% to the prices of the plans and shipping fees.

An Important Note About Building Code Requirements:

All plans are drawn to conform to one or more of the industry's major national building standards. However, due to the variety of local building regulations, your plan may need to be modified to comply with local requirements — snow loads, energy loads, seismic zones, etc. Do check them fully and consult your local building officials.

A few states require that all building plans used be drawn by an architect registered in that state. While having your plans reviewed and stamped by such an architect may be prudent, laws requiring non-conforming plans like ours to be completely redrawn forces you to unnecessarily pay very large fees. If your state has such a law, we strongly recommend you contact your state representative to protest.

The rendering, floor plans, and technical information contained within this publication are not guaranteed to be totally accurate. Consequently, no information from this publication should be used either as a guide to constructing a home or for estimating the cost of building a home. Complete blueprints must be purchased for such purposes.

rlinghouse 1998 Blueprint Price Code Schedule

Additional sets with original order $30

PRICE CODE	A	B	C	D	E	F	G	H
8 SETS OF SAME PLAN	$375	$415	$455	$495	$535	$575	$615	$655
4 SETS OF SAME PLAN	$325	$365	$405	$445	$485	$525	$565	$605
1 SINGLE SET OF PLANS	$275	$315	$355	$395	$435	$475	$515	$555
VELLUMS	$485	$530	$575	$620	$665	$710	$755	$800
MATERIALS LIST	$40	$40	$45	$45	$50	$50	$55	$55
ITEMIZED ZIP QUOTE	$75	$80	$85	$85	$90	$90	$95	$95

Shipping — (Plans 1-84999)

	1-3 Sets	4-6 Sets	7+ & Vellums
Standard Delivery (UPS 2-Day)	$15.00	$20.00	$25.00
Overnight Delivery	$30.00	$35.00	$40.00

Shipping — (Plans 85000-99999)

	1-3 Sets	4-6 Sets	7+ & Vellums
Ground Delivery (7-10 Days)	$9.00	$18.00	$20.00
Express Delivery (3-5 Days)	$15.00	$20.00	$25.00

International Shipping & Handling

	1-3 Sets	4-6 Sets	7+ & Vellums
Regular Delivery Canada (7-10 Days)	$14.00	$17.00	$20.00
Express Delivery Canada (5-6 Days)	$35.00	$40.00	$45.00
Overseas Delivery Airmail (2-3 Weeks)	$45.00	$52.00	$60.00

Option Key

Zip Quote Available   R Right Reading Reverse
Duplex Plan   Materials List Available

Index

TOP SELLING
GARAGE PLANS

Save money by Doing-It-Yourself using our Easy-To-Follow plans. Whether you intend to build your own garage or contract it out to a building professional, the Garlinghouse garage plans provide you with everything you need to price out your project and get started. Put our 90+ years of experience to work for you. *Order now!!*

No. 06016C $86.00
Apartment Garage With One Bedroom

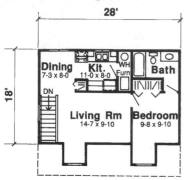

- 24' x 28' Overall Dimensions
- 544 Square Foot Apartment
- 12/12 Gable Roof with Dormers
- Slab or Stem Wall Foundation Options

No. 06015C $86.00
Apartment Garage With Two Bedrooms

- 26' x 28' Overall Dimensions
- 728 Square Foot Apartment
- 4/12 Pitch Gable Roof
- Slab or Stem Wall Foundation Options

No. 06012C $54.00
30' Deep Gable &/or Eave Jumbo Garages

- 4/12 Pitch Gable Roof
- Available Options for Extra Tall Walls, Garage & Personnel Doors, Foundation, Window, & Sidings
- Package contains 4 Different Sizes
- 30' x 28'   • 30' x 32'   • 30' x 36'   • 30' x 40'

No. 06013C $68.00
Two-Car Garage With Mudroom/Breezeway

- Attaches to Any House
- 24' x 24' Eave Entry
- Available Options for Utility Room with Bath, Mudroom, Screened-In Breezeway, Roof, Foundation, Garage & Personnel Doors, Window, & Sidings

No. 06001C $48.00

2', 14' & 16' Wide-Gable 1-Car Garages

Available Options for Roof, Foundation, Window, Door, & Sidings

Package contains 8 Different Sizes

12' x 20' Mini-Garage	• 14' x 22'	• 16' x 20'	• 16' x 24'
14' x 20'	• 14' x 24'	• 16' x 22'	• 16' x 26'

No. 06003C $48.00

24' Wide-Gable 2-Car Garages

- Available Options for Side Shed, Roof, Foundation, Garage & Personnel Doors, Window, & Sidings
- Package contains 5 Different Sizes
- 24' x 22' • 24' x 24' • 24' x 26'
- 24' x 28' • 24' x 32'

No. 06007C $60.00

Gable 2-Car Gambrel Roof Garages

Interior Rear Stairs to Loft Workshop

Front Loft Cargo Door With Pulley Lift

Available Options for Foundation, Garage & Personnel Doors, Window, & Sidings

Package contains 5 Different Sizes

22' x 26' • 22' x 28' • 24' x 28' • 24' x 30' • 24' x 32'

No. 06006C $48.00

22' & 24' Deep Eave 2 & 3-Car Garages

- Can Be Built Stand-Alone or Attached to House
- Available Options for Roof, Foundation, Garage & Personnel Doors, Window, & Sidings
- Package contains 6 Different Sizes
- 22' x 28' • 22' x 32' • 24' x 32'
- 22' x 30' • 24' x 30' • 24' x 36'

No. 06002C $48.00

0' & 22' Wide-Gable 2-Car Garages

Available Options for Roof, Foundation, Garage & Personnel Doors, Window, & Sidings

Package contains 7 Different Sizes

20' x 20'	• 20' x 24'	• 22' x 22'	• 22' x 28'
20' x 22'	• 20' x 28'	• 22' x 24'	

No. 06008C $60.00

Eave 2 & 3-Car Clerestory Roof Garages

- Interior Side Stairs to Loft Workshop
- Available Options for Engine Lift, Foundation, Garage & Personnel Doors, Window, & Sidings
- Package contains 4 Different Sizes
- 24' x 26' • 24' x 28' • 24' x 32' • 24' x 36'

Here's What You Get

- Three complete sets of drawings for each plan ordered

- Detailed step-by-step instructions with easy-to-follow diagrams on how to build your garage (not available with apartment garages)

- For each garage style, a variety of size and garage door configuration options

- Variety of roof styles and/or pitch options for most garages

- Complete materials list

- Choice between three foundation options:
Monolithic Slab, Concrete Stem Wall or Concrete Block Stem Wall

- Full framing plans, elevations and cross-sectionals for each garage size and configuration

Build-It-Yourself PROJECT PLAN

Order Information For Garage Plans:

All garage plan orders contain three complete sets of drawings with instructions and are priced as listed next to the illustration Additional sets of plans may be obtained for $10.00 each with your original order. UPS shipping is used unless otherwise requested Please include the proper amount for shipping.

Garage Order Form

Order Code No. **G8SM8**

Please send me 3 complete sets of the following GARAGE PLAN:

Item no. & description	Price
_____	$ _____

Additional Sets

_____ (@ $10.00 each) $ _____

Shipping Charges: UPS-$3.75, First Class- $4.50 $ _____

Subtotal: $ _____

Resident sales tax: KS-6.15%, CT-6% (NOT REQUIRED FOR OTHER STATES) $ _____

Total Enclosed: $ _____

My Billing Address is:

Name _____

Address _____

City _____

State _____ Zip_____

Daytime Phone No. _____

My Shipping Address is:

Name _____

Address _____
(UPS will not ship to P.O. Boxes)

City _____

State _____ Zip _____

Send your order to:
(With check or money order payable in U.S. funds only)
The Garlinghouse Company
P.O. Box 1717
Middletown, CT 06457

For Faster Service...Charge It!
U.S. & Canada Call
1(800)235-5700
All foreign residents call 1(860)343-5977
❏ Mastercard ❏ Visa

Card # | | | | | | | | | | | | | | | | | | |

Signature _____ Exp.___/___

If paying by credit card, to avoid delays:
billing address must be as it appears on credit card statement

or FAX us at (860) 343-5984

No C.O.D. orders accepted; U.S. funds only. UPS will not ship to Post Office boxes, FPO boxes, APO boxes, Alaska or Hawaii.
Canadian orders must be shipped First Class.

Prices subject to change without notice.